REAL WORLD
DIGITAL
PHOTOGRAPHY

DEKE McCLELLAND
KATRIN EISMANN

PEACHPIT PRESS
BERKELEY, CALIFORNIA

REAL WORLD DIGITAL PHOTOGRAPHY

Deke McClelland
Katrin Eismann

Peachpit Press
1249 Eighth Street
Berkeley, CA 94710
510/524-2178
800/283-9444
510/524-2221 (fax)

Find us on the World Wide Web at:
www.peachpit.com

Peachpit Press is a division of Addison Wesley Longman

Editor: Corbin Collins
Production Coordinator: Amy Changar
Editor-at-large: Tom Baer
Copyeditor: Felicity O'Meara
Compositor: Owen Wolfson
Interior Designer: Mimi Heft
Technical Editor: Andrew Rodney
Cover Designer: Lynn Brofsky Design
Cover Illustration Photo: Deke McClelland
Cover Illustration Production: Jeff McCord

ISBN 0-201-35402-0

9 8 7 6 5 4 3

Printed and bound in the United States of America

*For the two Johns who supported me throughout this
entire project: St. John's Wort and John McIntosh.
I can imagine living without one, but not the other.*

Writing a book about technology would be an impossible endeavor without
the support and insights from the brilliant people that develop and build the
cameras—such as Stephen Noble from Eastman Kodak, Michael Collette from
Better Light, and Ken Boydston and Richard Chang from MegaVision. I am also
indebted to the many professionals at Nikon, Olympus, Agfa, Ricoh, Fujifilm,
Kodak, Kaidan, and Roundhouse Publications who overnighted me many pieces
of equipment and looked the other way when I kept them a bit longer than
promised. Thank you: Dave Podwicka, Gus Radayminski, and Joe Rundy all from
Kodak, Bob Rose from Bogen, and Andrew Rodney (aka the digitaldog) for
answering yet another Katrin question. Finally, this book would never have seen
the light of day without the persistent help of the Peachpit team and my co-author
Deke McClelland who never lost his cool when explaining yet another aspect of
book publishing to me.

—*Katrin*

CONTENTS AT A GLANCE

TABLE OF CONTENTS

FOREWORD

This last decade of the century has witnessed the unfolding of the most profound revolution in imaging since the invention of flexible film. Digital photography—the creation of photographs encoded as binary data—has blossomed from the rarefied domain of military and space applications. First it made inroads in commercial catalog and studio photography and then it entered a broadening range of publishing, documentation, and general business uses. Today, the digital camera is on the verge of becoming a mass market product, and digital photography is becoming as commonplace as digital music was after the advent of the CD. "On the verge" because, although price/performance improvements to digital photography products have arrived at a dizzying rate in recent years, understanding and using digital photography still requires specialized knowledge.

That's where this book comes in. *Real World Digital Photography* makes a key contribution to closing that knowledge gap by building a practical, user-focused bridge between understanding the tools available and learning to intuit their real-world possibilities. Thus, the book enables readers to participate not only in an diverting new activities but also in a major societal transformation. Beyond the new technologies and their associated growing pains, the bigger picture is that digital photography has brought us to the edge of something potentially much greater than just exciting new tools. Provided we have the wisdom to seize the opportunity, it offers the chance to create new, richer, and more flexible models for human interaction in a globalized, information-based society.

I'm aware that such a sweeping statement may seem overstated—especially when compared to the relatively mundane uses the technology is being put to today. At first glance, there's nothing earth-shaking about pasting a photograph into a newsletter or flyer or emailing it to a relative or client across the country. Seeing a picture on a screen immediately after it was taken may be the ultimate in instant photography, but calling it a harbinger of a new age is an overstatement. Or is it?

There is in fact much more going on here than meets the eye. When we develop technology that changes our lives, we are like tradesmen, each working on a small part of a construction project whose overall plan is not available to us. We can only interpret what we're doing in light of what we've done before and can barely glimpse where our own footsteps are leading us. This is why works of science fiction are so often revealed, with hindsight, to be not so much predictions of the future than they are reflections of their own time. Digital photography is evolving within a pattern that all new media follow: Early stages of development reference and imitate previous media; only in later stages is the new idiom's intrinsic character revealed.

Digital photography is emerging from years of nose-to-the-grindstone struggles against technical limitations that constrained it into delivering results inferior to film photography. Now, those "quality wars" are all but over. Yet digital photography still lags conventional photography in other critically important respects. For example, it lacks the mass-market convenience of the film-based photo service infrastructure built over a century, and the ease of use that comes from iterating and refining products based on observing customer usage patterns. Digital photography is the medium of the future, but it is still striving to meet standards set by traditional photography. Largely for those reasons, it delivers an experience that is little more than a mimicking of traditional photography.

Simultaneously (and to a great degree invisibly), we are even now laying the foundation for our own future exploration of that new medium. The pieces of the puzzle we're struggling to assemble today—be it products, value propositions, business models, distribution channels, or service infrastructures—are the beginnnings of the reinvention of photography. And we will reinvent it. Not so much because digital technology enables us to, but because the transformation of the world fostered by digital technology over the last 30 years requires us to improve not just the network we use to communicate, but, even more importantly, the content of those communications. In this respect, pictures hold unique promise.

Of all the forms of expression our species has devised, still images deliver the best combination of content and bandwidth: Pictures can communicate staggering amounts of information and emotional content in compact form. Perhaps even more importantly, in an age of information overload, photos allow viewers to decide for themselves how much time and energy to invest in acquiring the message. Unlike linear media such as text, sound, and motion images, still photos allow choice between absorbing the key contents of a picture in a fraction of a second or spending the time to examine it for additional information and nuances. Because of those qualities, still images are the ideal match to the global telecommunications and computing infrastructures that have been transforming our societies and economies. Over the next ten years, the convergence of telecommunications, personal information technology, and digital imaging will be realized and will give birth to powerful new forms of communication.

The shape these new forms evolve into will be vastly more influenced by users than by engineers. The technological foundations, from image sensors to the Internet, have been in place for many years (many were inherited from Cold War research). For today's corporations who are commercializing these technologies, the crucial issue is to correctly anticipate and identify emerging customer usage patterns. Tomorrow's photographers will be digital, but will they want cameras that record motion as well as stills, or will they prefer separate devices for motion? Given an affordable and convenient option, will they print their pictures themselves or will they still chose to have what is after all a mindless activity done by a service provider? For that matter, will they print at all, or will most images be viewed only on screens? Will the Internet become the service infrastructure of choice, or will we preserve the "water cooler effect" of in-person interaction?

Your actions, dear reader, as you embrace digital photography and the advice offered in this book, are the all-powerful votes that will influence how the custodians of the technology will choose to serve you so as to profit by doing so. By demanding that the imaging revolution make you more connected, aware, and empowered, you can harness technological progress to enrich the quality of our collective lives rather than just mindlessly accelerating them (as too much technology does today). When you take up a digital camera, you are inventing the future. Seize the moment.

— Alexis Gerard, President, Future Image Inc.

About Alexis Gerard Mr. Gerard ranks among the visionaries whose contributions have shaped today's digital imaging industry. Future Image Inc. (*www.futureimage.com*), which he founded in 1991, is the leading publisher of business-to-business information and analysis for the digital imaging industry. Its publication *The Future Image Report* is read by executives and entrepreneurs in more than 50 countries. In 1993, Mr. Gerard produced and chaired Photography in the Digital Age, the first digital photography executive conference. He is a director and past president of the Digital Imaging Group, a consortium founded by Adobe, Canon, Eastman Kodak, Fuji, Hewlett-Packard, IBM, Intel, Live Picture, and Microsoft to promote the growth of digital imaging. His involvement in the imaging industry spans more than 20 years, during which he authored or directed ground-breaking studies forecasting the impact and adoption patterns of new imaging technologies such as Photo CD, royalty-free stock images, and digital cameras. He is a columnist and speaker with numerous conference and television appearances to his credit. A native of Switzerland, Mr. Gerard holds an MA from the Graduate Institute of International Studies in Geneva.

PREFACE

Normally, I hate trade shows. But when *Macworld Japan* magazine flew me out to the 1994 Tokyo Macworld Expo to give a short presentation on digital imaging, I saw a perfect opportunity to duck out after my session and have fun. Given that no one was paying me to cover the show, and I didn't understand the language, I imagined myself forgoing aisles of ephemeral products in favor of sushi, sake, and other time-tested pleasures of Japan.

But if you've ever been to Makuhari—where the Expo was held—you know it's about as representative of Japan as Super Mario. Essentially a cluster of high-rise hotels circling a coliseum, Makuhari feels less like a Tokyo suburb than an office park on the moon. Except for the selection of dried seaweed at the local drug store and the inventive use of English ("Let's kiosk" and "a salty snack food of the crunchy type" come to mind), I would have sworn my plane never left Los Angeles.

So without anything better to do, I begrudgingly attended the Expo. And it's a good thing I did, for it was there that Apple introduced its QuickTake 100. The first full-color digital camera priced under $1,000, the QuickTake captured up to eight 640-by-480-pixel pictures directly to computer memory. No film, no developing, no scanning. At a time when nearly every other digital camera on the market cost as much as a Lexus, the QuickTake was unique in delivering electronic photographs for the relatively modest price of $749.

Although Makuhari provided an atmosphere bereft of distractions, I knew I couldn't judge the merits of this wondrous device until I used it for myself. So few months later, I reviewed the camera for *Macworld* in the States. Sure enough, the QuickTake lived up to only half its hype. You could shoot a picture and view it onscreen inside of five minutes, but in every other way it was inferior to any film camera costing one third as much. To quote myself at the time: "Thanks to significant compression and interpolation requirements, the image detail is disappointingly coarse. The camera can take only eight pictures at a time when set to the more passable of the two image resolutions, and it doesn't even have a focus ring or zoom option. All things considered, it's one of the best gadgets of its kind, but it doesn't yet qualify as a practical tool." In other words, it's a great toy for rich people and reviewers, but I don't advise that you buy it.

But although the QuickTake was the kind of invention only a trade show could love, it ushered in an industry of affordable cameras that will (if they haven't already) change the way you capture photographs. In the years since Apple dropped out of the market, virtually every major photographic supply manufacturer—including such familiar names such as Agfa, Canon, Fuji, Kodak, Nikon, and Olympus—has released a digital camera that is not only several times superior to the original QuickTake but qualifies as a solid investment to boot. While the market remains in a state of positive transition, today's tools deliver the results that professionals expect at prices they can reasonably afford. Makuhari may not be anything to look at, but it changed the way we see the world.

Whom This Book Is For

Real World Digital Photography is by no means the first book to cover digital cameras. Although the industry is still young, we've seen a half dozen books on the topic and we imagine many more are on their way. Digital imaging sells books, and publishers are rarely remiss in their duties to print them.

Most of the books we've seen, though, focus on consumers: Mom and Pop taking pictures of Junior and emailing the images to Grandma. Naturally, we're all for consumers; we've even been known to consume a little ourselves, at times conspicuously. But such a strict diet of consumerism creates the impression that digital cameras are nothing more than electronic playthings, and we very much disagree.

This is why Katrin Eismann and I decided to write a book to satisfy the needs of working professionals. By that, we don't *necessarily* mean professional photographers, although Katrin is well-versed in this area, having studied fine-art photography at the Rochester Institute of Technology. Rather, we mean people such as yourself who purchased a digital camera or have plans to make such a purchase in hopes of making a businesses run more efficiently. Among these professionals, we count graphic artists, designers, prepress professionals, editors, real estate agents, insurance adjusters, health-care professionals, and, yes, photographers. We also mean teachers and students, the latter of which undoubtedly have professional aspirations in mind.

This may sound like a large collection of people to accommodate in a single book, but no matter which of these groups you fall into, you require an objective and authoritative discussion of the material. You need to know how these cameras work, how to buy a camera that will best serve your needs, how to shoot pictures like a pro, how to edit digital images to make them look their best, and what to do with your images after you've shot them. We know of no other book that covers each and every one of these essential criteria. And it's our hope that if and when such a book comes along, we will have covered the topic with sufficient scope and accuracy that ours will be the one and only book you ever need.

If you should decide to toss the camera in the luggage the next time you take a break and fly to a tropical island, then the information in this book will serve you in your role as an enthusiast as well. Just like you, we take breaks as professionals and put in our time as consumers. The difference is that when you wear your professional's hat, you need serious information—the kind of information that this book has been uniquely crafted to provide. Readability and attention to the detail are what *Real World Digital Photography* is all about.

Names You Can Trust

The other question we would have, were we in your shoes, is: who are you and why should we trust you? For my part, I've been writing books on computer graphics and electronic publishing since 1986, when I started as art director at one of the earliest all-digital service bureaus in the United States. In addition to selling more books on digital imaging than any other author, I review digital cameras for *Macworld* and *Newsweek* magazines. Since first laying hands on the QuickTake, I've worked with more than 100 different digital camera models, including nearly every one priced under $5,000.

If my background is writing and design, Katrin's is photography through and through. After studying electronic still photography beginning in its infancy (starting in 1989), Katrin served as the first intern at the Kodak Center for Imaging in Camden, Maine. In addition to her work as a fine-art photographer, she is perhaps the foremost lecturer and teacher on digital photography, with regular engagements throughout North America, Europe, and Asia. Throughout the book, she balances my digital ramblings with concrete guidelines for shooting better images, with special attention to high-end cameras in the $5,000 and up range.

It's my belief that I chose the perfect partner to create the foremost guide on digital photography and that I didn't make a mistake by including myself in the bargain. As always, we'd like to know what you think. To write me, visit my Web site at *www.dekemc.com* and click on the Contact Deke button. You can visit Katrin at *www.photoshopdiva.com*.

Please bear in mind that we get far more email than we can reasonably handle, so don't be surprised if we don't respond to your email in a timely fashion or even in the same calendar year. If you have a question that requires quick action, we're probably not the right people to turn to. Also, please—and we beg you—do not write us to ask why your camera isn't working properly or to get our opinion on a camera that you're thinking of buying. Despite our pleas, we get a hundred or more questions just like that every month; to answer them all, we would have to clone ourselves. (If you happen to have developed a reliable cloning machine, please send along the schematics at your earliest convenience and we'll see what we can work out in trade.)

Other Criteria

If we were to offer additional advice for judging the merits of this book, we would urge you to examine the table of contents to make sure that we cover the areas of digital photography that matter to you most. You might also care to look up questions in the index to see if they're answered to your satisfaction. Finally, check out the quality of the figures and color plates to make sure our standards match your own.

We sincerely hope you'll agree that *Real World Digital Photography* is the best book of its kind on the market. If you have thoughts for improving our content, please don't hesitate to let us know. In the meantime, sit back, relax, and let us show you how to capture and enhance first-rate photographs without once going to film. We guarantee you won't find this information on any trade show floor—in this or any other country.

—Deke McClelland

CHAPTER ONE

Why Use a Digital Camera?

The stereotypical view of digital cameras is not a flattering one. According to prevalent wisdom, the cameras are astronomically expensive. They lack the controls that professionals and adept amateurs have come to expect. And, most damning, digital photographs don't hold up when compared with those shot to film.

There's no denying that digital photography has earned this criticism. Like any emerging technology, its first tottering steps were awkward, even comical, when compared with the graceful strides of the entrenched standard—in this case, film.

But as time progresses, the stereotypes are growing less and less relevant. The field of digital photography is less than ten years old, and yet it's already every bit as viable as its film-based forerunner. Nowadays you can select from dozens of digital cameras priced under $500, and even purchase a serviceable refurbished model for less than $100. Many affordable models offer zoom lenses, manual focus over-rides, and exposure controls, not to mention image compression and other options that have no equivalent in traditional photography. At the very high end, digital produces unparalleled quality, capturing minute levels of detail without the grain inherent in film.

And it's only just begun. Prices are dropping, capabilities are expanding, and quality is improving. Whatever your feelings about film, it's a fairly sedentary technology, unlikely to change dramatically in the next century. In contrast, digital imaging is evolving at a pace that very nearly exceeds our ability to report on it. Deke imagines that most computer and design professionals will swear off film in the next five to ten years and never go back. Katrin believes film will continue to have a place for several decades to come, especially among professional photographers. But we both agree that digital imaging is a potent force that will earn its way into all walks of life, from weekend snapshots to studio photography.

So to answer our question, why use a digital camera?—because it's simply the best solution for the widest range of applications and occupations. This chapter explores the many areas in which digital photography excels, the few where it continues to fall short, and how digital is likely to improve in the future.

AFFORDABILITY AND IMAGE QUALITY

Our enthusiasm for digital technology is in no way intended as an epitaph for film. For the record, film is *not* dead. Its role is likely to grow significantly less commonplace and more specialized as time goes on. But for the present, it continues to enjoy a few important advantages.

For example, it's little surprise that as a mature technology, film offers the better performance-to-price ratio. Let's say you've budgeted $500—to our minds, a sizable but ultimately affordable chunk of change. For that price, you can purchase a very capable 35mm *single-lens reflex* (SLR) film camera that accepts interchangeable lenses and captures sharply focused, highly detailed photographs. But switch to digital, and $500 buys you a point-and-shoot device with a fixed lens. Extras like zoom functions and exposure controls are typically reserved for the $750 to $1,000 range.

But where the price of a film camera escalates as you add features, the price of a digital camera is inexorably linked to image quality. More money buys you sharper focus, greater clarity, more-accurate color, and all-around better-looking photographs. For $10,000 or more, you can purchase a digital camera that captures sharper pictures than film does. But unless you're a professional studio photographer (or a super-rich trust-fund baby), you may have to make do with something less.

Digital Quality On the Mend

The amount of image quality that $500 buys is improving rapidly. The following brief walk down memory lane demonstrates how film still reigns supreme in this price range but won't for much longer:

- **A couple of years ago** One of the earliest digital cameras in this price range was the easy to use but incapable Casio QV-10, introduced in the relatively ancient days of 1996. As shown with alarming accuracy in Figure 1-1, pictures shot with this camera suffered from gummy details, indistinct focus, and exaggerated contrast. They looked less like photographs than third-generation photocopies of photographs. But because of its low price, the QV-10 was very popular, doing much to create a negative impression of digital cameras as a whole.

- **Last year** The positive legacy of the QV-10 and other bargain devices was that they drove down prices. Prior to 1996, the asking price of an entry-level digital camera was $800; afterward, $500 was about the most a savvy shopper could expect to pay. The picture quality of this new round of affordable cameras was much improved, with more-stable details and smoothly modeled surfaces. But outlines of objects often appeared jagged, as the enlarged detail in Figure 1-2 shows.

Figure 1-1 This image captured with a Casio QV-10 represents a low point for digital picture quality.

Figure 1-2 Within a year, cameras like the Canon PowerShot 350 combined improved picture quality with affordability.

- **Now** If you have $500 burning a hole in your pocket today, settle for nothing less than a so-called *megapixel* camera, which captures significantly more digital information than similarly priced cameras a year ago. Shot with a Kodak DC200, the photograph in Figure 1-3 contains three times as much detail as the one in Figure 1-2, and 12 times as much as the image in Figure 1-1. More detail translates to crisper edges, sharper focus, and more-realistic texturing.

Figure 1-3 At the time of this writing, $500 buys you the megapixel Kodak DC200, which begins to approximate the quality of film.

Film is still better, though precisely how much better is difficult to say due to different film types. Although there isn't a direct correlation between the amount of data captured by film and the amount captured by digital, it's safe to say that a 35mm color negative—like the one used to capture the image in Figure 1-4—contains roughly six times as much detail as the digital image in Figure 1-3. That's a significant gap, but at the present rate of improvement, it's easy to imagine affordable digital cameras catching up to film in the next couple of years.

The ability of $500 digital cameras to capture accurate colors has also increased dramatically over the past few years. Color Plate 1-1 on page C1 offers full-color examples of pumpkin images captured with the Casio QV-10, the Canon PowerShot 350, the Kodak DC200, and 35mm film. The Casio can't manage to paint colors inside the lines, let alone make an even marginally believable stab at the right hues and shades. The Canon colors are garish, verging on a neon intensity not normally found in nature. But the Kodak gets the color very close to exactly right. In fact, at present, the color response of even affordable digital cameras matches that of film under normal light. Only under low light does film retain a significant edge.

Figure 1-4 This image from a stock photo library was shot to 35mm film and digitized with a flatbed scanner.

Factoring In the Other Costs

Not all digital-versus-film myths favor film. The most common myth put forth by digital camera vendors is that digital photography saves you money in the long run. But as Table 1-1 demonstrates, even assuming that the prices of digital and film cameras are fixed at $500, this is hardly the case.

	Digital	Film
Camera	$500	$500
Per-photo fees (1,000 photos)	125	250
Computer	2,000	NA
Printer	500	NA
TOTAL	$3,125	$750

All costs are rough ballpark figures, based on the assumption of a $500 camera. Your costs will surely vary.

Table 1-1 Digital Versus Film, the Real Costs

The argument for the myth goes something like this: Buying a film camera is like joining an expensive club. The $500 you spend for the camera itself is merely the entry fee. Then you pay the equivalent of a subscription in the film and development costs, which may translate to hundreds of dollars per year. Meanwhile, digital cameras—bless their hearts—require neither film nor development, so the one and only cost is the initial investment.

Er, not quite. First, you have to have someplace to store your vast library of digital images, which requires that you periodically purchase media like Zip disks or recordable CD-ROMs. Second, if you have any desire to print your photographs, you incur ink and paper costs. And third, digital cameras burn through batteries, so you need to stock up on those.

Correctly managed, those periodic costs are small—about 10 cents to store an image and 15 cents to print it, for a total of 25 cents per picture. (Printing costs vary widely depending on the printer and paper, but 15 cents is a safe average.) Halfway decent film and developing costs run about 50 cents per picture, about $4 for a 24-exposure roll of film and $8 for developing. So while the incremental costs favor digital, they aren't so wildly different that they're likely to have a dramatic impact on your pocketbook.

Where the argument breaks down is in the supposition that the cost of the digital camera is your only entrance fee. To use a film camera, all you need is the camera and a roll of film. To use a digital camera, you need a fairly powerful computer stocked with 32MB or more of RAM, a large enough hard drive to hold the image-editing software and a hundred or more images (about 1GB will get you by), some sort of removable media device to store last year's pictures, and optionally, a printer. If you already have these prerequisites, then the price of the camera is your only obligatory fee. But if you don't own a computer, or if your computer is more than, say, three or four years old, then you're looking at another $2,000 to $3,000 worth of investment.

> **NOTE:** *A few vendors balk at factoring a computer into the costs of a digital camera. After all, you can cable the camera directly to a printer or view the photographs on your television. These techniques qualify as diverting party tricks, and no serious user would regularly rely on either. And without a computer, it's difficult to archive the images for later retrieval.*

So when push comes to shove, you get more for less with film. Prices will go down, quality will go up, but the computer will always be a cost factor. And as any technically proficient person knows, computers demand regular upgrades and repairs whose costs are matched only by those of luxury automobiles.

STORAGE AND DUPLICATION

When you shoot a picture with a film camera, the film serves two purposes. It captures the photograph and then stores it for later development. Even after you develop the film, the exposed negative stands as the one true original from which future prints can be made. See Figure 1-5.

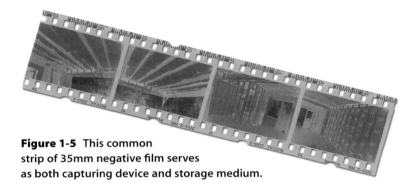

Figure 1-5 This common strip of 35mm negative film serves as both capturing device and storage medium.

Not so with digital cameras. As we explain in intricate detail in Chapter 3, an image sensor captures the photograph and transfers it to a separate storage medium. Most cameras costing less than $1,000 store images to cards the size of small Post-it notes, like those shown in Figure 1-6. The $10,000-and-higher variety store images on larger hard drives. Or, in the most extreme cases, the camera has to be tethered directly to a computer.

Obviously, film has the upper hand compared with the clunky hard drives and cables associated with high-end, professional-level digital cameras. But the dapper cards from Figure 1-6 provide some key advantages that put them at least on a par with film, if not ahead.

Figure 1-6 Measuring about 1.5 inches across, these electronic cards hold photographs until you can transfer them to a computer.

Availability and Flexibility

The main advantage of film as a storage device is that it's commonly available. Visit the most meagerly equipped drugstore in the deepest, darkest corner of the world and you'll find a dozen rolls of 35mm film. Not so with digital camera cards. Most folks have never laid eyes on the items in Figure 1-6, and yet these are *the* standards in digital photography. If you happen to fill up a card in downtown Manhattan near one of those stuffed-to-the-gills, closet-size electronics stores, you might be able to purchase another card. Otherwise, what you brought is what you got.

But where you can expose a roll of film just once, you can use a digital storage card over and over again. After you shoot a cardful of pictures, you transfer the pictures to your computer. Then erase the card and it's fresh as an electronic daisy, ready to use again. We suspect that each card has a finite life, but in two or three years of using them, we haven't managed to wear one out.

The upshot is that you can take many more pictures than you could afford to take with film. Back in Table 1-1, we claimed that the average cost of a digital photo is 25 cents. But we also mentioned that this quarter-a-picture value hinges on the assumption that you want to print the image. If your needs don't involve printing, it costs at most 10 cents to store the picture. And if you take a picture you don't like and end up throwing it away, the cost is almost nil.

A digital camera transforms the common shutterbug into a radiant, nimble shutterfly. No need to worry about whether that picture will turn out. Shoot it five to ten times from different angles, flash on, flash off, zoomed in, zoomed out, and you're bound to get the shot you want, as in Figure 1-7.

Figure 1-7 Reusable storage cards free you up to shoot a picture again and again until you get it right.

Surviving the Destructive Forces of Time

As storage mediums go, film is quite durable. Properly cared for, it can last 100 years or more (as much film already has). But last though it may, film does age.

The photograph of the Eiffel Tower on the left side of Figure 1-8 looks great, considering that it dates back to World War II. But in all probability, it looked more like the digitally restored version on the right when it was first captured in 1944. Even meticulously preserved, film can't help but fade over time.

Figure 1-8 Film is every bit as rugged as computer media. But it does fade over time, as witnessed by the original (left) and restored (right) versions of this 55-year-old photo.

Sadly, *care* and *meticulous* are not words that apply to the way most of us treat our old prints and negatives. Furthermore, consumer-grade film stock was never designed to be handed down as a family heirloom. If you can find a picture you shot in the 1970s that looks as good as Eiffel Tower #1 in Figure 1-8, you're beating the odds. Color shift, yellowing, scratches, and even rot are par for the course.

Digital media is no more impervious to the ravages of time than film is. The half-life of a typical magnetic disk may be as short as 10 years; after that, the chances of your being able to retrieve information decrease exponentially. Optical disks and CD-ROMs should last longer, but given the recent introduction of these technologies, it's too early to be sure.

However, we can be sure of two things, both of which work to the advantage of digital cameras:

- A digital photo stored to disk will never fade, yellow, wrinkle, rip, scratch, or rot. The disk might fail—in which case that particular version is lost—but if you can recover a digital photo, it will look as good as the day you shot it.

- With film, there is one and only one original. Every copy made from the original is just that—a copy, infinitesimally (if not dramatically) inferior to the original. Furthermore, duplicating film can actually harm the original. But when you copy a digital photo from one disk to another, the copy is *exactly identical* to the original. The copy, therefore, serves as a new original.

The upshot is that a moderately diligent person can preserve a digital photo as long as it's needed simply by making periodic backup copies as infrequently as once a decade. As a result, the original version of a digital image shot in the year 2000 could survive entirely intact, without a single flaw, until the year 5000, a claim you can't make for film or any other medium. To learn how to make your photos outlast the human race, read Chapter 14, "Archiving Digital Images."

SPEED AND CONVENIENCE

Speed is a hands-down advantage to digital photography. Unlike with film, you don't have to develop digital images. Seconds after you press the shutter release, the picture is ready to go. Within minutes of shooting a digital photograph, you can drop it into a newsletter, add it to a Web page, or print it and hand it off to a colleague. There's simply no waiting.

But digital photography goes beyond the mere gimme-gimme thrill of instant gratification. You can also preview images to make sure you like the lighting and composition before you waste time on a bad camera angle or idea. Virtually all digital cameras manufactured since 1996 let you preview any image in memory on an LCD screen, as in the case of the Kodak DC260 shown in Figure 1-9. If the LCD isn't big enough for you to see details and you aren't near a computer, you can connect the camera to a TV and examine on a grander scale.

Also, by capturing digital photographs, you send your images where the money is. Most high-paying jobs require you to be compatible with a digital workflow. You can either shoot to film, develop slides or prints, and then scan the images to a computer, or you can eliminate the middleman and shoot directly to disk. Why waste time and resources when all financial incentives favor efficiency and conservation?

Figure 1-9 The DC260's LCD screen lets you preview pictures in memory, delete images you don't like, and even zoom in on details.

Finally, digital makes photography convenient. Need a quick picture of a dog? There's no need to search through catalogs of stock art when the world is your stock library. Take Fido outside and snap a few spontaneous canine moments. You not only get the job done, but you squeeze in some quality time. Need a wood texture? Shoot a table. Some clouds? Shoot the sky. Your boss needs a quick head shot? Take her picture. When you can produce a picture from beginning to end in a matter of minutes, there's no need to plan, consider, or hesitate. Just grab the camera and get to work.

To prove our point, Deke took the thermos that holds his daily ration of morning enthusiasm and turned it into the product shot featured in Figure 1-10. To make things scientific, he timed his actions and rounded them to the nearest minute:

1. Wipe fingerprints off thermos, 1 minute.

2. Set up tripod and camera (Nikon CoolPix 900), 3 minutes.

3. Snap 12 pictures of thermos, 5 minutes.

4. Transfer 12 pictures to computer, 1 minute.

5. Cull through photos, select best shot, 2 minutes.

6. Edit photograph and add text in Adobe Photoshop, 27 minutes.

7. E-mail completed figure to editor, 4 minutes.

Grand total, 43 minutes.

You may notice that more than half of the time, 27 minutes, was spent editing the photograph in Photoshop, a professional image-editing program. Without the editing, the process took just 16 minutes. Even if we had a relay team with an on-site darkroom, we couldn't work that quickly with film.

Figure 1-10 From inception to delivery, this digital product shot took 43 minutes, a fraction of the time it would have taken with film.

COLOR AND FOCUS MODIFICATIONS

If you operate your own darkroom, you know the value of controlling the development and printing process. You can bring out highlights, details, and colors that you know are there because you saw them in person when you shot the photo. It's a lot more work than passing your film off to a commercial developer, but the results usually justify the effort.

On the other hand, if you're like most people, you drop off your exposed film at a drugstore or one-hour photo lab and let them develop the photos. It's easy and relatively inexpensive, but it's also risky. The one-size-fits-all approach of commercial development favors quantity over quality. This isn't to say your pictures necessarily come out bad, but they probably would've emerged brighter, crisper, and more colorful if you had been in charge.

Digital photography puts you in charge of the darkroom—only in this case, the darkroom is a computer, not a dimly lit room full of toxic chemicals. Naturally, you don't have to take advantage of this newfound capability; if you're in a rush, you can accept what the camera gives you and be done with it. But if you spend 10 to 15 minutes correcting color and focus, you can turn a drab, lackluster photograph into something special.

Figure 1-11 shows an image captured with a Fuji MX-700. This little point-and-shoot camera is small enough to fit in your pocket, but as the figure shows, it has a tendency to deliver dark pictures. Our photo also happens to be crooked, with the tower leaning slightly to the right—an error on the part of the photographer, not the camera.

Thankfully, both problems can be corrected. Most digital cameras costing less than $1,000 include some kind of image-editing software, all of which offer controls for lightening and rotating images. You can also crop a photo—great for homing in on the central subject—and heighten the focus to give it a sharper look. All these operations were employed to achieve the corrected image in Figure 1-12. Time spent: less than 15 minutes.

Figure 1-11 Shot with a Fuji MX-700, this Puerto Rican *garitas* is dark, soft, and crooked—three simple problems to remedy.

Figure 1-12 By lightening the colors, sharpening the focus, rotating the image 1 degree counterclockwise, and cropping away some of the wall and sky, we arrive at this more representative photograph.

The differences between Figures 1-11 and 1-12 are a bit subtle because the images are printed in black and white. But switch to color, and both problems and corrections become much more pronounced, as illustrated by Color Plates 1-2 and 1-3 on page C2. Again shot with a Fuji MX-700, Color Plate 1-2 is overly dark with a yellow tint—or *color cast*—typical of the camera. The clarity is good, but the image appears to have contracted an advanced case of jaundice.

Color Plate 1-3 shows how great the image can look if properly corrected. By applying four commands, we've managed to counteract the yellow cast, brighten the colors, sharpen the focus, and crop the horizontal image to create a more balanced vertical composition.

> **NOTE:** Not all problems are correctable. For example, although you can enhance the focus of an image by sharpening edges that are already in good shape, you can't bring a blurry image into focus. Similarly, if you shoot into the sun and the sky turns bright white, you can't darken the sky and draw out the clouds because all the camera captured was a bunch of white. Computers can't create something out of nothing; they can merely rearrange information that's already there. Fortunately, rearranging is all a well-photographed image needs.

With a little practice, you can learn to correct the color and focus of an image with relatively little effort. Chapter 12 explains the process in detail.

OTHER CONSIDERATIONS

Film cameras currently outsell digital cameras by a factor of about 20 to one. So it stands to reason that supplies favor the film camera owner. Thus far, we've seen underwater housings for only two digital cameras under $1,000, the Sony Mavica and the Hitachi MPEG Cam (neither of which we recommend, incidentally). Also, as a rule, digital cameras under $1,000 don't support 35mm lenses, and only a few models permit you to hot-sync to a studio flash. On the plus side, most digital cameras subscribe to the same basic look-and-feel as film cameras, all but a very few mount on standard tripods, and you can always load up on new accessories if you have a mind to.

Possibly the worst aspect of digital cameras is that they require you to update your skills and learn new approaches, particularly if you have only limited knowledge of computers. But hopefully this is cause for anticipation, not concern. After all, you wisely purchased this book, and we promise to make your education as engaging and effortless as possible.

Film or digital, it's still photography. This permits us to benefit from more than 150 years of hard-won and widely shared knowledge. Regardless of the medium, the photographic skills we learned yesterday continue to provide the foundation for the photographs we shoot tomorrow. Digital photography doesn't supplant film. Rather, it ushers us into a new chapter of visual and artistic expression.

CHAPTER TWO

Types of Digital Cameras

No matter how you use photography — as a hobbyist, small business owner, real estate agent, graphic designer, new media artist, educator, doctor, or even as a professional photographer — a digital camera that can meet your needs exists today. Consider what you need a camera to do, and that will help you decide which type to buy.

Are you a graphic designer who needs a camera to plan page layouts? A real estate agent who wants to be able to take good pictures both indoors and outdoors? A professional photographer looking for a camera that works with studio lights or flash equipment and delivers the highest quality available?

This chapter starts by asking four questions to help you to define what you need a camera to do. Then we discuss five general categories of digital cameras and show how people just like you are using cameras from each category on a daily basis to take great pictures.

Before you buy anything, think about what you want, what you need, and what you can afford. Deciding on the right digital camera will be a lot easier if you ask and answer the following four questions.

- **Why do you take pictures?** People take photographs for different reasons. Some work with photographs on a daily basis, others want to capture and share that special family moment, and then there are the curious people (like us) who enjoy experimenting with the latest digital technology. No matter what your reasons for taking pictures, identifying what you do with the photographs is the first step in finding the best digital camera. How will you use your photographs? Will they be shared with family and friends, used professionally in a magazine or on the Web, or needed at work or school?

- **What image quality do you need?** The ideal image quality is the one that is enough for your needs. It's like being hungry: Sometimes you're just a little hungry, and a piece of fruit is satisfying; other times you could eat everything in sight. The entry-level cameras are like the fruit, whereas the professional-level cameras can serve a feast of image information. With digital cameras, if you bite off more than you can chew, you not only get digital file indigestion—you will have spent way too much money.

- **What are you going to photograph?** Different subjects pose different challenges. For example, taking pictures of fast-moving sports action or close-ups of your stamp collection requires cameras that are designed to do two completely different things. For action pictures, the camera needs to respond instantly as the shutter is pressed. For pictures of postage stamps, the camera must be able to focus and frame accurately at extreme close-up range.

- **How experienced are you?** Are you the type of person who wants to control the lighting, exposure, and focus like a professional photographer does, or do you just want to point the camera and shoot great pictures? Each digital camera features different controls and options—ranging from full automatic to manual mode—and knowing how much control you want plays an important role in making the right purchasing decision.

The answers to those four questions are the first steps toward deciding what is the best digital camera for you. Next we'll look at the types of cameras.

To help you decide on the best camera, we've broken digital cameras down into five categories. Each camera type is classified according to cost, quality, and ease-of-use, as well as the kind of photography it's best suited for. Table 2-1 gives you a cheat sheet of the categories.

- **Entry-level** Basic digital cameras with few features and limited image quality.

- **Deluxe point-and-shoot** These cameras offer more controls and produce better images than the entry-level ones do.

- **Professional lite** Features, quality, and ease-of-use make these cameras ideal for many different jobs, ranging from graphic and Web design to insurance and real estate documentation to producing in-house catalogs.

- **Professional** The Ferraris of digital cameras, producing images that meet or exceed the quality of film.

- **Gadget** Toy cameras, and cameras that are built into computers.

Camera Type	Image Quality	Features	Price	Best Used for
Entry-level	low	none	$100–400	snapshots, Web
Deluxe point-and-shoot	good	Few	$400–800	low-end catalog, training manuals, education
Professional lite	very good	good variety	$800–2,000	real estate, insurance, documentation
Professional	excellent	many*	$5,000–50,000	advertising, art reproduction, photojournalism, fashion
Gadget	low	none	$60-200	having fun

*This category includes five subcategories, which will be addressed throughout the book.

Table 2-1 Types/Benefits of Digital Cameras.

Each digital camera category has its advantages, disadvantages, and appropriate uses. You will learn that you don't always need the most expensive digital camera to do the best job. For example, using a professional-quality camera to take pictures at the company picnic would be like taking the Concorde to go across town—a waste of technology and money.

ENTRY-LEVEL DIGITAL CAMERAS

Digital cameras in the $100 to $400 range tend to be simple devices that are good enough for snapshots and suitable for very small prints and Web images. Some people also refer to these cameras as PHD cameras (*push here, dummy*) because they don't have features like exposure controls, zoom lenses, or built-in LCD screens for you to see your pictures right away. Think of them as the Instamatics of digital cameras.

Entry-level digital cameras work with pictures of simple subjects where the success of the picture doesn't rely on showing detail. As Figure 2-1 shows, the picture of the American flag works well because the subject is very bold and clear. On the other hand, the picture of the flattened beer bottle (Figure 2-2), a picture with many fine details, fails miserably because the simple entry-level camera just cannot show fine details.

Figure 2-1 Large, simple, highly graphical subjects look good when photographed with entry-level digital cameras.

Figure 2-2 Entry-level digital cameras don't handle fine detail very well.

Who Is Using Entry-Level Digital Cameras?

The snapshot taker, graphic designer, insurance claims adjuster, and educator whose image-quality expectations aren't too high can use these cameras to take pictures for in-house reports and Web presentations. Many entry-level digital cameras, such as the Agfa ePhoto 307, Apple QuickTake 150 or 200, Canon PowerShot 350, Kodak DC-40 and DC-50, and Olympus D-220L may no longer be available for sale, but if you have one you can still use it—if you keep your pictures simple.

- **Are you a graphic or Web designer?** Even though the image quality is very low, you can still use an entry-level camera to take pictures of products, people, or locations "For Position Only" in a page layout. After the client has approved the concept, you can hire a professional photographer to compose, light, and photograph the subject to your specifications.

- **Did you have an accident?** Work with an entry-level camera to document your insurance claims reports. These cameras provide more then enough image quality to prove that there is a dent in the right rear bumper of a car (Figure 2-3). Professional insurance adjusters use entry-level digital cameras to take pictures of automobile and property damage claims on a daily basis.

Figure 2-3 Shot with a Kodak DC-50, this photo can be attached to an insurance claim by the claims adjuster.

- **Do you have a point to make?** Teachers work with entry-level cameras to document class projects and add excitement to their classes. The relative low cost of these cameras reduces some of the anxiety of letting an excited student handle them. Some cameras, such as the Sony Mavica MVC-FD71, store the photos on an ordinary floppy disk so the students can easily take their pictures home to show their parents.

Why Wouldn't You Buy Entry-Level?

After the novelty of these cameras wears off, and the reality of the lower image quality sets in, many people put these cameras in the "to be forgotten" drawer right beside that broken Walkman. If this might be you—if you think you need to show more detail, or you want better color and overall picture quality—you can avoid disappointment and frustration by spending a little more money and buying a deluxe point-and-shoot digital camera.

DELUXE POINT-AND-SHOOT DIGITAL CAMERAS

Deluxe point-and-shoot digital cameras cost $400 to $800 and offer nearly the same quality as a single-use disposable film camera. Delivering higher image quality than the entry-level digital cameras, they also typically offer some of the following features: a zoom lens, LCD screen, removable storage, the ability to do time-lapse photography, manual camera controls. These cameras are best used for in-house publications, low-end product catalogs, training manuals, and Web work. As with the entry-level digital cameras, taking pictures of highly graphical subjects produces good results, as seen in Figure 2-4. Examples of good deluxe point-and-shoot digital cameras include the Canon PowerShot A5, Kodak DC 210, Toshiba PDR-M3, and Ricoh RDC-4300.

Figure 2-4 This picture was taken with a deluxe point-and-shoot camera, an Olympus D-300L.

Use these cameras when the photograph will not be printed any larger than about 3 by 5 inches. Many of the deluxe point-and-shoot digital cameras have very good image quality, as seen in the images taken with the Ricoh RDC-4300 in Figure 2-5.

Figure 2-5 Taken with the Ricoh RDC-4300, these photos offer enough image quality to be used in a Web site catalog or for an in-house publication.

Is a Deluxe Point-and-Shoot Right for You?

For the graphic designer, real estate agent, educator, and for some professional applications, these cameras offer a legitimate alternative to snapping pictures with film and waiting for the film to be processed and printed.

- **Are you designing online catalogs or sales brochures?** Use a deluxe point-and-shoot camera to take the pictures quickly and easily. Experiment with the camera to photograph textures, skies, colors, shapes, and so on, to create original backgrounds and elements for design projects.

- **Does your business need photographs for inventory, sales catalogs, or employee ID cards?** The deluxe point-and-shoot digital cameras are ideal for these purposes. Real estate and travel agencies use them to take pictures of properties and resorts all the time. In Figure 2-6, an antique dealer photographed an enamel tray that a customer wanted to see. If the antique dealer had used a film camera, he would have had to take the picture, wait for processing and printing, photocopy the photo (losing detail and color), and fax it to the customer—who would not be very impressed with a fax of a black square on white paper. With a deluxe point-and-shoot camera, the dealer can just snap the picture, load the picture into the computer, and within minutes e-mail the picture to the client —and voila! the antique tray has found a new home.

Figure 2-6 Working with the Ricoh RDC-4300, an antique dealer can take the photo and e-mail the image to an interested customer within minutes.

- **Do you need to make student facebooks, track a student's progress, or document a school project?** If so, working with a deluxe point-and-shoot digital camera is a natural. In Figure 2-7 an elementary school teacher used the Ricoh RDC-4300 to take pictures of science and social studies projects. And for students, working with a digital camera is a great way to add excitement to a class report about the field trip to the Statue of Liberty (Figure 2-8) or a local museum.

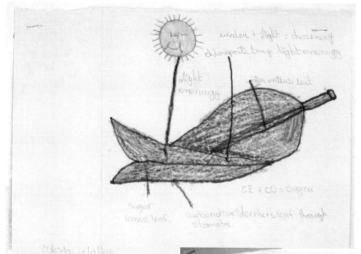

Figure 2-7 Both images were taken with the Ricoh RDC-4300, with automatic flash. The image on the top is from a science project on photosynthesis, and the image on the bottom says no to drugs. Both originals were 11 by 17 inches in size.

Figure 2-8 Working with a deluxe point-and-shoot digital camera is a great way to document a class field trip.

- **Want to liven up your next party?** If you're an amateur photographer, bringing a deluxe point-and-shoot digital camera to a party guarantees that you'll be the center of attention. Once you take a few pictures and start showing them around on the LCD screen, you'll be getting more party invitations than you'll know what to do with, because at a party everyone wants to have a picture taken (Figure 2-9).

- **Do you need to scout locations or take visual notes?** A professional photographer can use deluxe point-and-shoot digital cameras to scout locations and collect prop ideas. Believe us, it beats making notes and trying to remember all that stuff. If we had to choose one camera in this category that a pro would gladly carry in a shirt pocket, it would be the Leica Digilux—the exact same camera as the Fuji MX-700, but with the Leica name and some added styling. It's easy to use, fits in a shirt pocket, and is great for note-taking.

Figure 2-9 This fun party picture was taken with a Kodak DC-200. *Photo by Janie Fitzgerald.*

Why Not Use a Deluxe Point-and-Shoot Digital Camera?

If you need to make prints larger than 4 x 6 inches or are looking for manual camera controls, then these deluxe point-and-shoot cameras are not the best for the job. For example, the medical professional who relies on accurate detail and the need to control lighting will not be happy with the deluxe point-and-shoot cameras. If you need more control and image quality, then the next category will interest you—the professional lite cameras offer amazing image quality, at prices that aren't too terribly high.

PROFESSIONAL LITE DIGITAL CAMERAS

Forget everything about the poor quality and expensive digital camera cliches that we talked about in Chapter 1. The professional lite digital cameras come in between $800 and $2,000, and they don't compromise on image quality, ease-of-use, or features. For advanced amateurs, graphic designers, small businesses, museums, and medical professionals, and yes, even for the critical professional photographer, these cameras deliver a solid one-two punch: ease-of-use and great-looking pictures.

The major feature that sets the professional lite cameras apart from the entry-level and deluxe point-and-shoot cameras is the amount of picture information they capture. Inside every digital camera is a chip that captures the picture, and in the pro lite group the quality and size of that chip increases. These cameras are sometimes called *megapixel* cameras, meaning that they have a chip called a *charge-coupled device* (CCD) that has more than one million sensors. More sensors means more image information, and that means better pictures. In Chapter 3, we go into all those nuts and bolts in great detail, but for now the important thing to learn is this: A bigger chip with more sensors gives you better pictures with clearer details, sharper edges, and better colors.

Good examples of professional lite digital cameras include the Fuji DS-330, Nikon CoolPix 900s, Kodak DC 260, Olympus D-620L, Canon PowerShot Pro70, and Sony DSC-D700. Many of these cameras offer manual and automatic exposure control and include an optical zoom lens, LCD screen, and flash sync connections.

These cameras capture images that are of extremely good quality (Figure 2-12) as long as you don't expect to print wall-size posters. Note: print quality is a subjective term that depends on the viewer's eye, experience, and need for quality, as well as the type of printer used to make the print. In this book, high photographic quality means a print that is so good in regard to color, saturation, detail, and sharpness that the average viewer will think it was made with film camera.

TWICE THE MEGAPIXELS

Just as we were going to press, professional lite cameras with CCDs offering two million pixels—two megapixel cameras—were being announced. The first models of this ilk to be released include the Fuji MX-2700, Toshiba PDE-M4, Ricoh RDC-5000, Olympus C-2000 Zoom, and Nikon CoolPix 950. The most important feature of these cameras is the higher resolution offered by the 2 million pixel CCD. Although we haven't had a chance to work with all of these cameras yet, our experience with preproduction models of the Fuji MX-2700 and Nikon CoolPix 950 have been very satisfying in terms of image quality and improved performance.

Figure 2-10 Working with the Fuji DC-300, the photographer was able to capture the subtle details of the orchids. See Color Plate 2-1 on page C3 for the full color and creative version of this image.

Who Uses Professional Lite Digital Cameras?

With the prices of digital cameras dropping, and the quality rising, professional lites offer the best quality and features that the small business owner, designer, doctor, and professional photographer require. Keep in mind that the quality these cameras deliver is in relationship to their CCD chip, features, and price. Even a pro lite camera can't beat the image quality of a well-exposed 35mm slide. But, as we mentioned in Chapter 1, the gap between the quality of digital cameras and film cameras is narrowing.

- **Doctors** use these cameras to monitor a patient's healing progress, and dentists document their work if the camera has good close-up capabilities and a flash that is not too harsh (Figure 2-11).

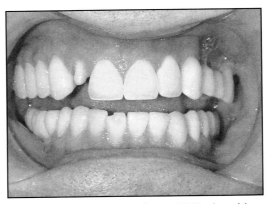

Figure 2-11 Dr. Vincent Celenza, DMD, shot this picture with a Nikon CoolPix 900s.

- **If you want to sell your house on the Web,** the combination of the Kodak DC 260 or Minolta Dimage EX 1500 Zoom (to shoot the pictures) and ScriptGenerator by Digitella (to produce the HTML code) makes putting pictures on the Web a cakewalk. This camera and script combination leads you through the picture-taking process, making sure that you get the best picture of the house and any rooms you want to highlight. While you're shooting, you can label each picture as the living room, bedroom, and so on, and tell the camera where to place the pictures on the Web page—left, right, or center. ScriptGenerator creates the HTML code for the Web page, complete with your pictures and labels. The combination of digital camera and scriptable software from Digitella or Flashpoint is changing cameras from picture-taking machines to computers that take, process, and produce images and a presentation framework for diverse uses.

- **Professional photographers** use pro lite digital cameras to document lighting, sets, props, and locations (Figure 2-12 and Color Plate 2-2 on page C3) and to shoot low-end catalogs. A photojournalist could use any of these cameras as a visual notetaker—and snapping a few photos of a hesitant subject and then playing them back on the LCD screen is a great icebreaker.

Figure 2-12 Working with the Nikon CoolPix 900s is a great way for a professional photographer to take location notes.

Why Not Use Pro Lite Digital Cameras?

If you need to make big prints, or if you're looking for a digital camera whose output equals that of images shot to Kodachrome film, then even the professional lite digital cameras don't offer the image quality you need. Considering how quickly the technology is improving, there will be a pro lite digital camera good enough for you in the near future. But at the time of this writing, if you're a museum or medical professional, or a professional photographer who needs to meet or exceed the quality of film and beat the deadline clock, then your only choice is to move up to the next category, professional digital cameras.

PROFESSIONAL DIGITAL CAMERAS

If you're not sitting down, we recommend that you take a seat and breathe deeply. All professional digital cameras share two attributes. First, they are expensive. These cameras cost $2,000 at the very low end, and prices climb from there into the many thousands, topping off at $50,000 for the Dicomed BigShot 4000. Second, the quality they deliver is astounding.

The professional digital camera category has five different types of technologies available: one-exposure, three-exposure, three-chip one-exposure, scanning, and piezoelectric. Each type does a specific type of photography very well. (See Chapter 3 for a description of each of these types of camera technology.)

Commercial, advertising, and portrait photographers, photojournalists, prepress folks, and museum personnel use professional digital cameras on a daily basis. As you might expect, these cameras offer precise control over exposure and composition, take advantage of interchangeable lenses, and deliver high-quality files that in many cases surpass the sharpness, color rendition, and resolution of comparable film formats, as seen in Color Plate 2-3 on page C4.

Who Uses Professional Digital Cameras?

People who shoot lots of pictures and require the highest quality possible are the primary users of professional digital cameras. The more pictures you take, the more time you save when you use a digital camera instead of film, and of course, time is money. Professional digital cameras don't show any bothersome film grain, and many deliver a wider dynamic range and better color fidelity than film. Many auction houses, museums, and high-end catalog photographers that demand the highest quality and the most accurate color have replaced their film cameras with digital cameras.

The painting in Figure 2-13 was shot with Fujichrome film and the Phase One Power Phase scanning camera. Both the film scan and digital camera captured 120MB of information—which is a lot of information.

Critical professionals, such as fashion photographers (Figure 2-14) and catalog photographers are working with professional digital cameras every day to produce high-quality work.

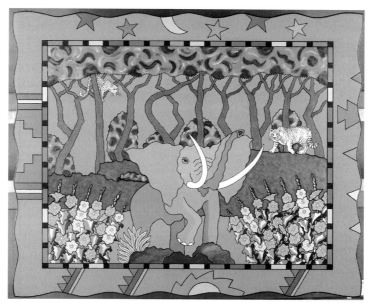

Figure 2-13 Working with a Phase One Power Phase scanning camera, the photographer captured 120MB of image information. *Photo by Andrew Rodney.*

Figure 2-14 Fashion photography by Kimberly Holcombe working with the Kodak DCS 460c, a portable, one-exposure camera based on a Nikon body. *Photos by Kimberly Holcombe.*

An additional benefit for a photojournalist (Figure 2-15) working with one-shot digital cameras such as the Kodak DCS 520 or Canon D2000 is the ability to get files to the newspaper picture editor via modem or portable phone. This beats having to drive back to the office to develop film. And more importantly, the photographer can stay with the story longer to take more pictures.

Figure 2-15 Being able to shoot quickly and stop fast action are imperative requirements for a photojournalist's digital camera. In this case, the image was captured with the AP-NC 2000e.
Photo by Rob Galbraith.

So, Why Isn't Everyone Using Professional Digital Cameras?

For many, professional digital cameras are an interesting exercise in technology, and we certainly hope that their prices will come within a range in which more of us can afford to buy them. Obviously, most people can't even think about spending $2,000 to $50,000 for *any* camera. Thankfully, most of the time you don't need the image quality that these cameras are capable of producing. Whereas deluxe point-and-shoot and professional lite cameras are like a perfect snack for the smaller image-quality appetite, the professional category is like a Thanksgiving feast. We hope you don't eat roast turkey with all the fixin's every single day.

GADGETS, JUST FOR FUN

Computer photo gadgets include computer "eye" cameras, toy cameras, and low-end videoconferencing cameras. We have worked and played—we call it research—with such items as the Nintendo Game Boy digital camera and Mattel's Barbie digital camera, as well as with videoconferencing cameras like the Logitek QuickCam, and our conclusion is that all of these gadgets are capable of capturing images.

A good example of a computer "eye" is featured on the Sony Vaio PCG-C1, a laptop computer that weighs in at a measly two pounds and offers plenty of computing features. The icing on the cake is a 270,000-pixel resolution digital camera that is mounted above the monitor. The camera can be used for videoconferencing, taking small still pictures, and even capturing video and sound.

Who Uses Gadget Cameras?

The digital toy camera's image quality is so quirky that only two kinds of people—enthusiastic kids and artists—can really appreciate it. The Nintendo Game Boy digital camera is actually an accessory to the original Game Boy. It uses a cartridge with a lens that turns 180 degrees and produces rudimentary electronic images on a liquid crystal display. The suggested retail price is $60 for the camera, and another $60 for a handheld black-and-white fax-quality printer.

The Mattel Barbie digital camera and CD-ROM is an effort to extend the popularity and novelty of the best-selling doll. The camera allows users to store a maximum of six 120 x 280-pixel pictures and then download them onto a Windows computer to make scrapbooks and postcards of Barbie's adventures with Ken. The suggested retail price is $70.

Artists are working with toy cameras to explore a new look or to get away from the pixel-perfect world of computer manipulation, as seen in two pictures (Figure 2-16) by Dan Burkholder, who is working with the Fisher-Price Photo Fun Maker digital camera. The Photo Fun Maker is a $45 digital camera that plays a tune as it spools the image from the video chip to the print head and then prints onto fax paper. The prints are crude and full of artifacts—which also means they can be beautiful and charming.

Why Wouldn't You Want a Gadget Camera?

At present, image quality from the computer photo gadget devices is pretty close to terrible. Gadgets are quirky and fun, and not meant for serious use or straightforward documentation. Yet they offer a glimpse into the future where entertainment, computer, phone, Internet, music, and image capture are all rolled into one package.

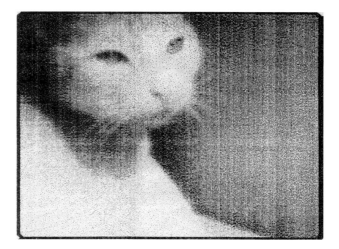

Figure 2-16 Both images were photographed with a Fisher-Price Photo Fun Maker digital camera. *Photos by Dan Burkholder.*

THE FIRST STEP IS HALF THE JOURNEY

Buying a digital camera can be a catch-22: "Should I buy or should I wait? But if I wait I can't work with the camera. But as soon as I buy one, a newer, better model will be released, so I'll wait. But then I can't work." We know what it feels like to buy a new piece of digital equipment, unwrap it, and then hear that the price has dropped or that a newer, better model was just announced. Because digital camera development is constantly speeding up, you might find yourself waiting and waiting and waiting for the next, better, newly improved model all the time. Meanwhile you'll never get a digital camera.

Although newer digital cameras are announced every day, the concepts presented in this chapter will definitely hold true for more than one model production cycle. Start by answering the four questions raised at the beginning of this chapter and learn about the different digital camera categories to identify the best one for you. After that, deciding on a specific digital camera shouldn't be a nerve-racking, budget-breaking experience.

Most important, the fact that a vendor has announced a new and improved digital camera doesn't mean that your camera's value suddenly vanishes. Both of us are still working with some digital cameras that aren't even on the market anymore. Of course it would be nice to always have the latest models—but it would be a full-time job just trying to keep up with the marketing hype, not to mention packing and unpacking new cameras every week. Besides, we're here to help you make the best decisions and get the most out of the cameras you already own or are about to buy.

CHAPTER THREE

How Digital Cameras Work (And Why You Should Care)

Where complex gadgetry is concerned, most people subscribe to the motto "work and let work." How the widget performs its magic is none of your business. Let the machine do its thing and you can do yours.

Normally, we're the first to agree. You don't have to know how your blender works to make a smoothie. You don't need to be able to reassemble a VCR to watch a movie. Fixing a device requires mechanical knowledge; using it does not.

But digital photography is a more demanding craft. For starters, a digital camera doesn't use film, so you can't expect it to respond like a film camera. While many aspects of digital photography mimic film photography, the device itself more closely resembles a video camera or a scanner. This has a profound effect on how a digital camera captures light, color, and movement.

Even more important, what you see is not necessarily what you get. When you peer through the viewfinder of a digital camera, you're looking not at the final photograph but rather at the basic composition on which the photograph will be based. The camera assembles the composition into a digital image according to a series of elements and operations that are common to all devices. If you take a moment to familiarize yourself with these elements and operations, you stand a better chance of predicting the outcome of your shots.

Like any creative tool, cameras respond best to informed use. Create a proper picture of digital cameras in your mind and you can get a digital camera to create proper pictures as well.

FROM LENS TO IMAGE SENSOR

A photograph enters a digital camera the same way it enters a film camera—through a series of lenses called the *lens element*. The lenses refract and focus light so it converges at a specific point, just as they do in a film camera. In fact, if you were to take apart a digital camera and examine its lens element—as we've done in Figure 3-1—it wouldn't look all that different from a film camera.

Infrared autofocus sensor   Primary lens element   Viewfinder

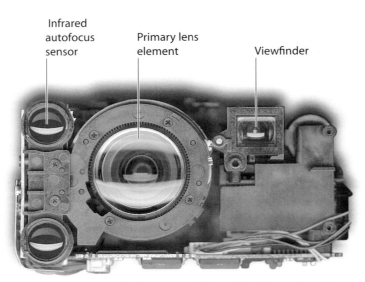

Figure 3-1 Stripped of its outer shell, Kodak's DC120 doesn't look like anything special when seen from the front...

The difference is that instead of refracting light onto film, digital camera lenses refract light onto specialized computer chips. Like any computerized device, a digital camera contains a logic board with the usual collection of microprocessors and transistors. Labeled in Figure 3-2, the main chip is the microcontroller unit (MCU). It directs the activities of the other processors and confirms the well-being of the camera during startup, much like the central processing unit (CPU) in a computer.

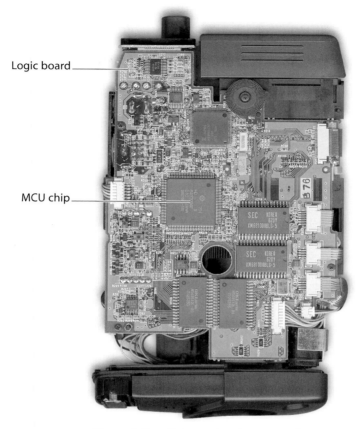

Logic board

MCU chip

Figure 3-2 ...But examine the camera from underneath and the DC120 reveals itself to be a miniature computer.

But while the CPU reigns supreme in a computer, the MCU is merely the operations manager for a digital camera, bossing around the other chips and making sure the photographic information gets where it needs to go. The chip that makes it all happen is known as the *image sensor*, pictured in Figure 3-3. Hidden deep inside a lightproof chamber, the image sensor is the "film" of the filmless camera, responding to the light that enters through the lens element. The quality of your photographs hinges on the performance of this one chip.

Figure 3-3 The image sensor converts light refracted by the lens element into a series of electrical charges. This particular image sensor comes from a Kodak camera.

Diaphragm and Shutter (Or Lack Thereof)

Light from the sun, a flash, or another light source reflects off objects in the real world. Some of that light passes through the lens element. Most lens elements contain a *diaphragm* that opens and closes like the iris of an eye to control the amount of light that enters the camera (Figure 3-4). The diameter of the opening in the diaphragm is called the *aperture*. At the time of this writing, only a few digital cameras in the $1,000 range permit you to adjust the aperture manually. More often, the diaphragm opens and closes automatically in response to the amount of available light.

Beyond the lens element and diaphragm, the setup varies a bit. Many $10,000-and-up models—as well as a few of the older point-and-shoot devices, such as Kodak's DC40—contain a traditional mechanical shutter. When you press the shutter release button the shutter snaps open and closes instantly, just as it does in a film camera.

But where a shutter is essential for film photography—controlling how long the film is exposed to light—it serves a significantly less important role in digital photography. With few exceptions, the light response of an image sensor is controlled electronically, whether the camera has a shutter or not. The shutter merely shields the image sensor from constant exposure, which might otherwise reduce the life of the chip.

To cut down on costs, most digital cameras forgo the shutter entirely. The diaphragm instead takes up the shutter's role, closing tight when the camera is not in use and opening only when previewing a scene or shooting a picture. A diaphragm opens and closes much more slowly than a shutter, but because protection is the only issue, speed isn't a factor.

NOTE: *When researching digital cameras, you might read that a particular model offers an "electronically shuttered sensor." This means that the image sensor controls the exposure time—or in other words, there is no shutter. Unless the company claims a "mechanical shutter," chances are the camera doesn't have a shutter.*

The absence of a shutter means no shutter noise. So when you press the shutter release, you don't hear the snap of the shutter opening and closing, the traditional audio cue that the camera is working. This may seem trivial, but you'd be surprised how much you rely on that cue. Without it, you're left wondering if an image has been captured or not. To compensate, many digital cameras beep, chirp, or play shutter noises. Others make no noise at all and instead require you to keep an eye on a digital readout or flashing indicator light.

This goes double when shooting long exposures under low light. For example, the image in Figure 3-5 required a 1-second exposure. If you were using a film camera, you would hear two distinct clicks—first the shutter opening, then the shutter

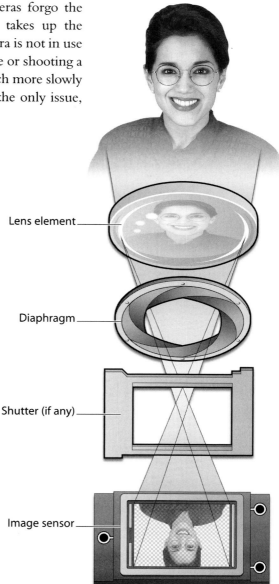

Lens element

Diaphragm

Shutter (if any)

Image sensor

Figure 3-4 The lens element refracts light from the natural world onto the image sensor. The diaphragm opens and closes to control the flow of light. In those few cases where a shutter exists, its main purpose is to protect the sensor chip.

closing. In between, you'd know to keep the camera stationary, preferably on a tripod. But in this case, the image sensor timed a 1-second exposure altogether silently, without moving parts. A chirp sounded the beginning of the exposure, but there was no sound at the end. You learn to keep your eye on the indicator lights, the LCD screen, and other visual cues.

Figure 3-5 Kodak's DC260 permits timed exposures. You know the shot is done when the image appears on the camera's LCD screen.

Focal Lengths

The lens element is as varied in digital cameras as it is in film cameras. Some digital cameras rely on a single lens, others use many. Some offer zoom lenses, so you can magnify or back off from a shot; others do not. Some include cheap plastic lenses, others boast polished glass. But while digital cameras rely heavily on the lens technology developed for film photography, they break with 35mm film cameras in their adaptation of *focal length*.

Measured in millimeters, the focal length is the distance from the point where the light makes its last bend after passing through the lens element (called the *rear nodal point*) to the point at which the light focuses perfectly onto the film (called the *focal plane*). In the simplified Figure 3-4, the focal length extends from the lens element to the image sensor.

More important than how the focal length is measured is what it means. The focal length explains both the *magnification* and the *angle of view* of a particular lens setting:

• **Magnification** A zoom lens permits you to magnify an image as it comes into the camera. Figures 3-6 and 3-7 demonstrate the difference between a fully zoomed-out and zoomed-in version of a fountain shot with a 3x zoom lens. That is, the image in Figure 3-7 is magnified 300 percent compared with Figure 3-6. The zoomed-out view is called a *wide-angle* shot, the zoomed-in view is *telephoto*.

Figure 3-6 A wide-angle lens setting not only backs you away from the scene, but also incrementally bends the image toward the viewer.

Figure 3-7 This 3x telephoto view both magnifies and flattens the image, eliminating the distortion, but also compressing the distances between objects, like the fountain and pillars.

• **Angle of view** A wide-angle lens creates a wider view of a scene. The effect is much like taking a few steps back from your subject, except that the view also expands to take in more of the background. To achieve this effect, the lens has to incrementally distort the scene, bending it slightly toward the viewer, as is visible in Figure 3-6. As the lens expands the angle of view, it bends the refracted light like an image reflected on the outside of a spoon. In contrast, a telephoto setting flattens the image. This means not only hammering the spoon into a flat mirror, but also bringing objects closer together. In Figure 3-7, for example, the fountain and pillars appear nearer to each other than they do in Figure 3-6.

In the world of 35mm film, a focal length of 50mm (f=50mm) is the *standard* view, neither wide-angle nor telephoto, free of distortion or flattening. This figure is approximately equal to the diagonal measurement (including sprocket holes) of one exposure of 35mm film negative, illustrated at the top of Figure 3-8. Focal lengths less than 50mm are wide-angle, focal lengths greater than 50mm are telephoto. The focal pictured in Figure 3-6 is equivalent to f=30mm; Figure 3-7 is equivalent to f=90mm.

We say *equivalent* because focal length is dependent on the size of the film medium. In the case of digital cameras, the image sensor is usually smaller than 35mm film. Figure 3-8 compares the Kodak KAF-1600 (typical of sensors in $1,000 digital cameras) with a piece of 35mm film negative. The standard focal length for this sensor is approximately f=16mm. To make matters more confusing, every image sensor is different. The standard focal length varies from less than f=5mm for very inexpensive cameras to f=50mm and up for the $10,000 and up crowd.

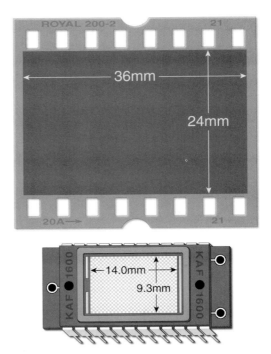

Figure 3-8 Although most image sensors (bottom) are much smaller than a piece of 35mm film negative (top), their sizes vary wildly. This means the definition of the standard focal length for digital cameras varies wildly as well.

As a result, most vendors specify the zoom capabilities of their cameras using two focal length ranges, both the real range and its equivalent in the world of 35mm film. The real range is meaningless unless you know the sensor size. So until image sensor manufacturers agree to a fixed size—which may never happen—the 35mm film equivalent will be the one focal length standard that everyone observes. Just remember than 50mm is the standard view and you're ready to judge the zoom capabilities of any device.

HOW THE IMAGE SENSOR WORKS

Like film, the image sensor responds to the light cast upon it by the lens element. But the mechanics of this response are as different as night and day:

- **Film responds chemically** The active ingredient in film is a layer of gelatinous emulsion filled with light-sensitive crystals. The crystals contain traces of silver. When light hits the film, impurities in the film crystals attract the silver atoms into microscopic clumps. Stronger light results in larger clumps (though still microscopic). The development process enlarges the clumps further, making them visible. Every step is irreversible, meaning that the film can be exposed and developed only once. From then on, the film serves as a storage medium.

- **An image sensor responds electronically** The sensor is composed of a layer of silicon covered with a grid of square electrodes. The silicon is rife with negatively charged particles, or *electrons*. When light passes through the electrodes, it sends the electrons scattering. Voltage applied to the electrodes attracts the free electrons into clusters called *photosites*. Stronger light and higher voltage at a specific electrode translates to more electrons per site. A digital converter counts the electrons at each site and sends the data out to the logic board for processing. The electrons are then released back into the silicon and the image sensor is ready to use all over again.

Admittedly, the last thing you want to worry about when shooting a photograph is the behavior of free electrons. But the unique proclivities of electrodes and silicon have a distinct effect on the performance of digital cameras.

Consider the aspect of speed. All this collecting and counting of electrons takes time, particularly if you're used to the immediate response of film. With film, the shutter opens, the shutter closes, the film advances, and you're ready for the next picture. The whole process can take as little as $1/8000$ second! This makes film cameras ideally suited to rapid-fire shooting.

In contrast, it typically takes a second or more for a digital camera to collect and store an image. Some digital cameras are capable of shooting multiple pictures per second, but they usually sacrifice data for the sake of speed. In normal situations, you can expect 5 to 10 seconds delay between snapping one picture and the next. This may not sound like much, but when working with lively subjects such as children and animals, it can mean the difference between getting and missing the shot.

A second element of speed is exposure. Despite their lack of a shutter, some digital cameras permit you to photograph long exposures. Rather than leaving the shutter open for a prolonged period of time, a digital camera controls exposure by applying a timed charge to the image sensor. The longer the charge, the greater the collection of electrons, which exaggerates the sensor's exposure to light. The downside is that present-day image sensors don't respond to low light as well as film does. As the 4-second exposure in Figure 3-9 shows, a prolonged exposure may result in arbitrary flecks of color, known as *noise*.

Figure 3-9 This 4-second exposure captured with a DC260 suffers from a pronounced case of digital noise, most obvious in the enlarged detail at top.

Pixels and Resolution

The biggest difference between image sensors and film stems from the electrodes themselves. Each electrode collects one square of image information. The camera likewise stores the image as a collection of tiny squares, much like the tiles in a highly detailed mosaic. These squares are called *pixels* (short for *picture elements*).

In most cases, the pixels are so small that they merge together to form a continuous photograph, as in Figure 3-10. But if you magnify the image—as illustrated in Figure 3-11—the image breaks down into a bunch of tiles, ruining the effect of the photograph. Therefore, the more pixels, the better.

Figure 3-10 With 267 pixels packed into every inch, this digital photograph is virtually indistinguishable from a film image.

Figure 3-11 But when we magnify a couple of areas to four times their normal size, the pixels become obvious.

The number of pixels captured by the image sensor is commonly known as the *resolution*. Strictly speaking, resolution refers to the number of pixels packed into a certain area. As demonstrated in Figure 3-12, an image printed at a resolution of 150 pixels per inch (ppi) will be twice the size but half as smooth as the same image printed at 300 ppi. In this context, resolution refers to the population density of the pixels.

But over time, the term *resolution* has fallen into less formal use to mean the sheer quantity of pixels in an image. For example, Canon's PowerShot Pro70 captures images that measure 1,536 pixels wide by 1,024 pixels tall, for a total of 1536 x 1024 = 1,572,864 pixels. Another Canon model, the PowerShot A5, captures

1,024 by 768 pixels, or a total of 786,432 pixels. Therefore, the PowerShot Pro70 offers twice the resolution of the PowerShot A5.

Figure 3-12
An image printed at 150 ppi (left) compared with the same image printed at 300 ppi (right). The image was captured with an Epson PhotoPC 550, a low-resolution camera that captures 640 by 480 pixels.

TIP: Most cameras shoot at multiple resolutions. For example, the Canon PowerShot A5 captures images at either 1,024 by 768 pixels (786,432 total) or 512 by 384 pixels (just 196,608). More pixels mean better-looking, smoother images with finer details, so always shoot at the highest resolution your camera has to offer. Otherwise, you're wasting the capabilities of your image sensor, the single most expensive component in the camera.

In addition to pixel and resolution, here are a few other vocabulary words to keep under your belt:

- **Megapixel** Unlike "ultra high resolution" and other meaningless marketing labels that find their way onto digital cameras, the insignia *megapixel* has a specific meaning. The prefix *mega* implies millions, so a megapixel camera is one that captures one million pixels or more. As we write this, megapixel devices cost anywhere between $500 and $1,000. But one day in the near future, all cameras will be megapixel or better. (By contrast, the resolution of consumer-grade 35mm film is estimated at about 6 million pixels.)

- **Masking** In most cases, each electrode on the image sensor translates to a pixel in the final image. The image sensor may, however, capture a few extra pixels that get thrown away. The image sensor in Kodak's DC260 contains 1,548 by 1,032 electrodes, but the maximum image resolution is 1,536 by 1,024 pixels. This means that a total of 24 thousand pixels are clipped away around the perimeter of the image. These trash pixels are said to be *masked* away.

- **Interpolation** The fact that the image sensor offers more electrodes than pixels is a good thing. In the rare cases where the opposite is true, it's a bad thing. The image sensor in Polaroid's PDC-3000 contains a total of 980,000 electrodes. But the camera claims a maximum image resolution of 1,600 by 1,200 pixels— a total of 1.9 million—twice as many pixels as electrodes! The PDC-3000 invents the extra pixels by averaging the colors captured by the electrodes, a process called *interpolation*. But whatever you call it, the pixels aren't authentic, so the process is a sham, as Figure 3-13 illustrates. Always check that the resolution of the image sensor is at least equal to the maximum advertised image resolution.

Figure 3-13 An image shot at the full resolution of the CCD (left) and another image shot at half the resolution and interpolated up (right).

Pixels are nothing more than little squares of color. But knowing how to use them, how many you need, and when to throw them away is one of the most confusing topics in digital photography. That's why we devote an entire chapter to the topic, namely Chapter 4, "The Mechanics of Digital Imagery."

Capturing Color

Like film emulsion, free electrons respond to the intensity of light, but not to its color. In that regard, both film and image sensors see the world in shades of black and white. Film gets around this by combining three layers of emulsion, each sensitive to a different part of the color spectrum. The emulsion layers are colorized with dyes built into the film.

Image sensors capture color using red, green, and blue filters. These filters are nothing more than dabs of translucent plastic applied directly to the electrodes, as you can see in the microscope photograph featured in Color Plate 3-1 on page C5. A red filter removes all nonred light, creating a red view of the world, as if you were wearing bright red sunglasses. The green and blue filters remove all nongreen and nonblue light, respectively. Red, green, and blue light mix to form white, which contains all the colors in the visible spectrum. So the layers of red, green, and blue pixels mix to form most (if not quite all) of the colors our eyes can see.

Although all digital cameras rely on red, green, and blue filters, the ways in which these filters are used vary, especially among professional-level cameras in the $10,000 and up range:

- **Trilinear scanning** Studio cameras, such as the Better Light 6000, scan a photograph line-by-line using a *trilinear* image sensor. The sensor contains just three rows of electrodes, the first line filtered red, the second line filtered green, and the third line filtered blue. This results in a very precise photograph. The problem is, both camera and subject have to remain perfectly still and the light has to remain constant. To scan an image 2,000 pixels tall, a *stepper motor* moves the image sensor parallel to the lens in 2,000 steps. A single photograph may take a minute or more to shoot, making it useful for still-life photography only.

- **Three-shot array** Another high-end solution (employed by the Leaf DCB II and MegaVision T2) is to shoot three separate pictures, one red, one green, and one blue. A separate filter rotates in front of the image sensor for each shot. The image sensor contains a grid of electrodes (hence the term *array*), permitting it to shoot the entire picture at once. Even so, the image sensor has to wait 5 to 10 seconds after capturing one filtered picture before it can shoot the next. The quality is outstanding, but as in the case of the scanning sensor, both camera and subject have to remain absolutely still. The exception is when shooting black-and-white photographs, which do not require filtering.

- **Piezo** A variation on the three-shot array is the so-called *piezo* device. Cameras such as the Carnival 2020 and the Eyelike rely on a grid of alternating red, green, and blue filters, each of which covers a single electrode, as demonstrated in Color Plate 3-2. When shooting a still photograph, the camera takes four exposures. In between each, a precise piezoelectric crystal moves the filter grid in single-pixel increments. This way, every electrode gets filtered with red, green, and blue. The four pictures are then merged to create the full-color image. Piezo devices also offer a single-shot mode in which the filter grid remains stationary—similar to the single-array system, described shortly.

- **Multiple-array** A fourth solution is the *multiple-array* camera, which involves two or more separate image sensors. A prism separates the light into its red, green, and blue components. (If you've ever seen a ray of light refracted through a crystal, you've seen a prism in action.) In most cases, the red and blue components are projected onto one image sensor and the green is projected onto a second. The camera captures both pictures simultaneously.

Of the various styles listed above, only the piezo and multiple-array cameras are *real-time* devices, meaning that you can take them out of the studio and shoot living, breathing subjects. But their reliance on complex electronics drives up costs. So if scanning and three-shot cameras are too slow, and piezo and multiple-array cameras are too expensive, what's the solution for affordable cameras costing $1,000 or less?

Far and away the most popular color filtering method is a simplified option called the *single-array* system. One image sensor is equipped with red, green, and blue filters, much like the piezo system. But instead of moving, the filters are fixed to the electrodes. A single electrode can respond to just one filter, so each electrode is filtered independently. One electrode is filtered red, its neighbor is green, and the next is blue, as in Color Plate 3-2 on page C5. The exact filtering pattern varies among sensors, but the upshot is the same—one chip captures a full-color photograph.

But while the single-array system is the standard in digital photography (including even $10,000-and-up professional models like the Kodak DCS560), it does have one drawback. The camera has to interpolate each set of filtered pixels to make a continuous picture—one in red, one in green, and one in blue. These colored pictures are called *channels*, and each channel much be complete before the camera can construct a full-color photograph.

The green channel is the easiest to interpolate, since there are usually twice as many green pixels as red or blue. Every other pixel is green, so the camera has to interpolate only half the pixels to finish off the green channel. But only one out of every four pixels in the red and blue channels is captured by the image sensor. The other 75 percent of the channel is interpolated, as demonstrated in Color Plate 3-3 on page C6.

And yet, as Color Plate 3-4 on page C6 shows, interpolated color channels come out looking much better than, say, an image that's been interpolated up from a lower resolution (Figure 3-13). There are three reasons for this:

- **The channels compensate for each other when mixed together** Point to any pixel, and that's exactly how it looked to a specific electrode.

- **The camera draws information from all three channels when interpolating any one of them** This means the colors of the green and blue pixels are mathematically factored in when the missing red ones are calculated. This is called *color interpolation*.

- **The image sensor mimics our eyes** Most image sensors favor green filters for a very good reason. Our eyes are more sensitive to green light than to red or blue. A highly detailed green channel tricks us into perceiving a highly detailed color photograph.

A few cameras permit you to shoot color and black and white photographs. If you'll print the final image in black and white, then shoot the image in black and white. Why? Because with a black-and-white photo, a digital camera ignores the filters, resulting in one channel of image data with no interpolation (Figure 3-14). It's all darks and lights, which the electrodes see without filtering.

Figure 3-14 This Kokopelli was captured in black-and-white using an Epson PhotoPC 700. The camera captures just 1,024 by 768 pixels, but every one of those pixels comes directly from the sensor electrodes free of interpolation.

CCD versus CMOS

Before we move on to livelier topics, there is one final item we should mention on the subject of image sensors. If you spend any time comparing different camera models, you'll hear two terms bandied about—*CCD* and *CMOS*. The two are competing types of image sensors:

- **CCD** The CCD, short for *charge-coupled device*, dates back to the late 1960s when it was developed as an alternative to the bulky, inefficient vacuum tubes originally used in TV cameras. CCDs now rank among the most common computer chips in production and are found in everything from camcorders and scanners to electronic telescopes and medical instruments. Virtually every optical recorder that doesn't use film relies on a CCD.

- **CMOS** Pronounced *sea-moss*, the *complementary metal-oxide semiconductor* sensor is a recent upstart. Found in only a handful of cameras, notably the SVmini and CMOS-Pro from Sound Vision, CMOS sensors represent thus-far-unproven technology that may drive down the price of digital cameras in the next two to three years.

CCD is the clear standard in digital photography. But CMOS sensors offer a couple of advantages. First, CMOS chips can be produced more economically because they require the same manufacturing processes used to create other kinds of computer processors. (By contrast, CCD production is highly specialized.) Second, a single CMOS chip can perform multiple duties, eliminating the need for the additional processing chips that currently riddle the logic boards of CCD-based cameras (as seen back in Figure 3-2). Together, these two factors mean cheaper cameras.

Well, at least, that's the theory. In practice, CCD still has the firm upper hand, both in cost and in quality. Currently, CMOS-based cameras under $1,000 rely on so-called *passive-pixel* sensors, which produce noisy images with random flecks of color, like the top example in Figure 3-15. *Active-pixel* CMOS sensors capture less noise, but still fail to measure up to equivalently priced CCD sensors.

In researching this book, we uncovered lots of press about the wonderful benefits of CMOS, but little evidence. (In fact, our experience with CMOS-based cameras usually proved quite the opposite.) We're not saying CMOS technology won't pay off, but as is so often the case, news of the next great wonder long precedes the actual event. Our guess is that mainstream camera vendors such as Kodak, Olympus, Nikon, and others will integrate CMOS sensors into their cameras when CMOS starts delivering quality comparable to that of CCD. In the meantime, it's a technology to squirrel away in the back of your mind for the day when it finally becomes worthy of consideration.

Figure 3-15 A detail from a sky captured with a CMOS sensor (top) compared with one captured with a CCD (bottom). The CCD sky is considerably cleaner, with less noise and smoother details.

STORING THE IMAGE

In a film camera, film both captures and stores the photograph. The camera merely focuses the light and keeps the film safe from further exposure. In a digital camera, the image sensor captures the image, and then it shuttles the data to the logic board and lets the MCU worry about storage and other details.

The storage medium in digital cameras is essentially some kind of computer memory. As with the image sensor, you can use the memory over and over again. No need to purchase more film, send the film to a developer, or perform any or the other tiresome chores associated with traditional cameras. When the camera memory fills up with pictures, just transfer the pictures to a computer, erase the memory, and you're ready to go out and shoot some more.

But while digital storage is in many ways miraculous, it demands that you grapple with new topics. First, you should be aware of the different kinds of storage media available to you. Second, you need to maximize your storage space so you never miss a shot. These key topics consume the rest of this chapter.

Media Capacity

The terms *medium* and its plural *media* refer to anything you can use to store information. Floppy disks are media. Computer chips are media. Even film qualifies as media. The challenge for digital photographers is selecting a type of media that is both portable and fast while at the same time capable of holding lots and lots of images.

The name for this last concern—the amount of storage space—is *capacity*. The capacity of a roll of film is measured in exposures, but the capacity of digital media is measured in *bytes*. A byte is nothing more than a sequence of 8 numbers. (This is where the word *digital* comes into play—the camera records images using digits.) A thousand bytes is a kilobyte, a million bytes is a megabyte, and a billion bytes is a gigabyte. The three are better known by their initials K, MB, and GB.

> **NOTE:** For discussing storage capacity aloud, we offer the following conventions to avoid embarrassment. You can pronounce K as either "kilobyte" or "kay." MB is either "megabyte" or "meg" (not "em-bee"); GB is either "gigabyte" or "gig." Now you can talk the talk, even if you're not always sure what the talk means.

Most forms of digital media are measured in megabytes. The smallest media hold a little more than 1MB of data; the largest hold several hundred MB, sometimes even more.

Types of Media

Now that you know how digital space is measured, we can look at a few of the specific kinds of media used in digital cameras:

- **Direct computer connection** High-end studio cameras capture very high resolution pictures that are often too large to fit on portable media. The solution is to cable the camera directly to a computer or external hard drive. Each photograph passes from the image sensor through the camera's internal circuitry and onto the computer's hard drive. The downside of this approach is that you can't easily take the camera with you on the road.

- **Portable hard disk** Field cameras costing $10,000 or more include portable hard disks with capacities of 100MB or more. About the size of a pack of cigarettes, this kind of hard disk uses a standard PC Card interface (technically known by one of the longest acronyms on earth, *PCMCIA*). Most portable computers produced since 1995 include PC Card slots. This means you can slide the hard disk out of the camera, stick it in your portable computer, and copy the images from the card to your computer's hard drive.

- **Internal memory** Megapixel cameras costing $1,000 or less don't require the same amount of storage capacity as their more expensive, higher-resolution cousins. Generally speaking, 16MB or less is sufficient. Some cameras in this class rely on internal memory soldered onto the logic board of the camera. Like the RAM built into computers, this memory contains no moving parts, making it incredibly fast. This kind of memory is sometimes called flash RAM because it retains photographs even when the camera is turned off. (In contrast, data stored in your computer's RAM is erased when you turn off the power.)

  The problem with built-in memory is that you have to connect your camera to a computer to transfer the images. The process is often very slow, and it requires special software. Worse, you can't expand the storage space. The moment you fill up the internal RAM, you have two options: erase some of the pictures you took so you can take some more, or return to your computer and transfer the pictures.

- **Floppy disk** The ultimate in expandability is the common floppy disk. Employed most notably by Sony's Digital Mavica (Figure 3-16), floppy disks are readily available in virtually every office supplies store on the face of the planet. So if you fill up one floppy, it's easy to find more. Floppies are also cheap, costing as little as 20 cents apiece. This means you can use them as permanent storage, as opposed to having to copy all the images to your computer's hard drive.

  But floppies aren't the ideal solution. First, they can hold only 1.4MB of data, making them suitable only for low-resolution cameras. (The Mavica maxes out at 640 by 480 pixels.) Second, floppies are among the slowest media available, adding a few seconds to every picture. Third, floppy disks are relatively huge by digital camera standards, and the drive mechanisms required to process them are even larger. The Mavica's internal floppy drive makes it one of the heaviest, bulkiest digital cameras on the market.

- **Floppy variations** In an attempt to invent a better floppy disk, Iomega has developed the tiny Clik disk, shown in Figure 3-17. A Clik disk holds 40MB of data, about 30 times as much as a floppy. A Clik is likewise several times faster and much smaller, measuring a scant 2 by 2 inches. As we write this, no camera uses Clik media. But Agfa plans to release the first Clik camera by the end of 1999. According to Iomega, Clik disks will cost about $10 apiece when purchased in quantities of 10 or more, making them the most affordable high-capacity media available for digital photographers.

Figure 3-16 Sony's Digital Mavica shoots pictures to inexpensive and readily available floppy disks. But the internal floppy drive makes this camera large, heavy, and slow.

Figure 3-17 Iomega's Clik disks measure just 2 by 2 inches and hold 40MB of data each.

• **Removable memory** Faster than Cliks and far more common is removable flash RAM, which offers an excellent combination of speed, flexibility, and capacity. Available in several different formats, removable memory cards have no moving parts, so they can save an image in a fraction of a second. They vary in size from half to a quarter of the size of a floppy disk, so you can carry several extras with you in your pocket. And they hold anywhere from 2MB to upwards of 100MB of data—and those numbers are climbing. The three most popular varieties of removable memory appear in Figure 3-18.

Figure 3-18 Three prevalent removable memory cards—PC Card (left), SmartMedia (top right), and CompactFlash (bottom right). All appear at their actual size.

Removable memory isn't nearly as common as floppy disks, nor is it as cheap. You can expect to pay $2 to $5 per MB of removable memory, compared with about one-tenth that price for floppies or Clik disks. On the other hand, removable memory is not limited in capacity in the same way as a disk. Iomega may one day release a Clik that holds, say, 100MB of data, but it would take a new drive mechanism—which means a new camera—to use it. With removable media, the capacity can grow without requiring new camera hardware. Also, a card is included with the camera; after you buy a couple of extras, you'll be set for years to come.

Of the various kinds of removable memory available today, our favorite is CompactFlash. Found in most cameras from Kodak, Nikon, and Canon, among others, CompactFlash cards are tiny and sturdy. SmartMedia cards—preferred by Olympus, Fuji, and Agfa—are even smaller. But the memory element (the grid with the wave in Figure 3-18) is exposed. As long as you keep your fingers off it, you're okay. But touch it, and you can destroy one of your pictures. Yet another medium, Memory Stick, is a proprietary Sony format. The jury is still out on how well it functions.

> **WARNING:** *Flash RAM is different from disks and other media in that once you erase data, it's gone for good. An electric charge destroys the data, and no program on earth can retrieve it. So if you have any doubt about whether or not to delete an image, don't. Only after you copy an image to a computer is it absolutely safe to delete it from camera memory.*

For more on copying your photos from removable memory and other media to a computer, see the "Downloading Directly from the Media" section of Chapter 5. For how to keep your photos safe well into the future, read Chapter 14.

Image Size and Compression

When you pop a roll of film into a camera, you know exactly how many pictures you'll be able to shoot. Not so with electronic media. The size of a digital image depends on its resolution. So a card that holds 16 low-resolution images may hold only one high-resolution image.

The formula for determining the size of a digital image is, on the face of it, quite straightforward. Each pixel in a black-and-white image takes up 1 byte; each pixel in a full-color image consumes 3 bytes (1 byte each for the red, green, and blue ingredients in the pixel). So to calculate the size of a color photograph, you multiply the number of pixels by 3. For example, Fuji's MX-700 shoots pictures measuring 1,280 by 1,024 pixels. Each image weighs in at 1280 x 1024 x 3 = 3,932,160 bytes, or 3.9MB.

But the MX-700 ships with a 2MB SmartMedia card, as pictured in Figure 3-19. That's enough to hold just half a picture! And yet, the MX-700 can store no fewer than two 1,280 x 1,024-pixel images pictures on a 2MB card, and as many as a dozen. How is this possible?

The answer is an added ingredient called *JPEG compression.* Pronounced "jay-peg," the JPEG standard is named for the people who designed it, the Joint

Photographic Experts Group. JPEG compression makes an image smaller by reorganizing its pixels so they can be expressed using less data. All the pixels are still there, but they're modified so they take up less space on disk.

JPEG works its magic by examining pixels in 8 x 8 blocks—that is, 64 pixels at a time. It averages the colors in the block and places that average in the upper left pixel. JPEG writes that one pixel in the block using the full 3 bytes of data, and then assigns the other 63 pixels truncated values based on how closely they resemble the average.

By itself, that mathematical trick saves a lot of data, but not enough. So JPEG examines the other 63 pixels in the block and tries to make them homogenous. If a pixel is close to the average color, JPEG says "what the heck" and changes it to the average color. If a pixel is far from the average, JPEG adjusts the color to make it a closer match. The result is a dramatic saving in bytes written to memory.

The definition of *close* is where you come in. If you examine the LCD screen on the MX-700 in Figure 3-19, you'll see a white line labeled Quality. Fuji asks you to select between three quality settings, Fine, Normal, and Basic. Other vendors use other setting names—Best, Better, Good; High, Medium, Low.

Still others offer stars or numbers. And while every camera we've seen offers three quality settings or fewer, JPEG supports up to 100. Whatever settings you may encounter, their purpose is the same:

- **High** A high quality setting applies less JPEG compression. This means JPEG changes only a few pixels to the average.

- **Low** By lowering the quality setting, you broaden JPEG's definition of *close*. At the lowest setting, JPEG changes every pixel in the block to some extent or other.

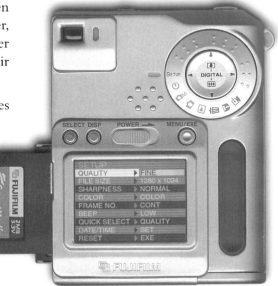

Figure 3-19 Like most megapixel cameras, Fuji's MX-700 lets you select between three quality settings that permit you to save images with varying degrees of JPEG compression.

Informally, JPEG is known as a *lossy* compression scheme because it modifies the definitions of pixels from the way the image sensor reported them, and some data is lost. But when you use JPEG compression with discretion, you won't notice the difference.

Figures 3-20, 3-21, and 3-22 show three MX-700 images, each subject to the Fine, Normal, or Basic compression setting. The differences are barely visible if you look at the vans, but you can pick out differences if you look closely at the enlarged text. The gray inside and outside the letter is smooth in Figure 3-20. But it grows slightly noisy in Figure 3-21 and very noisy in Figure 3-22. These random pixels of noise are known as JPEG artifacts.

Figure 3-20 The image was shot with the MX-700 with the quality option set to Fine. In color, this image consumes 722K.

Figure 3-21 The image shows the effect of a quality setting of Normal. The image is only half as large, taking up 356K.

Figure 3-22 The MX-700's final quality setting, Basic, produces this effect. Again the file size drops by half, this time to a scant 170K.

TIP: *If your camera offers three quality settings, we recommend that you try to stick with the highest of the three as much as possible. This will make your photographs easier to sharpen and correct, as we discuss in Chapter 15. However, if you're low on storage capacity and you want to take more pictures, you can get away with the medium setting. As for the lowest setting, avoid it at all costs.*

Some cameras let you save to images as TIFF files. TIFF may compress an image slightly by simplifying pixel definitions, but it never changes pixels. Hence, its compression is said to be *lossless*. Other cameras let you save raw, uncompressed image data in other formats. But we recommend that you apply at least the highest-quality JPEG compression, if JPEG is available. We have yet to meet anyone who can distinguish a high-quality JPEG image from an uncompressed image when the two are printed side-by-side, and we doubt you'll notice a difference either.

CHAPTER FOUR

The Mechanics of Digital Imagery

The number one question we hear from people who are interested in digital cameras is, "Can you print the photos?" Most of us are so used to the metaphor of film that our first and foremost expectation of a camera is that it delivers an envelope of printed pictures.

If that were all there was to digital photography, it would be nothing more than a fleeting novelty. The purpose of any worthwhile innovation is to go where no technology has gone before, and digital cameras are no exception. Yes, you can print your photographs, hand them off to colleagues, collect them in albums, and do all those wonderful things you've been doing with film prints for decades. But digital cameras afford merely so much added control that the simple act of printing is little more than a footnote. Wherever computers are the dominant tools of production —periodicals, books, video, the Internet—digital photography is ready to serve.

Digital cameras derive their power from the fact that they are digital through and through. Where film-based photos must be first developed and then scanned before a computer can interpret them, digital cameras see the world in the same way your computer does without any additional processing. Unlike a film print, a digital image is infinitely reproducible and equally malleable. You can accept the picture produced by the camera or adjust it to create an entirely different effect. You can duplicate a picture several times over—with no loss of quality whatsoever —and share it with others so they can modify it to fit their needs.

Film is a real-world substance and therefore is subject to natural laws, which (although generous) have their limits. A digital image is an ephemeral collection of colored pixels that are bound only by your ability to master certain software routines. This "unreal" quality of computer imagery goes to the heart of the digital process. Simply put, if you know how computer image files work, you can see what you can do with them. This chapter explores the underlying structure of the image file so you know exactly what sort of opportunities are open to you—well beyond the mundane chore of printing.

PIXELS AND BITS

Man created computers, but he didn't create them in his own image. In fact, computers and humans are so unlike, you'd swear they came from opposite ends of the universe. We communicate differently, we sense the world differently, we think differently. Digital images are a case in point. Though clearly part of the computer's domain, the image exists for the express enjoyment of you, the human viewer. And yet, the way the computer conjures up the image and the way you see it are two very different things.

The Math Behind the Pixels

You see a digital image as a collection of pixels. If you magnify the image, you can distinguish each pixel as a separate square of color, as in the first example in Figure 4-1. If you reduce the pixels so that more are visible at a time, they merge to form a continuous image, as increasingly evident in Figure 4-1.

But to the computer, the image is a file full of numbers. Because a computer's brain is merely a succession of switches—albeit an exceedingly long succession of switches—each digit in a file can be either a 0 or a 1, off or on. This special digit is called a *bit*, short for binary digit. In an image file, 0 indicates a black pixel, 1 indicates white. Hence, many computer artists refer to digital images as *bitmaps*.

The problem with equating a pixel with a single bit of data is that you don't have any intermediate colors to work with. You have black, you have white, end of story. As shown in Figure 4-2, black and white pixels are fine for representing line art, but they can't measure up to the task of digital photography.

The solution is to string a series of bits together. For example, if you use 2 bits to define a pixel, then you have room for two gray values. The value 00 is black, 01 is dark gray, 10 is light gray, and 11 is white. That's a total of 2 x 2 = 4 variations.

If 2 bits are better than 1, why not add more? The standard for grayscale imagery is 8 bits (or 1 byte) per pixel. If you multiply 2 by itself 8 times (2 to the 8th power), you get a total of 256 possible gray values in an image—black, white, and 254 others. That's why a grayscale photo is sometimes called an 8-bit image.

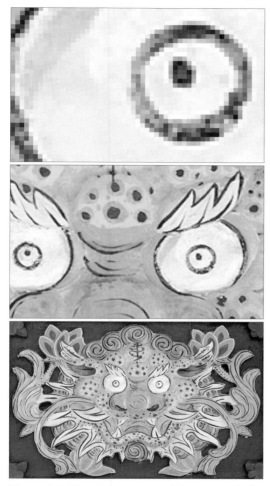

Figure 4-1 Three images containing 2,000 pixels (top), 30,000 pixels (middle), and 480,000 pixels (bottom) apiece.

Figure 4-2 A woodcut from the Kelmscott *Canterbury Tales*, scanned as a black-and-white bitmap, with enlarged detail at bottom.

NOTE: *As it so happens, a word processor uses 8 bits to express a character of type. For example, 01000001 is a capital A, 01100001 is a lowercase a. This means that each pixel in a grayscale image consumes the same space in your computer's memory as a character of type. The image at the bottom of Figure 4-1 contains 480,000 pixels, about as many letters as in this entire book. If you disregard all the formatting, the text in this book takes up about as much room in RAM as that single figure. And you thought that bit about a picture being worth a thousand words was just a cliché.*

Incidentally, the colloquial name assigned to a grayscale image is "black-and-white photo." But in computer imaging, "black and white" specifically refers to a 1-bit graphic, like the first example in Figure 4-3. If you're talking about an 8-bit photograph—like the second example in the figure—be sure to say *grayscale* to avoid confusion.

Figure 4-3 A 1-bit photograph is black-and-white (left), an 8-bit photograph is grayscale (right). Both images are derived from a single photograph captured with an Agfa ePhoto 1680.

Recipes for Color

A decade ago, all digital images—even color ones—were expressed using 8 bits per pixel. At first blush, 256 colors may seem more than sufficient. After all, thousands of traditional artists have managed on a fraction of that number. But there are two big differences:

- First, traditional artists mix their colors to create several thousand variations. In contrast, each of the 256 colors available to an 8-bit image is discrete and unmixable.

- Second, the purpose of digital photographs is to represent the world the way you see it. Your eyes can perceive millions, if not billions, of color permutations. As demonstrated in Color Plate 4-1 on page C7, 256 colors isn't nearly enough to produce a believable photographic image.

To human eyes, a photograph with 256 colors produces roughly the same visual effect as a grayscale image with a mere 6 shades of gray. Compare Figure 4-4 to Color Plate 4-1 and you'll see some striking similarities. This effect of harsh transitions between one color and the next is called *posterization*.

Figure 4-4 Equipped with a paltry 6 shades of gray, this boat suffers no worse posterization than it does when rendered with 256 colors (compare to Color Plate 4-1).

Although posterization may be an interesting effect, it isn't photographic. You need more colors. The obvious way to add more colors is to pile on more bits. The problem is, how? In a grayscale image, larger numbers are lighter. But when you add color to the mix, that simple rule doesn't work. You have to distinguish not only light from dark, but also vivid from drab, yellow from purple, and so on.

The solution is to divide color into its root components. There are several recipes for color, but by far the most popular is *RGB*, employed by all digital cameras, camcorders, scanners, and a host of other devices. The initials RGB stand for red, green, and blue—the primary colors of light. The idea is based on the behavior of light: If you shine three spotlights at the same point on a stage—one brilliant red, another bright green, and a third deep blue—you'll get a circle of neutral white. By alternately reducing the amount of light cast from one of the three spotlights, you can produce nearly all the colors in the visible spectrum, running the gamut from red to violet. As you dim a spotlight, the color grows darker; as you turn it up, the color grows lighter. This is why RGB is also known as the *additive color model*—you add light to get brighter colors.

Now imagine that instead of shining spotlights, you have three slide projectors. One contains a red slide, another a green version of that same image, and the third a blue version of the image. Shine the projectors at the same spot on the screen and—assuming the three slides were shot properly—you get the full-color photograph in all its glory.

This is precisely how digital images work, except that in place of slides, you have channels. Each channel is an independent 8-bit image, as shown in Figure 4-5. To generate the full-color photograph, the computer colorizes the channels and mixes them together, as illustrated in Color Plate 4-2 on page C7. Where the red channel is light—as along the top of the boat—red predominates. Where the green channel is light—the bottom of the boat—green comes through loud and clear. To see how other RGB combinations work, see Color Plate 4-3 on page C8, which shows how combinations of red, green, and blue mix to form yellow, violet, and white.

Three channels of 8-bit data means it takes 24 bits (or 3 bytes) to define each pixel. Hence, an RGB photograph is called a 24-bit image.

Figure 4-5 Computers produce full-color images by combining three channels—one for red (top), one for green (middle), and one for blue (bottom).

With three channels at its disposal, the image may contain up to 256 x 256 x 256 = 16.8 million colors. (You get this same value by taking 2 to the 24th power.) Some cameras can capture even more color—as high as 16 bits per channel, or 48 bits per pixel—but only the very high-end devices preserve all this data. For the present, every device costing less than $10,000 delivers 24-bit photographs. In other words, even if the image sensor is capable of capturing 10 bits or more per channel, the camera interpolates the data down to 8 bits. Given that most printers can reproduce at most a few thousand colors, 16 million is more than enough to suit most professionals' needs.

Converting Between Color Modes

To recap: A black-and-white image contains 1 bit per pixel, a grayscale image contains 8 bits per pixel, and a full-color image contains 24 bits per pixel.

The name given to the number of bits assigned to a pixel is *bit depth*. The term *depth* comes from the fact that 8-bit and 24-bit pixels carry long strings of data. As far as your computer is concerned, this extra data carries with it the additional dimension of depth, as fancifully illustrated in Figure 4-6.

Higher bit depths increase the size of an image, making it more difficult to open and edit. Fortunately, if you don't need all that depth, you can get rid of it. Suppose you shoot a full-color image, and now you want to place it in a newsletter that you intend to print in black-and-white.

Figure 4-6 An image shown head-on (top) and as the computer sees it (bottom), with colors mapped into a third dimension.

You have two options:

- **Place the color image in the newsletter as is.** Each and every time you print the newsletter, the software will send the printer three times as much data as it really needs, and the printer will have to spend extra time converting the colors to black and white. Best-case scenario, you waste time; worst case, the document refuses to print.

- **Convert the image from color to grayscale before placing it in the newsletter.** This is the smart choice. The software sends only the data that the printer needs, and the printer prints the data as it receives it. Faster print time, better reliability.

Every image editing program that we've seen lets you convert color photographs to grayscale. Sophisticated software such as Adobe Photoshop gives you even more control, permitting you to either merge the color channels to produce a grayscale composite or simply keep the channel you think looks best and throw away the other two.

TIP: *The quality of an individual color channel varies from photograph to photograph. But as a general rule of thumb, the red channel contains much of the color information, with the widest contrast between darks and lights. The green channel typically excels in image detail, which means sharp focus and clarity. Our eyes are least sensitive to blue light, so the blue channel is often dark and in relatively poor condition, as demonstrated in Figure 4-7. Of the three, the green channel is usually the best suited for conversion to grayscale.*

Figure 4-7 In this picture captured with a Toshiba PDR-M1, the green channel (middle) fares the best; the blue channel (bottom) fares worst.

The most important point is that bit depth—like any digital attribute—is an editable commodity. Never hesitate to change it to better meet your needs.

PIXEL COUNT AND RESOLUTION

In addition to bit depth, the other element that adds to file size and complexity is the sheer number of pixels in the image. In Chapter 3, we explained how you can calculate the size of an image by multiplying the height and width of the image in pixels by the bit depth in bytes. Bearing in mind that there are 8 bits in a byte:

- The size of a grayscale image that measures 1,280 by 960 pixels is 1280 x 960 x 1 = 1,228,800 bytes. There are 1,024 bytes in a kilobyte, and 1,024K in a megabyte. So 1,228,800 bytes = 1,200K = 1.17MB.

- A full-color image measuring 1,536 by 1,024 pixels consumes 1536 x 1024 x 3 = 4,718,592 bytes, which is equivalent to 4,608K or 4.5MB.

Just as you can reduce the bit depth of an image, you can reduce the number of pixels in an image. There are two ways to do this:

- **Downsampling** When a digital camera or other device captures a pixel of light, it is sometimes said to be *sampling* the data. Although you rarely hear this use of the word *sample* anymore, a derivative word—*downsample*—is very common. Downsample means to reduce the number of pixels by interpolating the colors of the existing pixels. In Figure 4-8, we downsampled an image shot with a Nikon CoolPix 900 to 50 percent of its original height and 50 percent of its original width. The resulting image consumes 25 percent (50 percent of 50 percent) as much memory as the original, yet it prints great at small sizes.

- **Cropping** If you want to home in on a specific detail in an image, you can *crop* away extraneous background elements, as in the lower right example of Figure 4-8. In the real world, cropping requires you to mark the boundaries for reprinting. But with a computer, you just throw away the pixels you don't need. Cropping is one of the easiest and most essential operations in all of computer imaging. We rarely publish a photo that we don't first crop.

All but a very few low-end image editors let you downsample and crop images. In Photoshop, for example, you downsample with the Image Size command and crop with the crop tool. Once you learn how, both operations are routine. Therefore, the question isn't so much *how* to downsample or crop, but *when*—which brings us to the nettlesome topic of *resolution*, both on-screen and in print.

Original

Downsampled   Cropped from original

Figure 4-8 If an image contains more pixels than you need (top), you can downsample the image (bottom left) or crop it (bottom right).

Screen Resolution

The one opportunity you have to see every pixel in a digital image is to view it on a computer screen. Like a digital image, a computer screen is composed of colored pixels. All monitors display colors by projecting combinations of red, green, and blue light. They even subscribe to the same bit depth settings. At the low end are 8-bit screens that display 256 colors; at the high end you have 24-bit screens capable of displaying 16.8 million colors. While color accuracy naturally varies from one monitor to the next, there is a one-to-one ratio between the way a digital camera captures an image and the way a computer monitor displays it.

NOTE: Most computers sold today ship with 4MB or more of VRAM, or video memory. This is enough to display 1,280 by 1,024 pixels in 24-bit color. As it so happens, you already know how to prove this: 1280 x 1024 x 3 = 3,932,160 bytes, or 3.75MB, which easily fits into the 4MB of VRAM. Not coincidentally, many cameras—including the Olympus D-620L, the Toshiba PDR-M3, and many others—shoot pictures that measure 1,280 by 1,024 pixels. These cameras are designed so you can see exactly what you shot on a standard computer screen.

To best view a digital image on-screen, you want each pixel in the image to take up exactly 1 pixel on the screen. Many image editing applications (including Photoshop) call this the 100% view; others (such as Jasc's Paint Shop Pro) call it the 1:1 zoom ratio. If you display the image any smaller, the software can't show you all the pixels. For example, at the 50% or 1:2 view size, you see only a quarter of the pixels in your image. The pixels are still there, but three out of four are temporarily hidden.

If part of your image is cut off when you view it at the 100% or 1:1 view size, you have two options:

- **Downsample or crop the image.** We frequently downsample images just to get a feel for how they look on-screen. This gives you a better idea of how the pixels look and what you can expect when printing the image. (Alternatively, you can zoom down the view size, but most image editors hide pixels instead of redrawing them, which produces a distorted screen image. Even in Photoshop, only certain view sizes—50%, 25%, and so on—are accurate.) The downsampling doesn't have to be permanent—after you get a sense of how the image looks, you can choose Undo to restore the image to its original size. Or you can save the downsampled image under a different name to avoid harming the original.

- **Change the monitor resolution.** Depending on your monitor and video card, you may be able to increase the resolution of your screen so that more pixels fit on-screen at a single time. Under Windows, open the Display control panel and click on the Settings tab. Then use the Screen Area slider bar (highlighted in Figure 4-9) to increase the pixel dimensions of the screen. On the Mac, choose the Monitors & Sound control panel. Then select a new setting from the Resolution list (also highlighted in Figure 4-9).

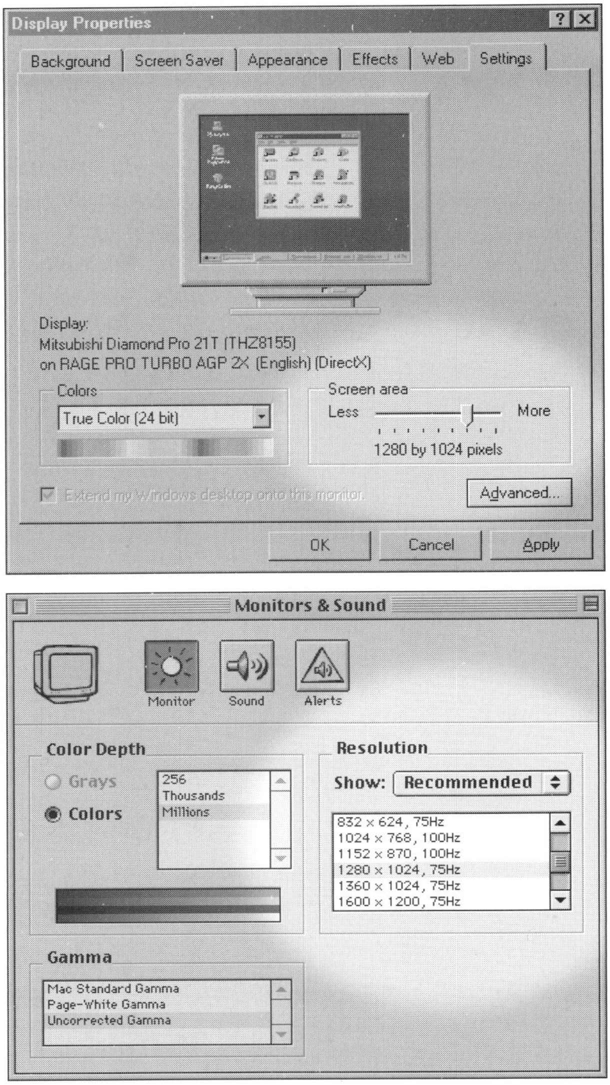

Figure 4-9 The Display control panel on the PC (top) and the Monitors & Sound control panel on the Mac (bottom) let you change the number of pixels displayed on-screen.

The disadvantage of setting your monitor resolution to an extreme resolution, such as 1,600 by 1,200 pixels or higher, is that it becomes hard to see text on-screen. Both Windows and the Mac OS permit you to increase the size of the text that appears in menus, title bars, dialog boxes, and so on. But many programs have a habit of labeling icons and other elements with tiny text that just gets tinier as the screen resolution increases. Rather than resorting to reading glasses, you may be able to change the screen resolution on the fly—say, to a higher setting when working in Photoshop and a lower setting when working in Microsoft Word. Under Windows 95 and later, look for a little monitor icon in the bottom right corner of the screen, like the one pictured in the top example of Figure 4-10. On the Mac, you can choose an option from the Control Strip, which resides at the bottom of the screen.

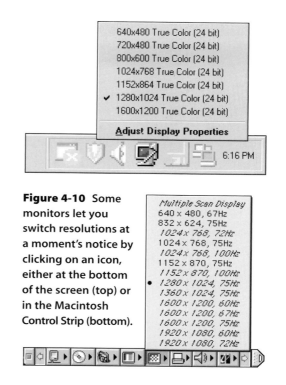

Figure 4-10 Some monitors let you switch resolutions at a moment's notice by clicking on an icon, either at the bottom of the screen (top) or in the Macintosh Control Strip (bottom).

Images for the Web

Another time when you'll most assuredly want to downsample or crop your images is when preparing them for inclusion on a Web site or other screen presentation. Even the 640 by 480-pixel images produced by the cheapest of entry-level cameras contain too many pixels for the Web. Thanks to overworked servers and the sluggish pace of phone connections, Web graphics have to be very small in order to transfer from one computer to the next in a reasonably timely manner. Therefore, they rarely contain more than 320 by 240 pixels, and frequently they're much smaller than that.

> **TIP:** When downsampling dramatically, it's a good idea to reduce the image in multiple steps. As a rule of thumb, avoid reducing the height or width of an image by more than 50 percent at a time. For example, to reduce an image to 30 percent of its original width, first downsample the image to 50 percent, then to 60 percent. (50% x 60% = 30%.) This way, you make sure that every pixel is calculated when interpolating the smaller image. Otherwise you run the risk of simply throwing away pixels, which may harm fine details in your image.

If the Web is your primary medium for displaying images, you may assume you can get away with purchasing the least expensive camera you can lay your hands on. But although 640 by 480-pixel cameras provide sufficient resolution for the Web, they don't necessarily provide sufficient quality.

Figure 4-11 shows two pictures shot in Disney's Epcot from approximately the same point in the park on similarly sunny days. The image on the left is the work of Kodak's first point-and-shoot camera, the DC40, which captures 768 by 504 pixels. The image on the right was shot three years later with a Kodak DC220, which delivers 1152 by 864 pixels, about two and a half times as many as the DC40. After cropping and downsampling the two images to a scant 190 by 140 pixels each, we end up with two very similar pictures suitable for the Web. But despite their identical size, the DC220 image still has the edge when it comes to clarity and detail. Higher-resolution CCD-based cameras not only capture more pixels, but often capture better image quality as well.

Figure 4-11 A picture shot in 1995 with a Kodak DC40 (left) and a similar picture taken in 1998 with a Kodak DC220 (right).

Figure 4-12 Even after downsampling the images to a size suitable for the Web, the DC220 image still conveys better clarity.

Where resolution is concerned, Web images are static. Browsers such as Netscape Communicator and Microsoft Internet Explorer always display images at a 1-to-1 zoom ratio. You see one image pixel for every screen pixel. If you use Photoshop or some other program to specify a resolution value, that value is ignored. All that counts are the image dimensions, as measured in pixels.

Print Resolution

Unlike on the Web, resolution is of critical importance when printing an image. The reason that the images in Figure 4-11 look so much smoother and more natural than their counterparts in Figure 4-12 is because the former are printed at a resolution of 300 ppi and the latter are printed at 115 ppi. With 680 percent as many pixels packed into every square inch, Figure 4-11 can't help but look better.

But there's a limit to how much resolution you want to use. Figure 4-13 shows an image printed at the same dimensions but at three different resolutions. The first image is printed at 150 ppi and measures 630 by 166 pixels; the second is 300 ppi and measures 1260 by 332 pixels; the third is 600 ppi and measures 2520 by 664 pixels. If you look closely, you can see a pretty obvious increase in quality and detail from an 150 ppi to 300 ppi. But despite the fact that the 600-ppi image contains four times the pixels as the 300-ppi version, it doesn't look that different.

As with bit depth, a printer can accommodate just so much resolution. Printers themselves output to pixels, known in the vernacular as *dots*. The resolution of printers is therefore specified in dots per inch, or *dpi*. (Some people likewise refer to image resolution in dpi, but we advocate ppi to clearly distinguish between image and print pixels.) Printer resolutions vary from 300 dpi for inexpensive laser printers to 2,400 dpi and higher for film-based imagesetters.

You'd think a 2,400-dpi printer like the one used to print this book could easily render each and every pixel in a 600-ppi image. But where your monitor displays pixels in any of 16 million colors, all but a very few printers can print just one color at a time. For example, a typical color ink-jet printer is armed with four colors of ink —cyan, magenta, yellow, and black, together known as CMYK. A page output by this printer appears to be a continuous full-color image. But if you scrutinize it closely, you can see tiny dots of ink. Each dot is either cyan, magenta, yellow, or black. Where the dots are smaller or more sparsely clustered, the color of the image appears lighter. Where the dots are large or densely packed, the image appears darker.

By and large, printers that are used to produce pages for commercial reproduction output their dots in very specific patterns called *halftone cells*. When enlarged, these cells appear as circles of color of varying size, as illustrated by the magnified detail in Figure 4-14. Bigger cells result in darker colors when the page is viewed normally.

Figure 4-13 Three images printed at increasingly higher resolutions, from 150 ppi (top), to 300 ppi (middle), to 600 ppi (bottom).

Just like image pixels and printer dots, halftone cells have their own resolution, called the *screen frequency* or *line screen*. This resolution is measured in lines per inch (or *lpi*), where a line is a row of halftone cells. The screen frequency of this book is 133 lpi—or 133 halftone cells per linear inch—which is typical of magazines and fine books.

At 133 lpi, there are more than 300 printer dots devoted to each halftone cell. This means that the halftone cells can vary in size by a few hundred increments, ensuring smooth color transitions. But it also limits the printer's ability to render image pixels. According to common wisdom, a single halftone cell can accurately represent up to four image pixels. That means two pixels horizontally and two vertically. So the resolution of an image should be approximately twice the screen frequency. Any less, and you're not taking sufficient advantage of the resolution of the printer; any higher, and you're sending the printer more pixels than it can use.

Figure 4-14 An enlarged version of the 600-ppi image from Figure 4-13, showing the individual halftone cells.

Table 4-1 offers specific recommendations for resolution settings to accommodate certain kinds of jobs. The Ideal Resolution setting represents a resolution of twice the screen frequency typical of this kind of device. The Good Enough setting is one and a half times the typical lpi and is designed to get you by during those times when you're low on pixels. Some professionals can see resolutions up to two and a half times the screen frequency, so we've added an Absolute Maximum category for those times when you want to show the most detail possible. Bear in mind, since we can't know exactly what kinds of printers and presses you'll be using, these are only estimates. If your commercial printer suggests different resolutions, it's probably a good idea to take heed.

Printer	Ideal Resolution	Good Enough	Absolute Maximum
300-ppi laser printer	120 ppi	90 ppi	150 ppi
600-ppi laser printer	180 ppi	135 ppi	225 ppi
Newsprint	180 ppi	135 ppi	225 ppi
Coated magazine stock	267 ppi	200 ppi	330 ppi
Super-fine coated stock	350 ppi	260 ppi	440 ppi

Based on industry-standard printer resolutions and screen frequencies.

Table 4-1 Recommended Resolutions for Various Print Jobs

Ink-jet printers and their cousins, the bubble jets, use random dot patterns called *dithering* to mix colors. These dither patterns don't subscribe to the same regimen as halftone cells, so measuring their frequency is difficult if not meaningless. Then again, because ink-jet pages are not commercially reproducible, there's not much reason to modify the resolution of an image to suit these devices. If you're using the device to proof a page that you intend to eventually print from a commercial imagesetter, then base the image resolution on the final device, not your ink-jet. If you're just printing snapshots, set the image resolution to about half the printer resolution. Or better still, don't worry about it.

If this discussion of halftone cells and dither patterns has whetted your appetite to learn more about printing technology, Peachpit Press has another great title called *Real World Scanning and Halftones, 2nd Edition* that tells all. We hear that the authors are members of a notorious Seattle commune, and that they travel the country wearing T-shirts decorated with cartoons of fallaciously labeled dinosaurs. Frankly, it's so weird, we're inclined to believe it.

IMAGE FILE FORMATS

We end our tour of digital imagery with a look at *file formats*, which are different ways to save files to disk. If you're new to digital imaging, the notion of file formats may seem a little strange. Computers save information in bits, and images are made of bits, so why not just write the bits to the hard disk and be done with it? Alas, the digital world is rife with innovation. Literally hundreds of file formats have come into being since the first painting programs arrived on the market in the early 1980s, all of which fulfill slightly different purposes. Thankfully, only a dozen or so formats are widely supported by image editing applications, and less than half of those merit your attention.

Conserving Disk Space with JPEG

As discussed in the previous chapter, JPEG is the format used by virtually every digital camera under $10,000. It accommodates 8-bit grayscale and 24-bit color images alike. More significantly, it minimizes the size of an image on disk by reorganizing pixels. This "lossy" compression results in images that consume anywhere from $1/2$ to $1/50$ as much space as they would if no compression were applied. (The exact savings varies from image to image.) This makes JPEG ideally suited to packing lots of pictures into small spaces. The caveat is: Compression comes at the expense of quality.

When you save an image in the JPEG format, most image editing programs present you with a slider bar labeled Compression or Quality:

- **Compression** If the slider is labeled Compression or the like—as in Paint Shop Pro and Micrografx Picture Publisher (Figure 4-15)—higher values apply more compression, which decreases the file size and image quality in kind.

- **Quality** If the slider is called Quality—as in Photoshop, Adobe PhotoDeluxe, and others—higher values apply less compression and preserve greater image quality.

Figure 4-15 Micrografx Picture Publisher presents an array of options when saving a JPEG image. But the one that counts is the Compression Factor slider bar.

Low compression or high quality settings result in larger but better images. As shown in Figure 4-16, high quality images look great even at low resolutions. They also hold up much better to image editing. As the compression value rises or the quality value drops, more and more of the fine details in the image get lost in the pixel shuffle, as demonstrated in Figure 4-17. If you push your luck too far, JPEG runs roughshod over clarity and quality, resulting in indistinct photographs like the one pictured in Figure 4-18.

Figure 4-16 Before cropping, the original version of this image consumed 2.8MB in memory. With a little JPEG compression, the file size dropped to 1.4MB, or 50 percent.

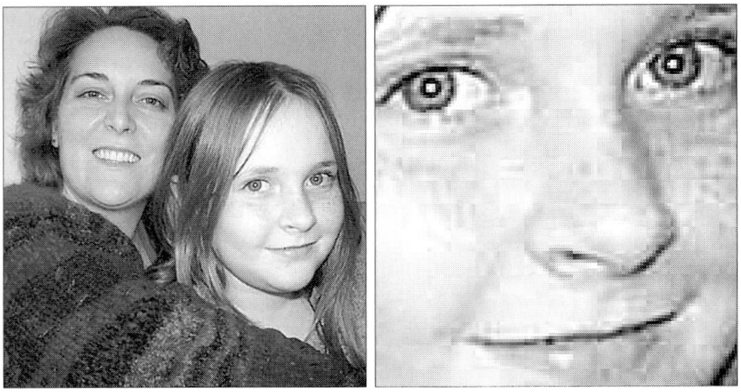

Figure 4-17 Increasing the JPEG compression reduces the file size to 890K, 30 percent of the original. But fine details like the freckles are beginning to break down.

Figure 4-18 Cranked up to full volume, JPEG gets this particular image down to 272K, less than 10 percent its uncompressed file size. But the pixels have turned to mush.

We recommend applying JPEG compression very conservatively. Programs like Photoshop are very good about preserving detail, especially at quality settings from 8 to 10. Other programs produce disastrous effects at the least provocation. In Paint Shop Pro, a compression setting of 20 (out of 99) applies more compression than does a rock-bottom quality setting of 0 in Photoshop. We recommend you keep an eye on file size. If JPEG reduces your image to less than 25 percent of its uncompressed size, it's probably a bad sign. (To remind yourself how to calculate the uncompressed size, see the section "Pixel Count and Resolution" earlier in this chapter.)

Two additional items to keep in mind about JPEG:

- Like any file format, JPEG affects the size of the image on disk—and only on disk. You cannot compress an image in RAM, which is where the image resides when you open it. Therefore, every time you open the image, it gets decompressed to its full size.

- If you make changes to the image and then save it to disk, the software reapplies the JPEG compression, which leads to further degradation of the image quality. Multiple applications of even conservative compression settings can destroy fine details. So if you're not sure what you're doing and you think you might be editing an image two or more times, it's a good idea to save the image to a lossless format such as TIFF.

To learn more about TIFF, keep reading.

Preserving Image Quality with TIFF

There are lots of file formats that save pixels exactly as you capture or edit them. But the most popular (and arguably most reliable) of them all is TIFF. Like JPEG, the TIFF format supports 8-bit grayscale and 24-bit color images. But it also supports 1-bit black and white, 8-bit color, and a variety of other color settings. TIFF is ideally suited to high-contrast photographs. It's also great for saving images that you intend to edit more than once or import into a publishing application.

Some image editors build lossless compression into the TIFF format. Depending on the image, this compression shaves 5 to 50 percent of the file size off an image without harming so much as a single pixel. TIFF achieves this amazing feat by simplifying neighboring blocks of pixels that are identical in color. Instead of individually recounting 10 black pixels in a row, for example, the compression itemizes the first pixel and then says "x 10."

A friend of ours suggested a pastoral analogy that we find helpful. Say you want to describe a flock of seven sheep:

- Using an uncompressed vocabulary, you must describe the flock as "sheep, sheep, sheep, sheep, sheep, sheep, sheep."

- By speaking lossless compression, you can take advantage of the more efficient phrase, "seven sheep." The original meaning is preserved but many breaths are saved.

- If you decide to speak JPEG, you merely say "sheep." You still convey the general idea, but some of the information is lost in the translation.

That's an exaggeration, of course. JPEG isn't quite that vague. But it gives you a general idea of how lossless and lossy compression differ.

The specific varieties of compression available to TIFF varies from program to program. Paint Shop Pro offers more compression varieties than any program we've seen, including CCITT, Huffman Encoding, LZW, and Packbits, all high-lighted in Figure 4-19. These different options are known as *compression algorithms*. Very briefly, here is how these particular algorithms work:

- **CCITT** Short (somehow) for International Telegraph and Telephone Committee, *CCITT* compression was developed as a way to accelerate the transmission of documents from one fax machine to another. CCITT is opti-mized for black-and-white images—which is all fax machines can send and receive—making it a poor choice for color and grayscale photographs.

- **Huffman Encoding** One of the earliest compression algorithms, *Huffman Encoding* was designed to compress text documents. As we mentioned back in the section "The Math Behind the Pixels" earlier in this chapter, a character of text occupies one byte of memory. Huffman searches for the most-common letters—A, E, and anything else that gets you 1 point in Scrabble—and replaces them with shorter codes. For example, a lowercase *a* changes from the 8-bit 01100001 to the 3-bit 010. Because it was originally intended for text, the effect of Huffman is unpredictable when applied to images. As likely as not, it can *increase* the size of an image.

- **LZW** Lempel-Ziv-Welch, or *LZW*, is the algorithm of choice for compressing grayscale and color images. In addition to replacing clusters of uniformly colored pixels (as in the sheep analogy), LZW looks for repeating patterns. For example, if LZW locates more than one instance of a red pixel followed by a white pixel and then a blue one, it replaces all instances with a simplified code. You'd be surprised how many times a combination of pixels repeats in a digital photograph.

- **Packbits** Apple Computer devised the *Packbits* routine to reduce the size of black-and-white MacPaint files. Like CCITT, it counts up consecutive pixels and substitutes them with smaller values. The only reason for a program to offer Packbits is to ensure compatibility with older software. For digital photography, Packbits is useless.

The compression algorithm of choice is LZW. Not only is LZW well suited to digital photography, but it is also the most widely supported means of TIFF compression. Some image editors—Photoshop among them—limit their support to LZW. If you compress a TIFF image with CCITT, Huffman, or Packbits, Photoshop won't be able to open it.

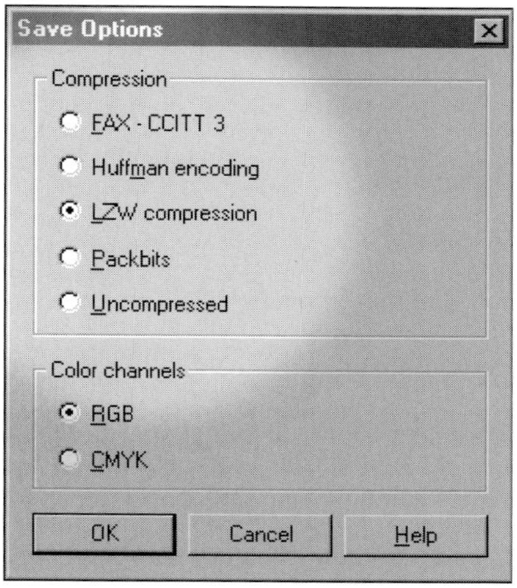

Figure 4-19 Paint Shop Pro offers several different compression options for TIFF.

Eight-Bit Images Choose GIF

Technically speaking, you can post images on the Internet using any file format you like. But unless a Web browser can read the format, your graphics can't be seen. We're always hoping that Netscape Communicator and Internet Explorer will broaden their support, but as we write this, only two formats can be read without the aid of third-party plug-ins. The first of these is JPEG, that ubiquitous format supported so widely among digital cameras. The second is *GIF*.

Short for Graphic Interchange Format, GIF is at once worse and better than JPEG.

- On the minus side, GIF images may contain at most 256 colors (and as few as two), compared with the 16 million permitted JPEG and TIFF.

- On the plus side, GIF includes lossless LZW compression, the same LZW included with TIFF. But unlike with TIFF, you can't turn the compression off. All GIF files rely on the same algorithm, so support from one application to the next is guaranteed.

The upshot is that GIF does a better job of representing high-contrast photographs, particularly those that include text. The images in Figure 4-20 are enlarged so you can see the pixels, as you can when viewing images on the Web. Both images take up about the same amount of room on disk—roughly 20K apiece. But whereas the JPEG image is infested with artifacts, the GIF image appears sharp and distinct—this despite the fact that the GIF image contains just 8 shades of gray.

Figure 4-20 A high-contrast Web image saved to JPEG (top) and GIF (bottom). GIF does a better job of maintaining the fine lines and sharp edges.

Although GIF images are limited to 256 colors, each of those colors may be any one of the 16 million available from the 24-bit color library. So although you can choose at most 256, you can choose any 256 you like. To communicate exactly which colors an image contains, the GIF file has to include an index. For example, the index may specify that Color 1 is dark blue, Color 2 is medium blue, Color 3 is bright yellow, and so on. For this reason, the process for downsizing the number of colors from 16 million to 256 or fewer is often called *indexing*. To learn how to best go about indexing, see Chapter 16, "Preparing Images for Print and the Web."

> **NOTE:** *On the off chance you find yourself needing to say GIF aloud, watch out. We usually say "jif," like the peanut butter, which is supposedly how the format's developers pronounced it. Others swear GIF begins with a hard g and should be pronounced like "gift" without the t. If we were linguists, we could probably come up with a rule of thumb for you—such as, use "gif" south of the Mason-Dixon Line and "jif" up north—but as we're not, we recommend that you say GIF any way you want.*

Other File Formats

JPEG, TIFF, and GIF are the most important file formats, but they aren't the only ones. Here are a few other formats to be aware of:

- **EPS** Based on the PostScript printing language, the Encapsulated PostScript (*EPS*) format combines a PostScript definition of an image with a screen preview so you can position the image in a page-layout program. Many prepress professionals advocate EPS because it streamlines the printing process. So long as you're printing to a PostScript printer, the software just sends the code to the printer and lets the printer do the work. The problem with EPS images is that they're huge, as much as two to three times as large as the uncompressed image size. So while you may on occasion want to save an image to EPS, it's a bad format for day-to-day use.

- **PDF** A derivative of EPS, the Portable Document Format (*PDF*) is a terrific format for exchanging documents on disk or over the Internet. If you send a PDF file to a colleague, he or she can open it in Adobe's free Acrobat Reader software. You can even embed fonts, ensuring that the document looks the same when opened on any computer. The only reason to save an image to the PDF format is to import it into Acrobat Exchange, a page-layout program for PDF files. If you prefer to export PDF files from some other program—such as QuarkXPress or Adobe Illustrator—then feel free to use TIFF or JPEG.

- **FlashPix** Resolution is one of the most bothersome concerns in digital photography. Wouldn't it be great if the software would automatically select the best resolution for you? That's the idea behind a format jointly developed by Kodak and Live Picture called *FlashPix*. The FlashPix format stores an image at multiple resolutions. When you open the file in an image editor, the software shows you the resolution that looks best on-screen. When you print, the software selects the resolution that is best suited to the printer. But for now, FlashPix is an interesting idea in search of support. Even Kodak's own cameras shoot to JPEG and then require you to make a separate conversion to FlashPix. It's a good format to be aware of, but we don't expect to see it in wide use for a few years.

• **PNG** Pronounced "ping," the Portable Network Graphics (*PNG*) format combines the best of both JPEG and GIF. In other words, you can save 24-bit graphics with lossless compression. PNG is also smart enough to adapt its compression to the specific kind of image you're saving. The problem is, neither Netscape Communicator nor Internet Explorer supports PNG without help from a plug-in. This means that if you post PNG images on a Web site, about 95 percent of your visitors won't be able to see your work. For the present, PNG is another good idea in need of support.

• **Native formats** Just about every program ever invented saves to a specialized format designed to track that program's special features. This custom format is called the *native format*. For example, Photoshop's native *PSD* (Photoshop document) format saves layers, masks, paths, and other items forbidden by standardized formats like JPEG. There's nothing wrong with saving an image to your software's native format; sometimes it's your only option. But if you hope to import the image into a different program, you'll need to save a copy of the image to JPEG, TIFF, or one of the others.

• **Platform-specific formats** Microsoft devised the BMP format to handle images at the Windows desktop level. Prior to that, Apple created PICT to serve the same purpose for the Mac OS. Both BMP and PICT have their purposes, but they have nothing to do with digital photographs. Unfortunately, BMP and PICT have a habit of popping up when they're not wanted. Some PC programs suggest BMP in lieu of a native format. If you connect your digital camera directly to a Mac, the software might urge you to save the images to the PICT format. We heard from one reader who used PICT over JPEG because he thought PICT would prohibit JPEG's lossy compression. In fact, PICT supports the same compression options as JPEG—it was just happening without his knowledge. By selecting PICT over JPEG, he was merely reducing the chance that the images would open properly if he ever transferred them to a PC.

- **Others** Over the years, other standards have experienced a brief period of fame, only long enough to make thousands of images unreadable by modern software. Formats to avoid at all costs include CUT (Dr. Halo), IFF (Amiga Interchange File Format), IMG (Gem Paint), LMB (Deluxe Paint), MAC or MPT (both MacPaint), MSP (Microsoft Paint), PIC (PC Paint), PCX (PC Paintbrush), PX1 (PixelPaint), RIFF (Fractal Design's Raster Image File Format), WMF (Windows Metafile), and WPG (WordPerfect Bitmap). There are others, of course, but those are the most common.

Color Plate 1-1 As recently as 1996 (the year of the Casio's debut), the color response of affordable digital cameras has improved several fold, though film still maintains a modest advantage. (See page 4 for more information.)

Casio QV-10

Canon PowerShot 350

Kodak DC200

35mm film

C1

Color Plate 1-2 Without correction, a photograph shot with the Fuji MX.700 appears dark with a yellow cast. But the detail is in good shape, and there are plenty of intermediate shades between the highlights and shadows. Therefore, it's possible—even easy—to correct this image. (See page 15 for more information.)

Color Plate 1-3 After 10 to 15 minutes of work in Photoshop, the scene is restored to the way it looked the day Deke shot it. Commands used include Variations, Levels, Unsharp Mask, and Crop. (See page 15 for more information.)

Color Plate 2-1 The original image on the left, captured with the Fuji DC.300 offers enough resolution to allow for creative image enhancement as seen on the right. (See page 29 for more information.)

(See page 29 for more information.)

C3

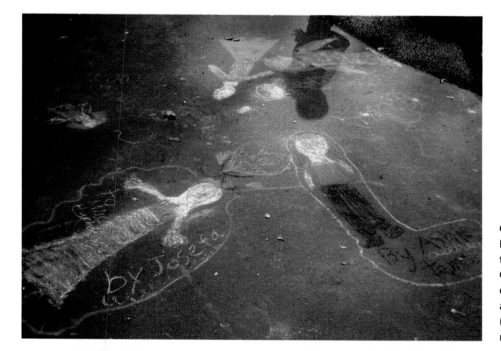

Color Plate 2-2 Both images were taken with the Nikon CoolPix 900s to document location and lighting. (See page 30 for more information.)

(See page 30 for more information.)

Color Plate 2-3 On the top left, an image captured with medium format Fujichrome 100. On the top right, an image captured with the MegaVision S2. On the bottom left, 300% image detail of film. And on the bottom right, 300% detail of digital capture. (See page 32 for more information.) *Photo by Andrew Rodney.*

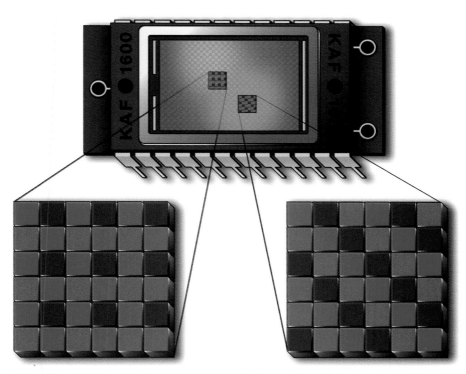

Color Plate 3-1 This detail from the surface of an image sensor was shot under a microscope. Each of the squares of color is a separate electrode. The colors are the results of red, green, and blue filters applied directly to the electrode. (See page 52 for more information.) *Photo by Dennis Walker.*

Color Plate 3-2 In a single array camera, each electrode on the image sensor is filtered differently than its neighbors. In most sensors, every other electrode is green, with every fourth electrode either red or blue (left). But a few sensors vary the filters in diagonal strips (right). Both systems produce a color image in one shot. (See page 53 for more information.)

Color Plate 3-3 These images illustrate the red channel as it appears raw from the image sensor (left) and after interpolation (right). On its own, the result looks gummy and soft. (See page 54 for more information.)

Color Plate 3-4 But mix the red, green, and blue channels together, and the raw (left) and interpolated (right) images look significantly better. This is because each pixel is accurate in at least one channel. (See page 54 for more information.)

Color Plate 4-1 This stock photo contains exactly 256 colors. The colors are brash; the transitions between colors are harsh. The effect is that of a silkscreen print—graphic but not photographic. (See page 68 for more information.)

C7

Color Plate 4-2 This full-color photograph contains three channels of image data in red, green, and blue (top). Each channel contains just 256 brightness values, but when mixed together they produce as many as 16 million unique colors. (See page 70 for more information.)

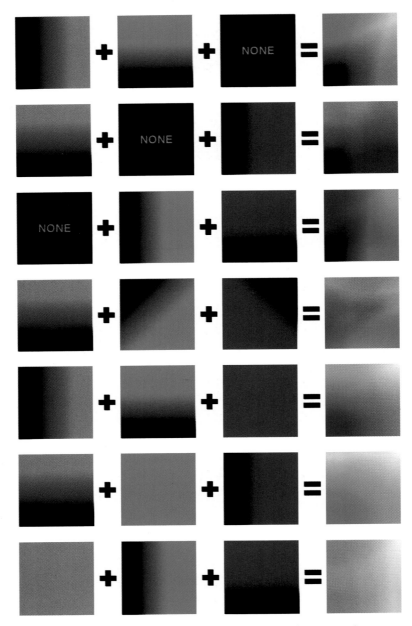

Color Plate 4-3 Each of these equations shows what happens when you add specific combinations of red, green, and blue light. As you can see, the more light you add, the lighter the colors get. (See page 70 for more information.)

CHAPTER FIVE

Bells and Whistles:
The Digital Camera Interface

The term *interface* commonly refers to the manner in which computer operating systems and other software elements communicate with their human users. But it can just as easily apply to any machine or invention. A dashboard contains most of the interface elements for a car. A remote control provides the interface for a television set. A pull chain is the interface for a lamp. Interface designs range from extremely simple to monumentally complex, and they exist all around us.

Digital cameras are no exception. From zoom levers to flash buttons, battery compartment latches to lens covers, focus controls to shutter releases, a digital camera offers more bells and whistles than most devices twice its size. It's that rare sort of gadget where you can find something to flick, twiddle, or poke on any of its six sides.

This chapter examines the interface elements and accessories that are the most essential to your enjoyment and mastery of digital photography. Whether you need to judge the merits of a camera that you think you might purchase or you're trying to grapple with the camera you already own, we help you identify and exploit the features that matter most.

VIEWFINDER AND LCD

As with a conventional camera, the most essential element of a digital camera's interface is the *viewfinder*. In case you're unfamiliar with the term, the viewfinder is the window you look through to line up the shot. It permits you to see what the camera sees. Without the viewfinder, you'd be shooting blind.

There are two kinds of viewfinders:

- **Optical** An optical viewfinder is the kind you'd expect to find in a conventional camera. You peer through one or more lenses that simulate the effects of the camera's lens element.

- **LCD screen** To give you a better sense of how your photograph will look when converted to pixels, many digital cameras include color LCD (liquid-crystal display) screens, like the one depicted in Figure 5-1. The LCD works like a small television, broadcasting the light refracted onto the image sensor.

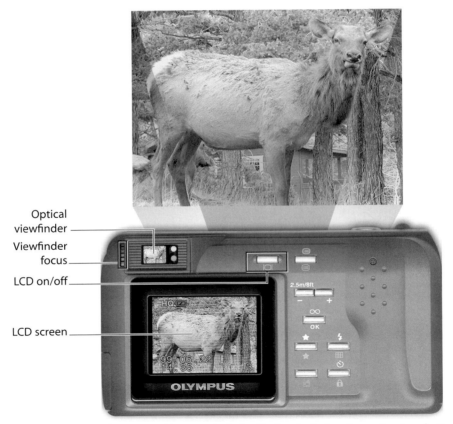

Figure 5-1 Many optical viewfinders include a focus ring to adapt the lens to your eye. The LCD screen includes an on/off switch so you can conserve batteries.

Because of its simple design, an optical viewfinder requires no power and works well under virtually any lighting condition. In contrast, an LCD draws heavily from the batteries and is very sensitive to lighting conditions. The LCD is too weak to compete with direct sunlight, and in a dimly lit room, the image sensor often captures too little light to be of much use. Cloudy days and shaded settings are most favorable to the LCD.

Rangefinder versus SLR

On the other hand, an LCD is often more accurate than an optical viewfinder, depending on how the camera is configured. Most digital cameras that cost $1,000 or less are *rangefinder* devices. This means you peer through one lens, and the camera shoots through another, as illustrated in Figure 5-2. The lenses are designed to be in sync for wide-angle shots. But when shooting close-up shots, the two views tend to drift apart, an effect known as a *parallax error.*

To get a sense of how dramatic this effect can be, try winking one eye and then the other. You'll notice that your view of the world shifts slightly back and forth. The shift grows more dramatic as you bring an object closer to your face. Scientists call this effect *binocular* parallax. The lenses of a rangefinder camera are about the same distance away from each other as your eyes. The only difference is that the viewfinder is situated above the main lens element instead of beside it.

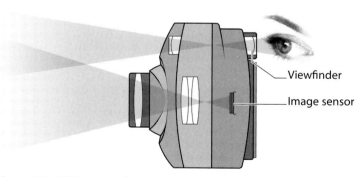

Figure 5-2 With a rangefinder camera, you look through one lens, and the camera looks through another.

A preferable option is to see the same image that the camera sees. In a *single-lens reflex* (SLR) camera, a mirror rests at a 45-degree angle in front of the image sensor. As shown in Figure 5-3, the light enters through the lens element, bounces off the mirror to another group of mirrors, and finally passes through the viewfinder. When you press the shutter release, the mirror pops out of the way and permits the light to hit the image sensor. This is why you see a flash of black when you shoot a picture with an SLR camera—for that split second, the mirror is not there to reflect the light.

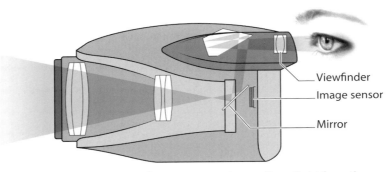

Figure 5-3 In a single-lens reflex camera, a mirror reflects light from the main lens element to the optical viewfinder.

LCD Preview and Playback

The LCD viewfinder is more accurate than a parallax viewfinder and may even enjoy a slight edge over SLR devices. This is because the LCD preview is fed directly from the image sensor. Where an SLR mirror may be slightly out of alignment, the LCD constantly tracks the image that the camera sees. Granted, the brightness and colors may be a bit out of whack—after all, a one-inch-tall LCD screen is hardly a match for a large desktop monitor—but if your subject is centered on the LCD screen, you can be sure it will appear centered in the final photo as well, as demonstrated fairly dramatically by the differences between Figures 5-4 and 5-5.

> **NOTE:** LCD previews are an exclusive function of rangefinder devices. When framing a shot, the mirror in an SLR camera blocks the light from the image sensor, so there is no image to convey to the LCD. The sole function of the LCD screen in an SLR camera is to look at images that have been captured, as explained next.

Katrin's feet

Figure 5-4 If you rely on a parallax viewfinder, your picture may come out differently than you expected. In this worse-case scenario, Katrin captured her own feet.

Figure 5-5 This is exactly what Katrin saw when she framed the shot using the LCD viewfinder.

After shooting one or more photographs with a digital camera, you can use the LCD to review your images. If you don't care for one of the pictures you took, you can simply delete it. Some cameras even offer slide show functions, so you can cycle through a cardful of images automatically. An LCD helps take some of the mystery out of the photographic process.

MEDIA AND CONNECTIVITY

The next most important features of a digital camera are its media and connectivity. In addition to determining how many images your camera can hold and how fast it captures them (as covered in the "Types of Media" section of Chapter 3), the media also defines the ways you can transfer images from the camera to the computer. You can either connect the camera directly to a computer using a cable or you can remove the card or disk from the camera and pop it into a special drive. After downloading the images, erase the camera media, and you're ready to take more pictures.

Serial: As Slow As It Gets

In the old days, digital point-and-shoot cameras captured pictures to memory that was hard-wired to the camera's circuit board. The only way to get the pictures from the camera's RAM to your computer—where you could edit and print them—was to connect camera and computer using a common serial cable, pictured in Figure 5-6. Because every computer manufactured since the mid-1980s includes a serial port, the cameras were universally compatible. But a serial connection is limited to speeds of 150 to 230 kilobits per second (Kbps), or three to four times as fast as a speedy modem connection. That might be fast for surfing the Web, but for transmitting photographs from a digital camera, it's maddeningly slow.

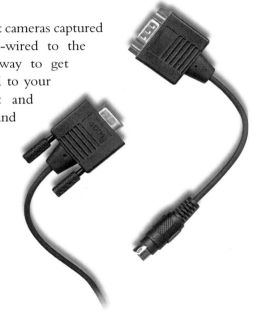

Figure 5-6 This PC serial cable (left) and Macintosh adapter (right) are a digital photographer's last and least satisfactory resort.

Relying on a serial connection also means you have to lug your computer around wherever you go. Deke likes to tell a story about the first time his wife, Elizabeth, used a DC40, Kodak's first point-and-shoot digital camera. In late 1995, Elizabeth agreed to field test the DC40 with a laptop computer at the Denver Zoo. After shooting 48 pictures—enough to fill up the DC40's memory—she took a break and downloaded the images to the laptop. In all, it took 17 minutes to download the pictures, which was about half as much time as she spent shooting the pictures in the first place. Imagine yourself sitting on a bench with a computer in your lap for nearly 20 minutes as the general public passes by gawking at you.

Modern cameras are faster. On a state-of-the-art PC, it takes about six minutes to download 8MB of images via a serial cable. But that's still several times slower than alternative methods. It also assumes that everything works according to plan, which is unfortunately rare. Serial connections require special software to download the images. Some programs require you to turn off networking; others make you restart your computer with the camera connected. In testing a Casio QV-5000SX, we couldn't get the software to recognize the camera on a PC at all, and it took us several minutes to get things up to speed every time we connected it to a Mac. We can live without such headaches, and we suspect you can, too.

To this day, virtually every camera priced under $1,000 includes a serial cable among its connection options. Serial is always there as a last resort, but there are better solutions.

USB: The Faster Connection

The newest trend in serial connections is *Universal Serial Bus* (USB). Included with just about every desktop computer manufactured from 1998 on, USB is the faster, smarter replacement for serial. If you're not sure whether your computer offers USB or not, look at the back of the machine and see if you can locate the symbol shown in Figure 5-7. If your computer lacks USB, for about $50 you can purchase a PCI board that adds two USB ports. You also need to be running a compatible operating system—either Windows 98 on the PC or OS 8 or later on the Mac. (Windows NT 4 does not support USB.)

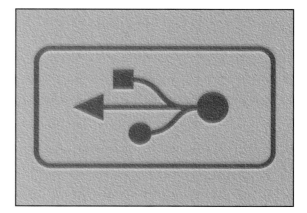

Figure 5-7 If your computer has this symbol on the back of the case, it supports USB.

If your computer is USB-ready, you might want to look for a camera that supports USB as well. To identify a USB device, look on the outside of the box for the symbol in Figure 5-8.

Figure 5-8 This symbol on the outside of a camera box tells you that you can connect the camera to your computer's USB port.

The primary advantage of USB over serial is that it's faster. USB can transfer data at speeds up to 12 Mbps—more than 50 times as fast as the speediest serial connection. This means that, in theory, you should be able to copy 8MB of images in a few seconds. In practice, our tests showed that it takes close to a minute. Undoubtedly, times will improve as vendors grow more familiar with USB, but it's already a significant time-saver.

The second advantage of a USB camera is that it's *hot swappable*. This means you can plug and unplug the camera in and out of the USB port while both computer and camera are turned on. The first time you plug a USB camera into your PC, Windows 98 immediately displays a dialog box, like the one in Figure 5-9, explaining that it has located a

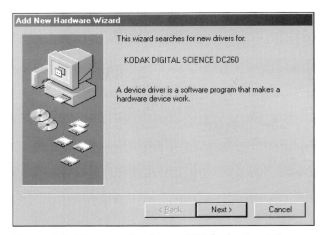

Figure 5-9 When you hook up a USB device to a PC running Windows 98, the operating system prompts you to load the driver.

new USB device and wants to load a driver. Just insert the disk or CD that came with the camera and follow the directions on-screen. (In some rare cases, you may have to load or update the driver manually from the Device Manager panel in the System control panel, as shown in Figure 5-10.) On the Mac, run the installation software that ships with the camera. In both cases, you'll be asked to restart your computer before using the camera for the first time.

From that point on, each time you connect the camera to the USB port and turn it on, your computer represents the camera to you as a disk drive. Double-click on the camera icon to browse through the pictures you've shot, as in Figure 5-11. You can open the pictures, copy them, or delete them, just as if they were files on a disk.

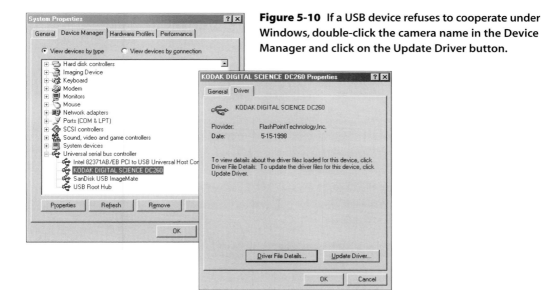

Figure 5-10 If a USB device refuses to cooperate under Windows, double-click the camera name in the Device Manager and click on the Update Driver button.

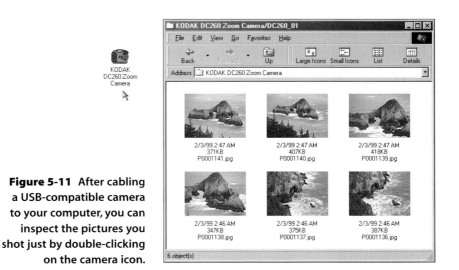

Figure 5-11 After cabling a USB-compatible camera to your computer, you can inspect the pictures you shot just by double-clicking on the camera icon.

Downloading Directly from the Media

If your camera relies on removable media such as CompactFlash or SmartMedia, you can take advantage of transfer options that are faster and more convenient than either serial or USB:

- **PC Card adapters** If you have a mobile computer such as a notebook PC, a PowerBook, or any of several handheld devices, the computer probably includes a PC Card port. Check your computer's documentation to see if it supports Type II cards (which are 5mm thick). If so, your best option is to purchase a PC Card adapter for either CompactFlash or SmartMedia (depending on your camera), as pictured in Figure 5-12. Insert the flash memory card into the adapter, insert the adapter into your PC, and it's available immediately. No driver or other software is required. And it's lightning fast—you can copy 8MB of images in a few seconds.

Figure 5-12 For about $20, you can buy a PC Card adapter for a CompactFlash memory card (left). An equivalent SmartMedia adapter (right) is more expensive to produce and costs about $80.

- **FlashPath adapter** For those who rely primarily on desktop computers—or whose mobile computers don't offer PC Card slots—alternatives abound. If your camera uses SmartMedia, you can purchase a FlashPath adapter, shown in Figure 5-13. Created by Toshiba and available from a variety of vendors including Fuji and Olympus, FlashPath inserts directly into your computer's floppy disk drive. Under Windows 95 and 98, you view and edit the contents of the FlashPath adapter just as if it were a floppy disk. On the Mac, you have to run a special utility that lets you copy files but not modify or erase them. As we write this, a Windows NT driver is still in the works. FlashPath is significantly slower than a PC Card adapter, particularly on the Mac, but it's still much faster than a serial connection. Several older-model SmartMedia cameras bundle FlashPath adapters for free.

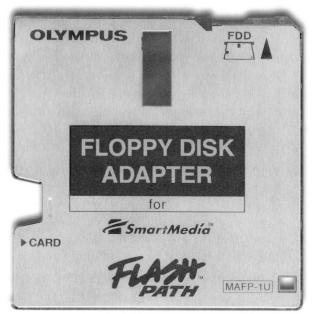

Figure 5-13 Insert a SmartMedia card into the left side of a FlashPath adapter, and then stick the FlashPath into your floppy drive.

- **ImageMate drive** The ImageMate drive from SanDisk lets you read and modify the contents of CompactFlash cards. Not only is it fast (copying 8MB of images in just over 10 seconds) but it's easy to fit on your desktop, weighing in at about the size and shape of a mouse (see Figure 5-14). PC owners can choose from either a parallel or USB model. If you own a Mac, USB is your only option (assuming, of course, that your Mac supports USB).

Figure 5-14
The $79 ImageMate CompactFlash drive connects to either the parallel or USB port on your computer.

- **Clik drive** When you're on the road—particularly when you're on vacation—it's not always convenient or desirable to take a computer with you. You can pack extra memory cards, but that gets expensive. Iomega offers an interesting solution: a drive that lets you copy images from CompactFlash or SmartMedia cards to inexpensive 40MB Clik disks without the aid of a computer. Shown in Figure 5-15, the Clik drive is less than 5 inches long and weighs under 7 ounces, making it highly portable. Armed with 10 to 20 disks, you have enough storage to last several weeks. Then, when you return home, you can plug the drive into your computer's parallel or PC Card port and copy the images off the Clik disks. At press time, the Clik drive is compatible with Windows computers only. Camera vendor Agfa plans to bundle the drive with its ePhoto 1680 camera.

Figure 5-15 For $249, you can purchase a Clik drive that lets you copy images from SmartMedia and CompactFlash cards to less expensive Clik disks.

Alternative Connections

Professional cameras in the $10,000-and-up price range capture several million pixels and use little or no compression. As a result, a single file may weigh in at anywhere from 12MB up to a whopping 300MB or more. Some of these cameras take advantage of removable Type III hard drives that you can swap into a portable computer's PC Card slot. Others use larger hard drives or require you to cable the camera directly to a computer. When a single photograph takes up as much space as 20 to 40 pictures captured by a $1,000 camera, serial and USB connections are simply too slow. Two connections transfer large files much more quickly:

- **SCSI** Pronounced "scuzzy," SCSI stands for *Small Computer System Interface.* Long a mainstay of Macintosh computers, SCSI transfers data at speeds ranging from 40 Mbps to 640 Mbps, or 3 to 53 times as fast as USB. But while SCSI grows faster every year, it's beginning to show its age. Every SCSI device must be connected and turned on before you start your computer. A single SCSI port can handle up to seven devices, but thanks to compatibility issues, you have to work to get much higher than three.Each device requires a separate address and you have to terminate the last device in a chain. Plus there are several different incarnations of SCSI, each of which requires different kinds of cables. It's fast, but it's sufficiently complicated to test the patience of even the most accomplished users.

- **FireWire** As USB is to serial, FireWire is to SCSI the faster, more convenient replacement. Designed in the late 1980s by Apple, FireWire also goes by names iLink and the less friendly IEEE 1394 (meaning that it's the 1394th standard of the Institute of Electrical and Electronic Engineers, not that you asked). Supporting speeds of 100 to 400 Mbps, FireWire permits up to 63 devices to be connected to one port, requires no addressing, and works without termination. And like USB, FireWire is hot swappable, so you can plug and unplug devices when your computer is running. FireWire is now standard issue on the colorful Power Mac G3 towers, but you can also purchase a third-party PCI expansion board. Our favorite is the $699 Adaptec Ultra HotConnect-8945, which includes two FireWire ports and one Wide Ultra SCSI, and works on both the Mac and the PC.

FireWire not only enjoys support from high-end cameras like Kodak's DC560 and DC620, but it's also the standard for digital video cameras, such as Canon's popular Optura. Pictured in Figure 5-16, the Optura captures video on hour-long Mini DV tapes. With this setup you can download video and audio over a single

FireWire cable—as opposed to using separate RCA and S-video cables, as with analog video—and you can also operate the camera via FireWire. Figure 5-17 shows Adaptec's DVDeck software for the PC, which lets you play, fast forward, and rewind a tape to a desired point and then record the movie to disk. And because the video and audio is already digitized at 720 by 480 pixels and 48kHz, respectively, there's no loss in quality when you transfer the movie from camera to computer.

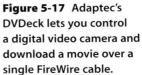

Figure 5-16 The Canon Optura digital video camera as it appears when connected to a computer with a FireWire cable.

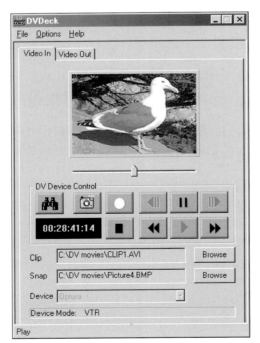

Figure 5-17 Adaptec's DVDeck lets you control a digital video camera and download a movie over a single FireWire cable.

The one caveat to keep in mind when editing digital video, however, is that the file sizes are massive. The 45-second clip pictured in Figure 5-18 takes up more than 160MB on disk. The 70-second segment pictured in Color Plate 5-1 on page C9 consumes more than 250MB. If you decide to record the entire contents of an hour-long Mini DV tape, you'll need nearly 13.5GB of open space on your hard drive—enough to fill 20 CD-ROMs! (In case you're wondering how DVD movies manage to pack two hours or more onto a single two-sided disk, the answer is compression. DV movies are slightly compressed, but DVD movies are compressed till it hurts.)

Figure 5-18 This 45-second, 720 by 480-pixel AVI movie with stereo sound weighs in at 160MB.

BATTERIES

Batteries may seem like a minor issue where photography is concerned. Unless you're a professional photographer who's used to working with lamps and strobes, it's likely that you take power largely for granted. If your film camera offers automated controls like date stamping and motorized film rewind, then you might need to replace the batteries once a year. If your camera is a decade or more old, it might not use batteries at all—the entire process is probably mechanical.

But digital cameras have ravenous appetites for power. If you make frequent use of your camera's telephoto function or LCD preview, it's not uncommon to churn through a set of batteries in less than an hour. Generally, a set of disposable batteries lasts long enough to fill one memory card— between 20 and 40 pictures.

That's why rechargeable batteries are so essential. Besides having the obvious advantage that you can use them over and over again, they also last several times longer per charge than alkaline disposables. Unless you relish the idea of keeping a 24-pack of AA cells in your camera bag at all times *and* you get a kick of making regular contributions to the city dump, then you should get rechargeable batteries.

> **TIP:** *Some digital cameras ship with rechargeable batteries, whereas others ship with the cheapest cells they can get away with. But even if your camera includes rechargeables, it's probably a good idea to purchase extras. That way, you can be sure you always have additional power ready in the wings.*

Kinds of Batteries

Deke's father shares a patent on the world's first sealed lead-acid battery, used to power everything from cars and commercial vehicles to Apple's original PowerBook 100. So you'd think we'd know everything there was to know on the subject. But, alas, Dad didn't bring his work home with him. So here's what we've learned for ourselves over the years:

- **NiCd versus NiMH** Most digital cameras rely on four AA cells, the kind that are about as big around as your pinky. The two most popular varieties of rechargeable AA are NiCd (pronounced "nicad") and NiMH, short for nickel cadmium and nickel metal-hydride, respectively. If you have a few rechargeables lying around from some other contraption, they're probably NiCds. But if you're in the market for new batteries, go with NiMH. According to industry tests, NiMH cells last about twice as long per charge.

• **Chargers** Every camera that includes rechargeable cells also includes a charger. Ideally, you want a small charger that plugs directly into the wall, like the one in Figure 5-19. Take our word for it, you don't want to be hassling with big, boxy chargers and cables on the road. If you somehow manage to accumulate more than one charger, be sure to use it with the correct batteries. Most chargers accommodate NiCd or NiMH cells but aren't designed for both. If you use a charger with the wrong kind of cells, it may work, but it may reduce the life of the batteries as well. If you're lucky enough to own a charger that works with both NiCd and NiMH—like the one in Figure 5-20—be sure to set the switch properly for the batteries you intend to charge.

Figure 5-19 Here we see the back of a charger that plugs directly into a wall socket without any messy cables. The entire unit fits in the palm of your hand.

Figure 5-20 Included with the Agfa ePhoto 1680, this unit provides a switch so you can charge either NiCd or NiMH cells.

- **Disposable varieties** All right, so not every battery you purchase has to be rechargeable. In fact, we like to keep a few fresh disposables around on the off chance that all of our rechargeables run out of juice. One advantage of disposables, after all, is that they take longer to lose their charge when they're not in use, so they're more likely to work when you need them. But rather than buying the cheapest batteries you can find, look for so-called "long life" cells, such as Kodak's PhotoLife brand. They cost a little more, but they last as much as three times as long. Not only does this make long life cells a better deal, it also ensures that you can take more pictures with fewer interruptions.

- **Specialized cells** Not all cameras use AA cells. Many ship with customized batteries that work only in one specific brand of camera. Virtually all cameras from Fuji and Sony fall into this camp; both rely on another variety of rechargeable battery, the Lithium Ion cell. The good news is that there's just one battery instead of four and, as likely as not, you can charge the battery without removing it from the camera. Just plug the camera into a wall socket when it runs low on power. Also, these batteries tend to be *zero memory* cells, which means you can recharge them without fully draining the power. The bad news is that if you run out of juice, you can't pop in some AAs to tide you over. Therefore, it's a good idea to purchase an extra battery from the camera vendor so you always have a spare.

Don't Be Too Frugal

One final note on the topic of batteries: When the camera complains that the cells are out of juice, they're out of juice. If the batteries are rechargeable, recharge them. If not, throw out *all* the batteries and replace them with fresh ones. Do *not* under any circumstance use one of those cheesy little testers—the kind where you squeeze a strip on both ends of the battery—to determine which cells are run down and which are not, and then switch out just the ones that test badly. Although this may sound like a smart and economical idea, those testers aren't all that reliable, and old batteries can really mess up some digital cameras.

Unfortunately, we learned this one the hard way. On a cruise to Alaska, Deke mixed and matched old and fresh cells in a Kodak DC120. The camera completely melted down and refused to function even after Deke inserted new cells. What should have been a fun day in Ketchikan turned into a nightmare of calling Kodak reps from pay phones, schlepping a computer to one of those rent-a-modem shops, spending an hour downloading new firmware from Kodak's site, and uploading the firmware to the camera by way of a slow serial connection. After that, the camera worked, but only barely. The autoexposure was completely blown, so that every picture looked like it was shot in a snowstorm.

Ultimately, these problems were the results of a design flaw with the DC120. But even so, they could have been avoided. Whatever model of camera you use, it's not worth running this risk to save a dollar or two on batteries.

THE TRADITIONAL STUFF: FOCUS, FLASH, AND MORE

LCD viewfinders, connectivity, and batteries are the issues that demand the most attention when working with digital cameras. They are the elements that most conspicuously distinguish digital cameras from their traditional cousins. But just because a camera is digital doesn't mean you don't have to pay attention to the traditional stuff as well. Here are some additional features that—while every bit as important as those we have discussed so far—should come as familiar friends to anyone who has a moderate amount of experience with film cameras:

- **Fixed focus** Every camera has to offer some means for focusing light onto the image sensor. In the early days, all digital cameras under $1,000 were "focus free," meaning that the focus was set at the factory and could not be changed. This is called *fixed focus*. A subject located 6 to 10 feet from the camera appeared in sharp focus, subjects closer or farther away appeared in acceptable focus, and anything closer than 4 feet was out of focus, or *soft*.

- **Autofocus** These days, most digital point-and-shoot cameras offer *autofocus*. Infinitely preferable to fixed focus, the autofocus feature automatically repositions lenses to bring a single subject into sharp focus. You can identify an autofocus camera by looking through the optical viewfinder. If you see a cross or circle, as illustrated in Figure 5-21, then the camera provides autofocus; otherwise, the focus is very likely fixed. To use autofocus, press and hold the shutter release halfway down to permit the camera to lock onto the subject inside the cross or circle. If the main subject of your photograph is not in the center of the frame, or the frame contains multiple subjects, align the cross or circle with the subject on which you want to focus, press the shutter release halfway, and then move the camera to take in the full image, as demonstrated in Figure 5-22. Pressing the button all the way down takes the picture.

Figure 5-21 A cross or circle in the optical viewfinder indicates that the camera offers autofocus.

Figure 5-22 If the subject is off center, align the circle with the subject (top), press the shutter release halfway, then frame the shot (bottom).

- **Manual focus** Autofocus is smart, but it's not smart enough to handle all situations. If the camera can't lock onto an object—as when shooting through leaves or in low light—the camera may shoot a soft picture or it may refuse to capture the image altogether. That's when you need manual focus. As things stand now, the only cameras that offer traditional manual focus rings are the $10,000-and-up professional models. Less-expensive models offer everything from a series of fixed-focus overrides—say, one for a subject 2 feet away, another for a subject 8 feet away—to incremental lens controls that you monitor on the LCD screen. Sadly, many cameras offer no backup for those times when the autofocus fails; the one you purchase should.

- **Macro function** If you have good eyesight, your far vision may be infinite. But no matter who you are, your near vision is limited. If you move this book closer to your face, for example, your eyes will at some point give up and the text will go fuzzy. The same is true for cameras. A typical digital camera can focus on a subject as close as 12 inches away. If you want to focus closer, you have to turn on a *macro* function (usually in the form of a button marked with a flower icon). Like a pair of reading glasses, the macro function shifts the focus abilities of the camera forward—say, from 4 to 20 inches. Again, not all cameras offer a macro function, but if you plan to do close-up work, you'll need one.

- **Automatic flash** Virtually all point-and-shoot devices include a built-in flash, also called a strobe. The best models mount the flash at the top of the camera so you don't accidentally place your finger over the flash when framing the shot. The flash automatically fires in low light, and automatically turns off in bright settings. You should also be able to turn the flash off, as when shooting close-ups or when shooting long exposures with a tripod.

- **Red-eye reduction** Because of the proximity of the flash and lens element in a point-and-shoot camera, red-eye is a common problem when photographing at night or indoors. In dim light, a person's pupils dilate. This allows the flash to pass into the eye and reflect off the back of the retina. The reflected light appears red to the camera. There are two ways to avoid this aptly named red-eye. One is to use a flash that's set high above the camera, such as the pop-up strobe included with the Olympus D-620L. The more common solution is a *red-eye reduction* function, which instructs the strobe to flash twice, with the first flash at low power to light the scene and shrink the pupils of the people in your photograph. In this way, the second full-power flash bounces harmlessly off the iris, as illustrated in Color Plate 5-2 on page C9. We include more information on red-eye in Chapter 9.

- **Fill flash** One of the best uses for flash is to fill in shadows in full daylight. When you shoot a person against a bright sky—a condition called *backlighting*—the camera averages the light from the person and the sky and comes up with an intermediate exposure. The problem is, that exposure is too brief for the person and too long for the sky, so you get a dark silhouette against a blindingly bright background, as in the first example in Figure 5-23. The solution is to turn on the flash (by pressing the flash button so a bolt appears on the LCD) so it fills in the shadow. This *fill flash* not only brightens the person, it also reduces the exposure so the sky appears less bright, as the second example in the figure shows.

Figure 5-23 With no flash, a subject shot in direct overhead light appears lost in shadow (left). Force-activating the flash helps fill in the shadow and even out the overall lighting (right).

- **Flash extras** Only a few cameras under $1,000 are set up to synchronize with external flash units or studio strobes. Notable examples are the D-620L from Olympus and the DC260 from Kodak, both of which provide industry-standard flash synchronization sockets. Cable the strobe to the camera, as in Figure 5-24, and it automatically flashes when the camera sends out the proper signal. We have yet to encounter any digital camera in this price range that offers a hot-shoe for mounting a flash on top of the camera, but we expect to see these as the cameras mature. Other cameras, such as Agfa's ePhoto1680, let you adjust the aperture for studio flashes, but you have to bounce the flash off a slave sensor. Chapter 9 includes more information about working with an external flash.

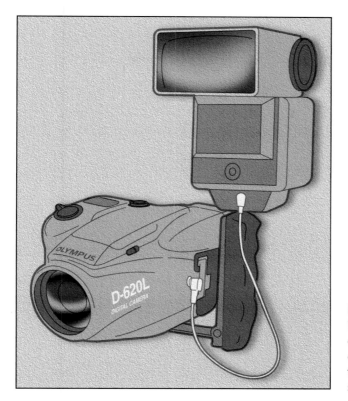

Figure 5-24 An enhanced image from the D-620L's documentation showing a cable (in white) attached to the flash synchronization socket.

- **Optical zoom** Lots of cameras make claims for zoom functions, but only a handful provide the real thing. Look for a camera that offers an *optical zoom*, in which a lens actually moves back and forth to magnify the scene. A camera that includes T and W buttons (telephoto and wide) uses a motor to move the lens element. Also acceptable is a lever to move the lens manually. Do not be misled by claims for a "digital zoom," which merely crops the image down to a smaller size and then interpolates it up, adding thousands of pixels that were never there in the first place. Figure 5-25 shows the difference between an optical 14x (1400 percent) zoom and the same scene captured with a camera that maxes out at 3x optically and then interpolates the remaining pixels. One is a true representation of the image, the other is not—it's as simple as that.

Figure 5-25 A still frame captured with the Optura digital video camera (top), which offers a 14x optical zoom, compared with the same scene captured using an equivalent digital zoom (bottom).

That pretty much sums up the features that you should expect from a digital camera interface. Obviously, you can expect a camera that provides all of these features to cost more than one that doesn't. In some cases, you may prefer to live without a feature or two if it means getting a great deal. Consider the Epson PhotoPC 550. It lacks an optical zoom, there's no flash or LCD screen, the lens is fixed focus, it ships with disposable batteries, and you have to download images via a serial cable. In other words, it lacks just about every feature covered in this chapter. But it takes decent pictures, is small enough to fit in your palm, and costs less than $200. It's a wonderful, compact, cheap device.

For our full range of advice on shopping for a digital camera—taking into account the many features covered in this chapter and more—stay tuned for the next chapter.

CHAPTER SIX

Shopping for a Digital Camera

Shopping for anything (for some of us anyway) is a difficult and not altogether enjoyable process. Maybe it's a fear of commitment, but we are always sure there's a better selection and a better deal just around the corner, and that if we just hold off making that purchase…

In the case of digital cameras, this is particularly true. First, they are part of a technology that's unfamiliar and a little intimidating. Second, the state of the art is advancing so rapidly that what was the most sophisticated and expensive camera last month is now only midlevel, and its price has dropped dramatically. But at some point we need to take the plunge, knowing that whatever we choose will be old news the day we buy it. We need to have something to work with.

In this chapter, we try to organize the decision-making process to make it a little less frightening. For those given to impulse buying, this chapter should help put on the brakes a little and allow reason a chance to tame the raw consumerism inflamed by shameless marketeers.

We have broken the process of making a decision down into the following manageable steps:

1. Determine what you'll be using your new camera for.

2. Turn this into a set of clear minimum requirements.

3. Decide what you can afford.

4. Make a list of desirable features (other than image quality) you'd choose if you could afford them.

5. Research and test what's available.

6. Finalize your decision and lay down your money.

WHAT WILL YOU BE USING THE CAMERA FOR?

Is your main purpose in buying a digital camera to send pictures of the kids to their grandparents (and this is certainly a noble cause)? Is it to snap photos for the company newsletter? To create a catalog of stuff on a Web site? To document the results of a research laboratory? To create small images for a mail-order catalog? To take photographs for newspapers and magazines?

Each of these purposes suggests a different group of cameras, once we have teased out their explicit requirements. Understanding your audience and how exacting they are also helps determine how much image quality you need. Will your images be seen by a fastidious art director who insists that you show every detail, or by the folks in the parts department who need to know which air cleaner to send the customer?

To narrow down the number of cameras you need to consider, start by evaluating your photographic needs. Figure out what you'll really be using your camera for. Yes, there are all kinds of things you might someday want to do with it; there's always the chance that if you had a high-end scanning camera you'd finally get around to seriously pursuing photography as an art form, but let's be realistic.

How will your work be published? How large will the final images be? Do you need to be able to shoot images in rapid succession? Will you be working where available light is limited? Will you be taking a large number of photographs at a time, or only a few?

WHAT DOES THE CAMERA HAVE TO DO?

At this point, you need to do a little soul-searching. Begin with the understanding that you may still be better served by conventional photography or that the right choice for you is a digital camera that is capable of meeting your needs only 80 percent of the time and that for the remaining 20 percent, you can use film, borrowed or rented digital equipment, or even have someone else do the photography for you. These are all issues no one can resolve for you; they ride as much on personal preference as on practical determinants.

Minimum Image-Quality Standards

The final presentation of your image determines what level of image resolution your new camera needs to produce. Higher resolution comes at a price, and if your requirements are not exacting, you can save money by buying only the capability you need. Look at the quality of the optical and digitizing systems, as well. If you need to make presentations that have accurate color and fine detail, take this into account when you select a camera. Table 6-1 summarizes the output resolutions required for a number of applications. It should help you narrow down your choices.

Final Purpose	Type of Output	Image Size	Camera Category
Internet	monitor display	160 x 120 pixels 320 x 240 pixels	entry-level deluxe point-and-shoot
Desktop color prints	ink-jet printer	3 x 5 inches 5 x 7 inches 8 x 10 inches	entry-level deluxe point-and-shoot professional lite
In-house newsletter	laser printer	3 x 5 inches 4 x 6 inches 8 x 10 inches	entry-level deluxe point-and-shoot professional lite
Advertisement	b&w newsprint 65/85 ls	3 x 5 inches 4 x 6 inches 8 x 10 inches	deluxe point-and-shoot professional lite professional
Advertisement	color magazine 133/150 ls	3 x 5 inches 4 x 6 inches 8 x 10 inches	professional lite professional professional
Commercial display prints	ink-jet , LED, CRT ink-jet, LED	up to 20 x 24 inches up to 40 x 60 inches larger than 40 x 60 inches	professional professional (one-shot or three-shot) professional (scanning)

Table 6-1 General Resolution Guidelines

Control

For many purposes, the combination of a fixed lens of reasonable quality with automatic metering, an on-camera flash, and a decent sensor and processor is perfectly adequate; most entry-level cameras take surprisingly good pictures under a range of lighting conditions. If you'll be working under more demanding conditions or you'll need a higher degree of image control, consider the various options available among the more advanced cameras: deluxe point-and-shoot, professional lite, or even professional.

Speed of operation

The next thing to consider is the speed at which you need to take pictures. Digital cameras are notably inferior to their film cousins when it comes to doing *anything* in a hurry. If you are going to need fast responses from your camera, make sure you choose a model that is up to the task—they do exist.

HOW MUCH CAN YOU AFFORD?

After you have narrowed down your search to a category of camera and decided on what features you really need it is time to determine what you can spend. As with all new technologies, sticker shock is part of the package, but weigh the cost of the camera against the savings on film and—more important—time.

If you are purchasing a camera for personal use, it will be a matter between you and your pocketbook how much the convenience and the vogue of digital photography are worth. If you are using the camera as part of your business, it is likely that the initial purchase price will quickly be offset by savings in film and processing costs. How long your digital camera takes to pay for itself depends on how often you use your camera.

Table 6-2 shows the relative costs of film and digital imaging for a working studio over time. Figured this way, the cost of professional digital photography is comparable to that of working with film, but 1) time is money and there should be real time savings here and 2) working digitally allows you to offer additional, billable services including digital retouching, compositing, proofing, and layout.

CONVENTIONAL FILM, LARGE FORMATS

Large-format film	Number per shot (exposure bracket)	Cost
4"x5" Ektachrome @ $1.70	5	$8.50
4"x5" color Polaroid @ $3.00	2	6.00
4"x5" b&w Polaroid @ $2.25	3	6.75
processing @ $1.50	5	7.50
Cost per shot		**$28.75**

CONVENTIONAL FILM, MEDIUM FORMATS

Medium-format film	Number per shot (exposure bracket)	Cost
roll 220 film @ $8.50	5 frames	$1.75
color Polaroid @ $23	2 frames	2.30
b&w Polaroid @ $17	2 frames	1.60
processing @ $12 Roll	5 frames	2.50
Cost per shot		**$8.15**

DIGITAL IMAGING AMORTIZED OVER 12, 24, AND 36 MONTHS

Initial equipment costs

Professional digital camera	$25,000
Mac or PC w/10GB hard drive & 64MB RAM	4,000
Additional 196MB RAM	1,000
20" Monitor	2,000
Photoshop & CMYK software	1,500
CD writer & software	500
Dye sublimation printer/proofer	8,000
Misc. media (backup and print)	2,000
Maintenance & upgrades	1,200
TOTAL	$45,200

Digital Imaging Costs per Shot	Over 12 months	Over 24 months	Over 36 months
Equipment cost Shooting days per month: 10	$3,767	$1,883	$1,256
Equipment cost per day Number of shots per day: 8	377	188	126
Cost per shot	**$47**	**$24**	**$16**

Table 6-2   Cost Comparison: Film versus Digital Imaging

WHAT FEATURES DO YOU REALLY WANT?

Even after you've decided on a category of camera, a price range, and your rock-bottom feature requirements, a lot of variables still exist. This is probably the hardest part of the decision: you have to choose among a large number of options that you'd like, but that aren't really deal breakers. How do you weigh a little more lens sharpness against a camera that feels right in your hands? Better customer service against slightly quicker editing functions?

Perhaps the best route is to make a laundry list of these discretionary items and try to keep track of the advantages and disadvantages of each model you investigate. You won't end up with a truly objective measure of the value of one camera over another, but such a list helps keep track of the evaluation process. Some of the following may be things you can't do without, and others probably aren't.

- **On-camera flash** Most cameras have an on-camera flash unit, but beyond that, there are many different features to choose among.

  Can you control the flash power? This feature is more likely to be found on higher-priced models.

  Does the camera offer a red-eye reduction feature? Many offer some version of this feature, which may or may not be something you need.

  Does the camera support external and/or studio flash equipment? We don't understand why hot shoes and flash synchronization jacks are not more common on digital cameras; in any case, the ability to use an external flash may be critical to your needs.

- **Color balance** Most cameras adjust the color balance by making the lightest part of the image white. Some allow you to control the white-balance feature.

- **Metering** How sophisticated is the metering system the camera employs? Low-end cameras usually rely on center-weighted metering. Another measurement pattern may be better suited to your needs. Some higher-end cameras have an exposure lock feature; some even allow you to use an external meter and manually set the exposure.

- **Shutter speed and aperture** If you need more direct control of the image, you want a camera that allows you to vary both the shutter speed and the aperture. Otherwise, the camera's tiny (and not very artistic) brain decides how to handle depth-of-field and moving subjects.

- **Focus** Similarly, you may want a camera that permits you to focus on the subject of your choice. Some let you lock the autofocus onto a particular subject in the frame. Only the most expensive have true manual focus.

- **Compression** Many, but not all, cameras let you set the compression used to store the image. You may have occasion to trade off image quality against the number of images stored on the disk.

- **Stop-action** Some cameras offer the option of taking 12 or 16 stop-action photos in a few seconds. The catch is that all the images share the resolution of one standard image, as shown in Figure 6-1. Stop-action images are not much good for reproduction, since each individual image is very small and has limited resolution.

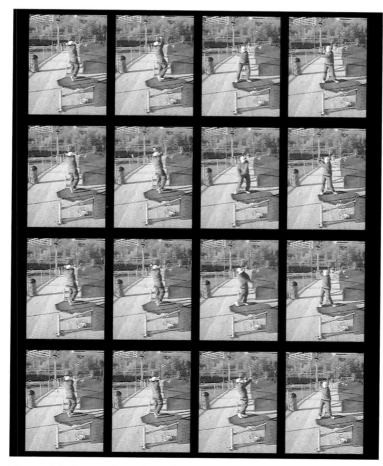

Figure 6-1 Stop-action of a golf swing captured with the Fuji MX-700.

- **Storage** A number of different systems exist for storing images. Each has its advantages and its drawbacks. You should take this into account when you choose a camera.

- **Viewfinder and LCD screen** Most cameras have a viewfinder with its own little optical system rather than through-the-lens viewing. Some also have an LCD screen (some larger than others) that previews and reviews images, and displays other information as well. This may well be something you will want.

- **Burst mode** Some cameras have a *burst mode* feature, which stores the unprocessed output of the CCD in a buffer and allows a number of shots in quick succession. The number of shots you can take at this rate is limited by the size of the buffer.

- **Camera RAM** How fast can you view, select, and delete images from disk? The camera's RAM and the type of storage medium it uses affect your ability to edit images in the camera.

- **Zoom** Many cameras offer zoom lenses of various descriptions; they are a nice feature and not prohibitively expensive. Do not confuse digital zoom (simply a reduction in the area of the sensor and hence of image resolution) with optical zoom, which is performed by the lens. Some cameras have interchangeable lenses and may even be compatible with equipment you already own. Consider also if the lens offers a macro setting to allow taking extreme close-ups.

- **Style** Digital cameras come in an inordinate variety of forms, some familiar, some more like cigarette packs or old Polaroid cameras. Some of these will be more comfortable for you than others.

Accessories: The Little Things in Life

We have evaluated dozens of digital cameras, and the manufacturers that paid attention to what they included in the initial price are the ones that we seem to remember and recommend. If you spend $500 to $1000 on a piece of equipment, the least the manufacturer can do is include a camera strap and a basic pouch to protect your investment. The following is a list of the little extras in a digital camera package that make it more economical and enjoyable to work with as it comes out of the box.

- All cameras come with guarantees and customer service plans; some are better than others.

- Digital cameras have a voracious appetite for batteries. Rechargeable batteries and charger make the camera more convenient, economical, and environmentally responsible.

- Being able to hook the camera up to an AC power supply while downloading files or when working in the studio saves batteries and spares the landfill.

- Kudos to the manufacturers that supply all of the above plus a set of standard batteries so that eager customers can unpack the camera and start shooting right away.

- Manufacturers that deliver cameras with the smallest storage disk or no disk at all are not on our Christmas list.

- Once your lens is damaged, there is nothing you can do to fix it. A lens cap, preferably one that attaches to the camera strap, should be included.

- A wrist or neck strap is the cheapest camera insurance you can buy. If the manufacturer includes one, attach it and use it.

- A bag or pouch to protect your camera from dirt, scratches, or being banged around is the second cheapest form of camera insurance. We especially like the bags that have separate pockets for extra memory cards and batteries, like the bag that comes with the Agfa ePhoto 1680.

- All cameras come with some type of documentation, either in booklet or CD form. We prefer well-written, well-translated instruction booklets that slip into a camera bag to be consulted when needed.

- Any and all additional information, such as a CD tutorial, is always welcome.

- Additional archiving, creative, or QTVR software gives you more options to work and play with your digital camera.

TIME TO TEST SOME CAMERAS

Once we have narrowed down the choice to a few contenders, it is important to carefully evaluate the quality of their output. Up to a certain point, it's fine to compare the relative merits of the equipment based on published specs. But in the final analysis, it is important to actually test it yourself, preferably under conditions as close to real-life as possible.

If you have the opportunity to test a camera before buying it, jump at it. Test the camera in your shooting environment and take pictures of the things that you plan to photograph. If you're a real estate professional, take pictures of houses; if you need to do a lot of close-up work, shoot close-ups.

Most likely, your chance to test a deluxe point-and-shoot or professional lite camera will come by borrowing a camera from a friend or by shooting files at a camera store. If you're in the market for a professional camera, most resellers will work with you in your studio to see how the camera performs in your shooting conditions.

Trade shows allow you see the cameras in action, handle them, and look at files coming straight off the cameras. When checking out a camera, hold it to feel how it lies in your hands, look through the viewfinder, and see if you are comfortable with the controls. Take a couple of exposures, ask the sales rep to put the files on a floppy or Zip disk that you brought with you, and take the files home to see how the files look printed on your printer.

Lens Performance

The lens gathers light coming from the subject and focuses it on the image plane. Even a perfect digital capture cannot compensate for corruption of the image at this stage. When buying a camera, therefore, pay close attention to the quality of the lens. Inexpensive entry-level cameras are likely to have inexpensive plastic entry-level lenses that will never give you the quality you need.

Examine files and prints (and *not* ones that have been worked on) for the following characteristics:

- **Sharpness** Check that the image is sharp—side to side and top to bottom (see Figure 6-2). If the image isn't sharp in the first place, there is nothing you can do to fix this. When judging sharpness, make sure that the image was captured at a high shutter speed ($1/25$ second or higher) and/or that the photographer used a tripod. The resolving power of a professional quality lens is approximately a 15-micron circle. If the lens resolves slightly better than the CCD's pixel size measured in microns, you should perceive the greatest degree of visual sharpness.

Figure 6-2 Notice that the image is sharp in the center and gets progressively softer toward the edges.

- **Exposure evenness** Look to see if the exposure is even over the entire image. Are the corners darker? Take a picture of a white wall and look at the corners of the image for exposure fall-off. Although this problem can be corrected in the digital darkroom, it's not something you want to fix on every picture you take.

- **Distortion** Does the image bow in (pincushioning) or out (barrel effect)? Don't mix this up with the widening effect that you get from shooting with a wide-angle lens.

- **Color fringing or chromatic aberration** means that the lens is not focusing all wavelengths uniformly onto the sensor. It shows up as slight red and green color fringes on dark lines, such as text, or around areas of high contrast. It cannot be corrected. See Color Plate 6-1 on page C10.

- **Flare** Shooting toward the light source can create flare, which appears as diffuse light areas, shutter-shaped blotches, and a general loss of contrast. This problem is minimized by quality coated optics that reduce the amount of light bouncing around inside the lens before it reaches the CCD. Figures 6-3 and 6-4 show the same shot with a flare and without.

Figure 6-3 Notice the string of light blotches caused by lens flare.

Figure 6-4 The same image taken with the Agfa ePhoto 1680— it has absolutely no telltale signs of lens flare.

• **Image Processing and Storage** Once the light has passed through the lens and focused on the sensor, a whole new set of issues come into play. The electronic portion of the process has its own limitations that have to be evaluated for their impact on the final image quality. No matter how perfect the optics, an inadequate sensor and/or processor will never give you the image quality you need.

Digitizing electronics are still changing daily and we need to pay close attention to them when we choose a camera. Image quality is determined by a number of factors, some of which are functions of the CCD (or the CMOS sensor), others of the analog-to-digital converter (A/D), still others of the system the camera uses to write the image to disk.

- **Resolution** is the ability of the camera to capture fine detail; it refers to the number of pixels on the sensor. This is not a strict definition of the word, but it is common usage; it can range from a Barbie camera's 120 by 280 pixels (33,600) up to an 8000 by 10,640 pixel, 244MB RGB file (85 million pixels in each channel) produced by the Better Light 8000 scanning camera. The resolution of your image determines how large you can print it without having it look like it's made up of little pixel squares (which, in fact, it is).

- **Dynamic (or tonal) range** refers to the camera's ability to capture detail in the highlights and the shadows of a photograph. It is a function of both the sensor and the processor and is an important variable in selecting a digital camera. Most cameras perform just fine when the light is diffuse and the contrast is low. But if you're going to be taking pictures in bright sun, for example, pay attention to this parameter if you need detail across the full range (see Figures 6-5 and 6-6).

- **Bit depth** is the number of bits assigned to describe the level of each pixel and refers to the data the sensor passes through the A/D converter to the processor, not to what the camera ultimately spits out as an image. It is not identical to dynamic range; with a poor-quality sensor and/or converter, you still get 8-bit data, but of the 256 levels, the shadow details all disappear into noise and the highlights are undifferentiated white, leaving only the middle levels to carry real information.

Unless you are looking at the extreme high or low ends of the digital camera market, it's all pretty much the same: three channels of 8 bits. This is likely to change, however, and increased bit depth will mean a general improvement in the quality of the final image.

In the most expensive cameras, however, you can access the individual channels (sometimes as deep as 16 bits) before they are processed and perform exacting corrections at that level before you go on with other manipulations.

Figure 6-5 This image, captured with the Nikon CoolPix 900s shows good detail in both the shadow and highlights.

Figure 6-6 This image, captured with the Ricoh RDC-4300, suffers from blocked-up shadows and highlights without detail.

Evaluating Digital Image Files

When you have the opportunity, look at a raw camera file—one that just came off the camera and hasn't been perfected with any Photoshop magic. Look for softness, jagged edges, compression artifacts, noise in the shadows, blown-out highlights, color casts and misregistration of the color channels, and noise in the blue channel. Color Plate 6-2 on page C10 shows the effect of compression damage, revealing compression artifacts and loss of detail in the picture inset.

Check image histograms for telltale white gaps of missing information. Figures 6-7 and 6-8 show the same image taken with two different cameras. Figure 6-7 reveals a spiky histogram where image information is missing; notice the noisy surfaces on the bows. In Figure 6-8, the evenly distributed histogram correlates with a lack of noise in the image.

Figure 6-7 White gaps in the histogram are symptomatic of poor image quality.

Figure 6-8 Solid histograms reveal more tonal information and a better image.

BUYING A PROFESSIONAL DIGITAL CAMERA

If you're in the market for a professional digital camera there are a few additional considerations to take into account.

- **High-bit-depth files** can be twice as large as standard 24-bit files, and working with them requires fast computers with more RAM and a larger hard drive. For the high-quality output demanded for advertising and museum work, the ability to access the high-bit data enables higher-quality results and the price is well worth it. Make sure you can access the high bit-depth.

  Many professional digital cameras use similar technology and produce similar-size files, but the software can make or break how well you work with the camera. Some professional cameras support third-party software that greatly improves the camera's performance, especially the quality of the RGB-to-CMYK transforms. The best example of this is how the Leaf Digital Camera Back I and II work with Scitex Colorshop. The software's ability to access the camera's 14-bit data and give the photographer great control over the file conversion results in spectacular separations that print very well.

  Left to its own devices, the CCD would allow the electrons in the brightest areas of the image to overflow the little pixel buckets that collect them and cause "blooming." This would look like streaking or blurring in the highlights. Most manufacturers control this problem in the electronics.

  CCDs are very sensitive to infrared radiation invisible to the human eye. To compensate, a filter is used to block these wavelengths, which can make the image look flat or give it a magenta color cast. You may want to be able to remove the filter for certain special purposes.

- **Antialiasing (blur) filters** are installed in many professional one-shot cameras to reduce the stairstep effect on diagonal lines and to control the color artifacts found in high-frequency image areas, such as finely woven cloth or hair. Some photographers feel that antialiasing filters soften too much and remove them.

  Does the company offer a good warranty? How much customer support is included with the camera? Does the company offer a replacement camera while yours is being repaired? Companies with excellent customer support include MegaVision, PhaseOne, and Better Light. You can often find a list of users on a company's Web site; e-mail a few of them and ask about the camera's reliability and the company's customer support.

- **Upgradeability** Before buying, ask about upgrades for both cameras and software. A good upgrade example is Better Light, which upgrades models 4000 and 6000—for a fee, of course—to the higher-performance models 6000 and 8000, respectively, at any time during their warranty (or extended warranty) period.

- **Color rendition** is a little more subjective. Problems here are can arise from any number of sources. The sensor may be responsible, the conversion from analog to digital data may be introducing inaccuracies, or the white balance may be off. The human eye is an extremely sensitive tool for seeing color differences, but when you're presented a number of different renderings of the same scene, it is often difficult to say which is better than another. Even images of a standard target can vary in so many ways that it is hard to rank them.

  Basically, two variables are at work here. Accuracy of color compares the spectrum of the image with that of the original. Saturation is the relationship between the hue and neutral gray. While pictures may look snappy with the saturation boosted a bit, it comes at the cost of tonal detail and may also increase the noise levels in the image. See Color Plates 6-3 and 6-4 on page C11 for examples.

  You need to choose carefully here. For snapshots, you may want to go for a camera that gives attractive images requiring little manipulation; for more critical work, you need to be sure that you're not losing detail or creating noise that will be impossible to correct in the digital darkroom.

- **Low-light performance** is a problem for digital cameras. Most CCDs have an effective ISO rating around 50. The long exposures needed to capture an image in weak light tend to introduce noise into the image. Turning up the gain to increase the effective speed of the sensor has a similar effect.

  As one might imagine, more expensive cameras suffer less from these failings; Kodak's DCS 520 and Canon's D2000 perform very well from 200–800 ISO and can even be pushed to 1600 ISO with good results. In some cameras, higher speeds are achieved by increasing pixel size at the price of lower resolution.

  If you will be using your camera under controlled lighting, this may not be an issue. Otherwise, how much you want to spend for the ability to shoot under difficult conditions may be a tough call.

- **Speed and responsiveness** Turn off the camera, wait ten seconds, and then turn it back on. A digital camera that turns on quickly, such as the Olympus D620L, will let you get the spontaneous pictures that a slow starter won't. We have missed shots when the digital camera we were working with just wouldn't start up fast enough.

How fast does the camera respond after you press the shutter? This is a huge issue if you plan to take pictures of just about any animate subject (see Figure 6-9 for an example of when it becomes an issue). When you push the shutter, you expect the camera to take the picture. Many entry-level and deluxe point-and-shoot, and even some professional lite cameras, hesitate one, two, or even four seconds before actually taking the picture. This is one of the most irritating flaws of many digital cameras and guarantees that you've just missed the expression, the light, or the action. Professional one-shot cameras use additional RAM and improved electronics to provide near instantaneous shutter response.

Figure 6-9 The photographer wanted a picture of the bicyclist but missed the shot because the shutter just didn't respond quickly enough.

How fast can you shoot consecutive pictures? If you photograph children, animals, or fast action, a camera requiring a three- to five-second delay between shots for processing, compressing, and then writing the file to disk is unacceptable. This is another problem common to all but the more expensive digital cameras. The Olympus D620L claims to shoot 3.3 images per second, but at the time of this writing it costs $1100.

INTERNET RESOURCES

As always, the Internet is an excellent resource for getting information about what products are available in a quickly changing market and finding out what people think about them. Visit *www.dcresource.com* for comprehensive listings of the latest cameras. The manufacturers' sites (*www.kodak.com, www.agfa.com, www.fujifilm.com, www.olympus.com, www.nikonusa.com,* and so on) offer useful information as well.

After you have found two to three cameras to consider seriously, it's time to start talking to as many people as possible that have experience with the cameras you're interested in. On the Web, visit the discussion groups for entry-level and professional lite cameras at *www.pcphotoforum.com;* for professional cameras and digital photography go to *www.peimag.com/Forums/forums.htm* and *www.prorental.com* to participate in active discussion groups.

At some point, you will have satisfied yourself that you have found the right one and all you need is a little reassurance that you're doing the right thing. You have chosen a reliable camera that does what it needs to do, has some features you like, and feels good in your hands.

Buy it.

CHAPTER SEVEN

The Digital Darkroom

For most folks, the difference between a film camera and a digital device is the difference between subscribing and owning. Unless you have a traditional darkroom in your basement, film photography adheres to a subscription metaphor. Your entry costs are limited to the price of the camera. But every time you take a picture, you have to pay a fee. Film, developing, slides, and enlargements may incur small expenses at any given moment, but they add up over time.

Fortunately, when you go digital, film and developing are things of the past. However, in return for little or nothing in the way of subscription fees, you have to make a huge purchase up front. It's up to you to build your own digital darkroom, one that can manage large images quickly and accurately, as well as keep your photographs safe and accessible for years to come.

If you purchased a computer in the last year or two, then a few modest investments may be all that stand between you and a state-of-the-art imaging system. If your computer is a bit older—particularly if it's a pre-Power Mac or a 486 PC—then you can probably get by, but a substantial upgrade will help you work faster and with fewer headaches. And if you don't own a computer at all, or the best you can dig up is some ancient hand-me-down that seems to do a good job of word processing and that's about it, then prepare to part with a couple of thousand dollars of hard-earned cash.

This chapter walks you through the essential ingredients of the digital darkroom, including the computer itself, the computer's memory, storage devices, monitor, and printer. It's a tall list of ingredients, but you don't necessarily have to break the bank. In fact, a base system can be had for as little as $2,000 to $2,500, or about what you'd expect to pay to shoot and develop 200 rolls of consumer-grade film. Then again, if you do by any chance have more money to spend, there are certainly lots of areas in which you can pay more and expect to gain a higher degree of sophistication in return. We'll keep you apprised of the highs and lows as we make our way through the list.

THE COMPUTER

A computer is basically a plastic box that holds a logic board and other hardware elements that make the computer run. The best kind of computer for day-to-day imaging chores is a tower, which is any computer in which the logic board is oriented vertically instead of horizontally. Towers are easily identifiable by the fact that they are taller than they are wide, like those in Figure 7-1.

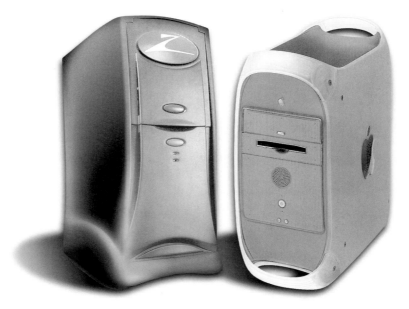

Figure 7-1 An ExtremeZ Windows NT tower from Intergraph
(left) and a Power Mac G3 tower from Apple (right).

The tower design provides two advantages over the old short and squat-style computer:

• First, a tower is large enough to hold a wealth of hardware elements inside its chassis. In addition to the logic board, power supply, and other necessities, a typical tower provides room for one or two internal hard drives; two to four removable storage devices including floppy, CD-ROM, and Zip drives; and three to six slots for expansion cards, in the very likely event that new technologies will hit the market before your computer becomes obsolete. In other words, a tower is designed to grow with you.

- Second, a tower can sit on the floor, underneath your desk, as illustrated in the snapshot from Deke's unkempt office in Figure 7-2. This frees up your desktop for the monitor, keyboard, mouse, manuals, pen holder, coffee cup, calculator, sticky notes, picture of the kids, and a million other items that are a lot more important to your ability to get work done than the hunk of plastic that is your computer.

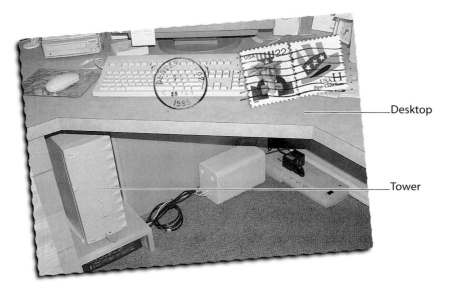

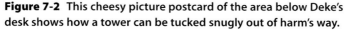

Figure 7-2 This cheesy picture postcard of the area below Deke's desk shows how a tower can be tucked snugly out of harm's way.

NOTE: Not long ago, Apple began a new trend in hardware design with its iMac, a computer and a monitor in one. These attractive machines cost about $1,200 and run as fast as machines costing twice as much. Given the iMac's popularity, we wouldn't be surprised to find PCs with similarly compact designs popping up all over the place. Be aware, however, that the iMac has one big drawback—limited expandability. You can't add a PCI board, RAM upgrades are expensive, and the only connectivity is USB. If you want a cheap machine, an iMac is fine. But if you need something that can grow with you, get a tower.

Regardless of what style of computer you buy—tower, short and squat, iMac-ish—bear in mind that not all computers of a particular style are equal. When shopping for a good imaging computer, here are a few items to look for:

- **The CPU** As a rule, it's a good idea to invest in the most modern CPU design available. As we write this, the fastest Macs rely on PowerPC G3 chips, while high-end PCs use Pentium IIs and IIIs. Clearly, the newest of new chip designs are invariably faster than their predecessors, but there's an even better reason to insist on them. Three to five years from now, you can bet that many software packages will run on nothing less than today's super-fast chip. By purchasing an older CPU, you risk quicker obsolescence.

- **Clock speed** One of the most widely touted and least important attributes of the CPU is its *clock speed*, which is the speed at which the chip can process instructions. Clock speed is measured in *MHz (megahertz)*, or millions of instructions per second. So, a 450MHz Pentium II chip can process 450,000,000 instructions per second. The problem is, very subtle differences in clock speed are quite expensive. Although you probably won't notice the difference between the performance of a 400MHz machine and a 450MHz one, you will notice that the former costs $300 to $500 less. Also, clock speed isn't the only measure of a CPU's ability. A 300MHz Macintosh CPU is typically faster at imaging chores than a 400MHz Pentium II. We don't recommend dropping much below 250MHz—that much of a slowdown you'll notice. But if you want to save money, you can safely skimp on 50MHz to 100MHz without making a significant difference.

- **Cache** In direct contrast to clock speed is an under-reported but critical component of the logic board called the *cache*. The idea behind the cache is this: Once an instruction completes, it takes less time to recall that instruction than to perform it from scratch. So to help speed things along, your computer continually stores completed instructions for reuse. In computer parlance, this is called *caching*. Instructions are cached all over the place—on the hard disk, in RAM—but the most common instructions go to a super-fast element of the logic board appropriately named the cache. Most computers offer two caches— a tiny one (about 32K) on the CPU and a second, larger cache elsewhere on the logic board. This secondary or L2 (Level 2) cache is the one to inquire about. Ideally, it should measure 512K or larger, and it needs to be fast. The L2 cache adheres to an independent clock speed from the speedier CPU, but the closer the two clock speeds are to matching, the faster the performance of the computer. To give you an idea, a 400MHz CPU with a 267MHz L2 cache (where the ratio is 3:2) is typically faster than a 450MHz CPU with a 225MHz L2 cache (with a lower ratio of 2:1). As with all things, a computer is no faster than its slowest component.

- **Expansion slots** No computer can anticipate the technologies that will emerge in the next three to five years. To permit you to add USB, FireWire, SCSI, and other options to your computer over time, a tower computer includes *expansion slots*, which permits you to plug *expansion cards* directly into the logic board, as illustrated in Figure 7-3. Diagramed in Figure 7-4, each card adds input and output ports to the back of the computer. The two most popular kinds of expansion slots are ISA (Industry Standard Architecture) and PCI (Peripheral Component Interconnect). Of the two, PCI is substantially faster and more prevalent. Meanwhile, ISA is being phased out of PCs and was never an option on the Mac. To adequately prepare for future trends in the imaging market, we suggest that you purchase a machine that has no fewer than three open PCI slots.

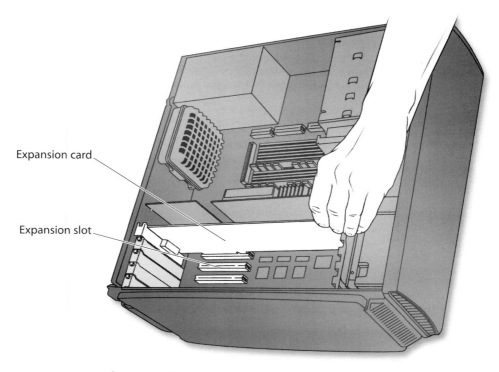

Expansion card

Expansion slot

Figure 7-3 This open tower reveals a series of expansion slots at the bottom of the logic board. Be sure you are grounded when installing such boards, as explained in your computer's documentation.

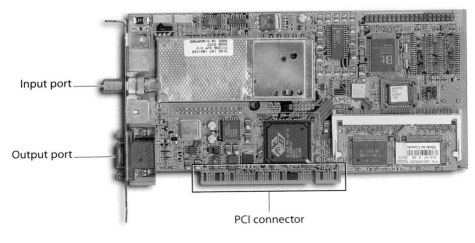

Input port

Output port

PCI connector

Figure 7-4 A photograph of a typical PCI expansion card, which adds input and output ports to the back of a computer.

The Laptop Option

Many digital photographers like to keep a laptop computer handy for field work. If you use a professional camera that has to be tethered to a computer, then a laptop model is essential if you ever hope to leave the studio. Otherwise, a laptop is most useful when you plan to be off-site for several days at a time. We tend to take laptops with us on most domestic trips, particularly if we're on business. That way, we always have a place to download our images when the camera's removable memory fills up.

Beyond portability, the best feature of the modern laptop from a digital photographer's standpoint is that it includes one or two PCMCIA (PC card) slots. Figure 7-5 shows a side view of Apple's PowerBook G3, which offers two Type II PC card slots, meaning that each opening is 5mm thick. Together, the two Type II slots add up to one Type III slot, which is 11mm thick. This means the computer can accommodate both Type II PC card adapters—like those featured in the "Downloading Directly from the Media" section of Chapter 5—as well as Type III hard drives found in a few professional still cameras and the occasional digital video device.

The downside of laptops is that they don't make very good day-to-day desktop computers. Although you can attach peripherals such as mice, monitors, and external drives to laptop computers, you can't expand them with PCI cards the way you can towers. In fact, the only way to expand a portable computer is by way of the PC card slot. A variety of vendors sell specialized PCMCIA expansion options. One of the more exotic that comes to mind is the FireWire card from Ratoc Systems, which lets you add IEEE 1394 connectivity to Macintosh and Windows laptops. But PC expansion cards aren't nearly as prevalent as their PCI equivalents, and some solutions simply don't exist. So while it's possible to rely exclusively on a laptop, you have to be prepared to make sacrifices.

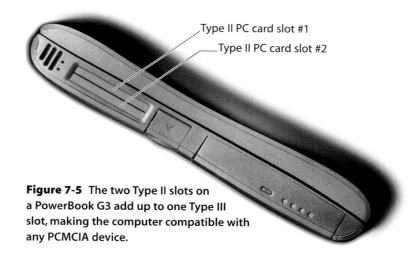

Type II PC card slot #1

Type II PC card slot #2

Figure 7-5 The two Type II slots on a PowerBook G3 add up to one Type III slot, making the computer compatible with any PCMCIA device.

Mac versus Windows: Which OS Is Better?

There are three topics you should never discuss in polite company: religion, politics, and operating systems. Some folks will tell you that Apple's Macintosh is the only platform for serious designers and imaging professionals. Others swear that anything less than Windows NT is fundamentally inefficient and unstable. But in truth, it's mostly a matter of taste. While both of the authors of this book spent many formative years working on the Mac, we have to admit that PCs are every bit as adept at most key tasks and more adept at others. This is not to say we feel any dislike for Macs—far from it. We both rely on Macintosh computers on an almost daily basis. But it's a cross-platform world and we see nothing wrong with relishing its diversity.

Suffice it to say that if you prefer the Mac, you should stick with it, and the same goes for Windows users. If you're not sure which you prefer, then here are a few very generalized observations:

- **Mac advantages**   It's very easy to connect two Macs together to form a network and share files between them. You can just as easily add printers and other devices to an AppleTalk network, so that you and another user can print images simultaneously. Many Macintosh models provide their CPUs on removable cards, permitting you to swap the CPU out for a different one when new technology emerges. And it's relatively simple to solve problems when something goes wrong on the Mac. Elements of the system are named logically and they all reside in a single group of folders, claims that can't always be made for the PC. Color management is also handled better on the Mac, a topic we explore in more detail in Chapter 13, "Preparing Images for Print and the Web."

- **Windows advantages**   Windows uses dynamic memory allocation, so you can run multiple applications without paying strict attention to how much RAM is assigned to each. Windows NT also includes protected memory, so that one application can crash without affecting others. Both Windows 98 and NT do a superb job of making sure you never have to wait for an operation to complete. Even when opening a series of files or starting up a program, you can invariably switch to another application and get work done. Windows makes easy work of connecting to the Internet via a modem. Finally, there's a much wider variety of software for the PC, although many of the best applications are available for both platforms.

Obviously, many of these relative advantages could change the next time a major version of the Mac or Windows operating system is released. And there are hundreds of minor advantages that we don't have the space or inclination to mention here. But the fact is, for every Macintosh advantage Katrin comes up with, Deke can think of something even better on the PC, and vice versa. Luckily, we refrain from engaging in such arguments. We use Macs when we feel like it, we use PCs when we don't, and we recommend that you do the same.

Windows 98 versus NT

If you're in the market for a PC, you may be less concerned with Mac versus Windows than Windows 98 versus Windows NT.

- **Windows NT**   Windows NT 4.0 offers superior memory management, so you can better control the performance of applications and concurrent tasks. NT is also faster, more stable, and more secure, designed specifically for multiple-user environments.

- **Windows 98** However, if you work in a private studio or small office, Windows 98 is the better choice. Unlike NT, Windows 98 supports USB, offers support for plug-and-play hardware, and supports a wider variety of applications.

In the near future—if it hasn't already happened by the time you read this—Microsoft will roll Windows 98 and NT into one operating system to be called Windows 2000. It promises to combine the power of NT and the ease of use of 98. Only time will tell if that promise comes true.

MEMORY

When you open a photograph in an image-editing application, it fully decompresses into memory. This means a full-color image takes up 3 bytes per each and every pixel—no ifs, ands, or buts. But that's just the tip of the iceberg. Very likely, you'll want to open more than one image at a time, which increases your memory needs further. The program also needs RAM to process the edits you apply. And don't forget that your computer requires memory to hold the image-editing application itself, along with any other programs you decide to run, including the operating system.

Consider this example of a typical hour you might spend editing images:

- Let's start with the computer turned off. Naturally, you press the power button to turn it on. As it starts up, the computer loads the operating system from the fixed memory (called the ROM, short for read-only memory) and the hard drive into RAM. These days, operating systems take up a lot of room. **Estimated memory consumed: 24MB.**

- After the computer starts up, you dial onto the Internet and check your email. **Estimated memory consumed: 24MB + 12MB = 36MB.**

- Somebody has sent you a large file, so you decide to take a look at a few images you shot while you're waiting. You start by launching the image editor. **Estimated memory consumed: 36MB + 16MB = 52MB.**

- The day before, you took five megapixel snapshots of a family member, and you want to see which one looks best. What better way to pick a winner than to open all five and compare them side-by-side? **Estimated memory consumed: 52MB + (4MB x 5 images) = 72MB.**

- Apply some edits. As you work, the image editor has to keep track of the last operation in case you decide to undo it. If the program permits multiple undos, it has to store several past versions of the image as you work along. Copying all or part of an image takes up still more RAM. **Estimated memory consumed: 72MB + (2MB x 20 edits) = 112MB.**

- Print an image or two. The image editor hands off the images to the operating system, which takes additional space in memory. **Estimated memory consumed: 112MB + (4MB x 2 images) = 120MB.**

- As you wait for your prints to come out, you notice that your email has finished coming in. A friend of yours has sent you a URL that she thinks you should check out. You click on the URL and the operating system automatically launches the browser. **Estimated memory consumed: 120MB + 8MB = 128MB.**

With very little effort, you've managed to fill a whopping 128MB of memory, which is about as much RAM as a typical high-end computer includes by default. This memory is not gone for good. RAM frees up whenever you close a file, quit a program, or complete a print job. And restarting the computer completely empties the RAM and starts the process all over again. But the fact of the matter is: image editing is one of the most memory-intensive activities that you can engage in.

To ensure that things run as smoothly as possible, you want to equip your computer with as much RAM as you can reasonably afford. Although you can get by with 64MB or even 32MB of RAM, we consider 128MB a good baseline for digital photography. If you intend to work with digital video or high-resolution images from professional cameras, then you should increase the RAM to 256MB or more. RAM is sold on little boards called DIMMs on modern machines and SIMMs on older ones, as shown in Figure 7-6. At the time of this writing, a 128MB upgrade costs about $250 depending on your computer and whether the logic board has a memory slot open. If not, you'll have to replace an existing DIMM or SIMM, which can make the upgrade more expensive.

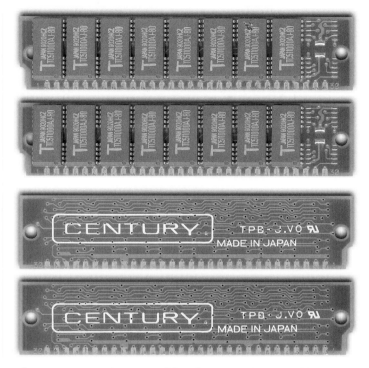

Figure 7-6 RAM chips are soldered onto small boards, like these old SIMMs, shown from the front and back.

Virtual Memory

Given the scenario we outlined, 128MB of RAM may sound like scarcely enough to get the job done. And certainly there are times when RAM by itself will not do the trick. Luckily, your operating system permits you to open applications and images beyond the confines of the physical RAM using a convention called *virtual memory* in which data is offloaded from RAM to an empty portion of the hard disk. The portion of the hard disk set aside for virtual memory is called the *scratch disk*. Because hard disks can be several times larger than the maximum RAM permitted by your computer, virtual memory allows you to open enough applications and perform enough operations to fill your RAM 10 or more times over. The downside is that a hard disk involves moving parts and is therefore 100 or so times slower than RAM. The more your operating system has to rely on virtual memory, the slower your computer responds to your instructions.

The moral is this: If you notice your computer becoming slower and slower as you work, listen to the machine for the *shicka shicka* sound of the hard disk. If the hard disk seems to be perpetually moving, there's a very good chance that you need more RAM.

Carving up RAM on the Mac

Windows 95, 98, and NT automatically assign RAM to applications using a process called *dynamic memory allocation*. When you open a large photograph in an image editor, the image editor tells Windows that it wants more RAM. Windows checks to see how much RAM is available, queries the other programs to see if they can spare some, and gives the image editor what it can. As the user, you don't have to give it a second thought.

On the Mac, you have to assign RAM to applications manually. On one hand, this is a pain in the neck because it means you have to take responsibility for how much memory each application consumes. And each program has to work inside the confines of the memory you give it. But like a stick shift on a car, manual memory management isn't all bad. It gives you absolute control over how the RAM gets divvied up.

To assign memory to an application, first quit the program if it is running. Then select the program icon at the Finder desktop level and choose the Get Info command from the File menu (⌘-I). Under OS 8.5, choose the Memory option from the Show pop-up menu. Look for the Preferred Size option in the Memory Requirements area. This option controls how much memory gets assigned to the application. When you change this value, be sure to raise it to a number equal to or larger than the Suggested Size value, which is the vendor's recommendation for the base amount of memory that the application needs to run. In Figure 7-7, we've raised the Preferred Size value for Photoshop to 120,000K of RAM (or 117.2MB), which gives us plenty of room to open and edit several large images at a time. If the application exceeds 117.2MB of RAM, it will have to resort to virtual memory.

To monitor how much RAM is being used at any one time, go to the Finder desktop and choose About This Computer from the Apple menu. A dialog box shows all the applications that are currently running, as well as how much RAM they're using, as in Figure 7-8. As the reining image editor on this system, we've assigned Photoshop the lion's share of memory, more than three times as much as the operating system. If we want to launch another application at this point, it has to be able to fit inside the remaining RAM, indicated by the Largest Unused Block value, 35.2 MB. More RAM may be free, but this is the biggest continuous block. On the Mac, an application may occupy only one uninterrupted block of memory at a time.

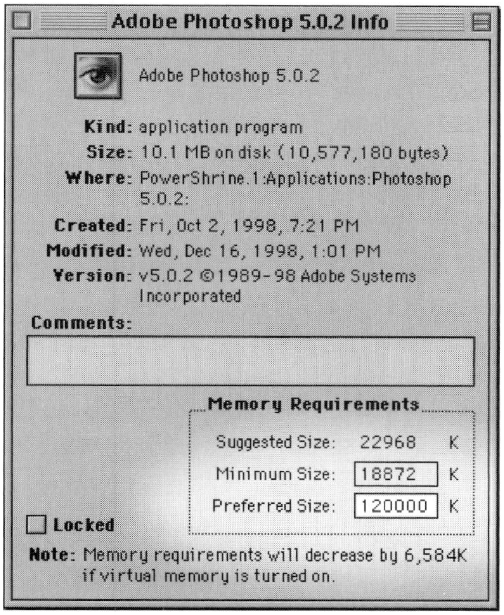

Figure 7-7 On the Mac, choose the Get Info command and assign memory to an application by adjusting the Preferred Size value.

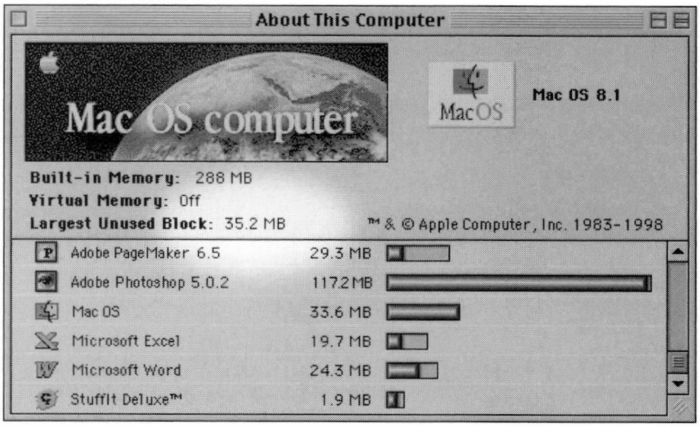

Figure 7-8 The Largest Unused Block indicates the biggest chunk of memory still open to run additional applications.

STORAGE

Storage is where software and other files go when they aren't open in RAM. There are two kinds of storage: fixed and removable:

- **Fixed storage** is your computer's hard disk. Along with the operating system and other software, the hard drive contains your day-to-day work. It's a good idea to always work from the hard drive, not from a removable device. If you want to open an image from, say, a floppy disk, first copy the image to the hard drive and then open it. With few exceptions, the hard drive is more reliable than removable media and can be several times faster.

- **Removable media** includes anything that you can insert into your computer and then eject without first rebooting the system. These include floppy disks, SmartMedia and CompactFlash, Zips, SuperDisks, CD-ROMs, and a host of others.

We discuss both kinds of storage in depth in the following sections.

The Hard Disk

Every computer comes with a hard disk built in. In modern computers, the capacity of the hard disk varies from 4GB to 16GB and up. Capacity is very important, of course, because it determines how many applications you can install and how many files you can create at any given time. But although arguably the highest priority for digital imaging, capacity is not the only criterion that deserves your attention.

- **Speed**   The speed of a hard drive is measured in several ways. First, there's the *seek time*, which is the average amount of time it takes for the head to move from one morsel of data to another inside the drive, as measured in milliseconds (ms). Next is the *rotational speed*, which is how fast the disk spins, measured in rotations per minute (rpm). Together, these two factors determine how fast the drive can locate data, somewhere in the neighborhood of 15ms at most. More important is the *transfer rate*, which is how fast the data can be conveyed to the CPU. The transfer rate is measured in megabytes per second (MBps).

- **Connectivity**   Transfer rate is largely a function of the way in which the hard drive is connected to the logic board. There are three basic kinds of connections, each of which varies in speed. The slowest is *IDE*, also known as *ATA*. (Exactly what these acronyms stand for isn't the least bit important, but just so you know, IDE is *Integrated Drive Electronics* and ATA is *Advanced Technology Attachment*.) IDE drives are limited to transfer rates of about 4 MBps. Next up the scale is EIDE, sometimes called Fast ATA, which starts at 11 MBps and tops out at about 16 MBps. Finally comes SCSI, which starts at about 10 MBps and goes much higher depending on what kind of SCSI you buy into. The drawback, of course, is that faster connections cost more money. Many imaging professionals will tell you that SCSI is the only way to go, but the objective testing we've seen suggests that EIDE or Fast ATA is sufficient for most applications.

- **Quantity** Most computers ship with just one hard drive, but you should seriously consider installing a second, even if its capacity is relatively small. Inside the hard drive, a single head reads and writes data. This means, no matter how many instructions you throw at your computer, one hard drive can read or write just one bit of data at a time. By equipping the machine with a second hard drive, you increase the potential of the system. By installing the operating system and software on the first hard drive and saving all your images and other data to the second, you set up a situation where the system can read software commands and write data at the same time. Granted, the CPU is limited to just one instruction at a time, but the CPU works several times faster than the hard drive—fast enough to keep several hard drives busy.

A second hard drive is especially helpful in speeding up virtual memory functions. We know designers who leave one entire hard drive blank so it can serve exclusively as the scratch disk. This way, the disk never becomes fragmented—with little pockets of data spread all over the place—so the system can read and write continuous streams of data without interruption.

> **TIP:** While setting aside an entire drive requires more resources—not to mention discipline—than most of us possess, it does make two important points. First, defragmented disks work more efficiently than fragmented ones. Microsoft includes a Disk Defragmenter utility with many versions of its Windows operating system (see Figure 7-9). On the Mac, you can purchase a commercial defragmenter such as the one included with Norton Utilities. Second, be sure to leave a generous amount of space open on your hard drive. Image editors such as Photoshop employ their virtual memory schemes in addition to the operating system's. If you fill up the hard disk, you make both system and application less stable by limiting them to the physical RAM. For best results, leave at least 25 percent of your hard disk space free at all times.

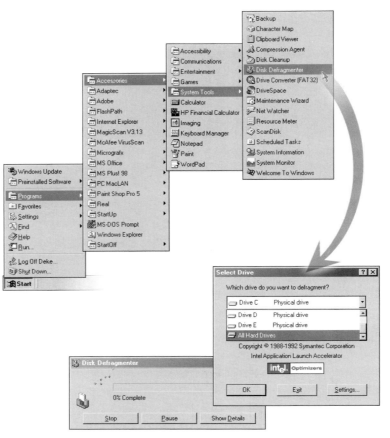

Figure 7-9 Choose Disk Defragmenter from the Start menu to optimize the performance of your hard drives under Windows 98.

Removable Media

Removable drives permit you to use disks, tapes, and cartridges to store your images. Although typically slower than an internal hard disk, removable media serves three purposes:

- **Backup** Removable media permits you to duplicate important files that are on your hard disk, so if the hard disk fails, you have a backup.

- **Archiving** When your hard disk starts to get full, or you're simply finished working with a group of images, you can copy the files for long-term storage. Make sure you have at least two copies of your data in case one medium goes bad—preferably using two different types of media in case one becomes more convenient or more reliable than the other. Then when you are double backed up, delete the files from your hard disk to save space.

• **File exchange** Removable media is also a great way to exchange files with other people. For example, the figures in this book were too large to email, so we spent a lot of time overnighting Zips and CDs filled with images to our editor.

Of the different kinds of removable media available to you, the most common and least useful is the ubiquitous 3.5-inch floppy disk. Simply put, floppies hold too little data and are too slow to serve much of a function for digital photographers. In a move that may prove to be trend, Apple has discontinued the floppy drive as a standard component of its PowerBook, iMac, and G3 tower series.

If you are in the market for a new Mac or a floppyless PC, don't be lured into purchasing a third-party floppy drive. If you suspect that you may need to use floppies on an occasional basis—to install some small piece of software, for example—get

a SuperDisk drive from Imation. Figure 7-10 shows the translucent USB drive designed to work with the new Macintosh computers. SuperDisk drives read the standard 1.44MB floppies as well as the new breed of 120MB disks. So, whereas two or three megapixel images might fit on a floppy, a SuperDisk provides room for 250 or more. Keep in mind, however, that only the new SuperDisks hold 128MB of data; your old floppies will still hold the same 1.4MB they ever did.

A more popular form of high-capacity floppy disk is Iomega's Zip. The common Zip holds 100MB of data; newer drives handle both 100MB and 250MB varieties. The downside is that Zip drives do not accommodate 3.5-inch floppy disks. But if your computer already includes a floppy drive—as do older-model Macs and virtually all PCs—then

Figure 7-10 Imation's SuperDisk drive accommodates standard 1.4MB floppies as well as new 128MB disks.

a Zip drive offers the advantage of wide market penetration. You can probably swap Zips with a colleague, where it's substantially less likely the colleague will have a SuperDisk drive. Zips are also available in a wide range of colors, as shown in Color Plate 7-1 on page C12. This may seem like a simple cosmetic issue, but if you're a visual thinker, you can use colors as an organizational aid. Personal photos go on yellow disks, business photos on blue, financial data on black, and so on.

> **TIP:** *If you decide to purchase an external Zip drive, get a SCSI or USB model. If a parallel connection is your only option, then purchase an internal drive instead. Our experience is that parallel drives are excruciatingly slow. It's not unusual for a single 100MB disk to take 15 minutes or more to copy, depending on how the parallel port is configured.*

For larger backup, you might consider a removable hard disk cartridge, such as Iomega's Jaz or SyQuest's SyJet, both featured in Figure 7-11. Both are exceedingly fast, claiming speeds that rival fixed drives, and they can hold anywhere from 1GB to 2GB of data. Jaz is more popular than SyJet, but it's also more expensive. A 1GB cartridge costs about $100, and a 2GB cartridge runs $125. (By comparison, SuperDisks and Zips costs about $10 apiece, making them similar deals. But at 1GB, you expect a quantity discount.) Also worth noting, the external drives have a tendency to overheat and burn out, as Deke learned from personal experience when his first, two-year-old drive melted down and had to be replaced to the tune of $200. SyJets are a much better deal, priced at $60 per 1.5GB cartridge. But now that SyQuest has filed for Chapter 11 and sold its remaining assets to Iomega, the future of SyJet doesn't look good.

Our preferred method for archiving large amounts of data is CD-ROM. You can purchase a CD recorder (CD-R drive) for as little as $300. And the media is astoundingly cheap, on average $1 for a 650MB CD like the one pictured in Figure 7-12. We've found that rebates are so prevalent that you can get the per CD price down to 50¢ or less. In one extreme case, Katrin actually *made* money on a box of CDs! The downside is that CD-R disks can be written to once and only once. (You can purchase CD-RW disks that can be erased and rerecorded, but they cost $15 to $25.) This means you have to have all your data organized before burning the CD. You also have to master a new piece of software, namely Adaptec's Toast on the Mac and Adaptec's Easy CD Creator on the PC. But in return, you get cheap, dependable, convenient storage that you can pop into just about any computer on the face of the planet. And if you send your CD out to a coworker and it never gets returned, who cares? You're only out a buck.

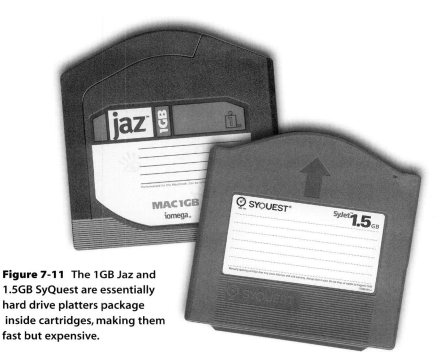

Figure 7-11 The 1GB Jaz and 1.5GB SyQuest are essentially hard drive platters package inside cartridges, making them fast but expensive.

Figure 7-12 Armed with a CD writer, you can archive images for as little as a penny per 10MB.

NOTE: *As we write this, DVD recorders are just starting to hit the market. The drives cost less than $1,000 and will undoubtedly drop if they become popular. But the media is pricey, about $60 for a two-sided 5.2GB disk (about 7 times as expensive per MB as a bargain CD). But for that price, you can erase and rerecord the DVD. We have yet to get our mitts on one of these drives, but we must confess to having lusted in our hearts.*

These aren't the only removable options. By the time you read this, Castlewood will have released a high-capacity disk dubbed Orb. Featured in Figure 7-13, Castlewood promises the 2.2GB disks will cost a mere $30 apiece, less than one quarter the price of the comparable 2GB Jaz. Magneto optical disks (or MOs) are also popular among artists and designers. Built like CDs inside disk casings, MOs range in capacity from 128MB to 5.2GB and cost anywhere from $8 to $100 apiece. There are also several varieties of tape-backup drives that archive 10GB to a whopping 70GB of data at per MB costs that rival CDs. But although tapes are great for archiving huge volumes of data—like the daily transactions of a corporation—they amount to overkill for independent photographers. Not only are the drives typically expensive, but retrieving data from tapes is exceedingly cumbersome. You can't just pop in a tape and examine its contents, as you can with a CD. Instead, you have to load log files and spend several minutes hunting down files using a program called Retrospect.

Figure 7-13
The upcoming 2.2GB Orb
disks promise to cost a mere
$30 piece. Will wonders never cease?

To learn more about storing your photographs to Zips, CDs, and other media, read Chapter 14, "Archiving Digital Images."

MONITOR AND VIDEO CARD

As we mentioned in Chapter 5, the computer screen is the best place to view your image because it uses the same color model as your digital camera. Layers of red, green, and blue intermix to display as many as 16.8 million color variations. And you can magnify images on screen to see each and every pixel in glorious detail. No other computer peripheral can make this claim.

Also integral to your enjoyment of the screen image is the *video card* (also called the *graphics card*), which conveys the color data to the monitor. Some computers hard-wire the video functions into the logic board; others include a separate PCI expansion card. Either way, you want to make sure that the video hardware offers enough memory to display your photographs as accurately as possible.

CRT versus LCD

Two prevalent styles of monitor are on the market:

- **CRT** The traditional computer screen that we've all come to know and love is the *cathode-ray tube* (CRT). An electron gun mounted at the far back of the screen fires beams at the inside of the glass facing. The beams excite red, green, and blue phosphors, which shine through the transparent glass to produce the screen image. Most monitors in use today—including even unusual designs such as Apple's monitor-in-computer iMac (Figure 7-14)—are CRT devices.

- **LCD** A recent development in monitor technology that's gaining a lot of attention these days is the flat-panel LCD (*liquid-crystal display*). As shown in Figure 7-15, these monitors take up very little desk space, measuring about 7 to 9 inches deep compared with twice that for a similar CRT screen. Like the LCD screen on a portable computer, flat-panel displays are actually three layers of liquid crystals and glass, each filtered with red, green, or blue film. A steady light passes through the layers. Electric current is applied to crystals to make them untwist. Less twist means darker colors, more twist means lighter ones.

Figure 7-14 Apple's popular iMac is essentially a computer built around a CRT monitor, reminiscent of the old Mac 128K design.

Figure 7-15 Mitsubishi's 18-inch LCD80 displays 1,280 by 1,024 pixels, but it takes up half the space on your desk as a CRT monitor.

LCD screens offer the obvious advantages of stylish looks and compact design. Also noteworthy, most LCD screens rely on an *active-matrix* design, which provides a constant signal to each screen pixel, resulting in a smooth and uninterrupted picture. (Avoid older *passive-matrix* screens, which experience periodic delays, making it difficult to track moving items like the mouse cursor.) By contrast, CRT monitors project an image by redrawing it several times a minute. This *refresh rate* is measured in *hertz* (Hz), or times per second. So a 75Hz display redraws the screen from top to bottom 75 times every second. While the visual effect is one of a continuous screen image, some experts claim that staring at a CRT screen results in more eye fatigue than the truly continuous LCD.

The obvious downside of LCDs is their expense. LCD screens may cost two or three times as much as their CRT counterparts. But that's not the only problem. Because of the position of the light inside the monitor, LCD screens suffer when viewed from different angles. You have to look straight at the device to see the colors clearly. Move your head side to side and the colors change; looking at a very acute angle produces the effect of inverted colors. Finally, LCDs are very sensitive to ambient light. If you have a window behind you that casts light over your shoulder, the glare can make the LCD screen virtually unreadable.

This is why, for the present, we have to come down on the side of CRT screens. Although considerably more bulky, they produce more reliable colors viewable from a variety of different angles. And although CRTs are likewise susceptible to ambient light and glare, you can always see the screen image, even if you may want to close the blinds to make the screen appear a bit brighter.

Variations on CRT

Choosing which kind of CRT screen to buy is a more complicated matter. There are two basic varieties of CRT display—tridot (also known as *shadow mask*) and Trinitron (*aperture grille*). If you look closely at a tridot screen, you can see a trio of dots—red, green, and blue—merging to form colors on the screen. The effect is analogous to a printed halftone pattern, except that the dots are much smaller and don't overlap. Colors on a Trinitron screen are arranged in vertical strips, uninterrupted from the top of the screen to the bottom. Look closely at the screen and you can see fine breaks between the columns of color. But it's virtually impossible to see any variance between the red, green, and blue phosphors.

Lots of folks work with tridot screens and have no problem with them. But our experience is that even the best tridot is awful when compared with Trinitron. The screen image on tridot is softer, and the screen itself bows outward horizontally and vertically, resulting in greater distortion. A Trinitron screen is significantly sharper, and though it bows slightly horizontally, it's absolutely flat vertically. Because Sony holds an exclusive patent on Trinitron technology, Trinitron screens also happen to cost more, but they're well worth it.

Another factor worth considering is screen calibration. If you're willing to part with some extra money—more than an LCD display, in fact—you can purchase a professional-level monitor with precise hardware calibration. By calibrating your monitor on a monthly basis, you ensure that the colors are displayed as accurately as possible. Two excellent examples are Mitsubishi's 17-inch SpectraView 700 and 21-inch SpectraView 1000, priced at about $1,600 and $2,500, respectively. Both monitors feature Diamondtron tubes—licensed from Sony but essentially a step up in brightness and clarity from Trinitron—and include calibration hardware and software. The calibration process itself is very simple. A sensor unit attaches to the screen with a suction cup, as shown in Figure 7-16. You then run the calibration utility and let the software do its thing. Monitor such as the SpectraView represent the height of accuracy for digital photographers.

Figure 7-16 To balance the colors on a Mitsubishi SpectraView monitor, you attach a sensor unit to the screen and run a calibration utility.

Video and VRAM

Contrary to popular misconception, the number of colors and pixels that you see on screen has little or nothing to do with the monitor. A typical monitor is just a big dumb tube that does what the computer tells it to do. The part of the computer that's in charge of pixels and colors is the video board (or the on-board video in the case of computers in which the video functions are hard-wired into the logic board).

The primary measurement of a video board is the amount of *VRAM* (video RAM) that it provides. These days, most boards include 4MB to 8MB of VRAM, although you can still find low-end boards equipped with just 2MB. More VRAM means more color at higher resolutions:

- A 2MB board provides 16 million colors up to 800 by 600 pixels (or 832 by 624 pixels on the Mac). If you raise the resolution of the monitor above that, you have to drop the number of colors that can be displayed at a time to 32,000 or fewer.

- 4MB of VRAM permits you to display 16 million colors at resolutions up to 1152 by 864 pixels (or 1152 by 870 on the Mac).

- Most boards top out at 8MB of VRAM, which permits 16 million colors at resolutions as high as 1600 by 1200 pixels.

How can you figure this out for yourself? You need enough VRAM to hold the entire screen image at once. For example, a 24-bit 832 by 624-pixel image weighs in at 832 x 624 x 3 bytes = 1.5MB, which fits easily into 2MB of VRAM. But if you raise the resolution to 1024 by 768 pixels—the next step up—a 24-bit image grows to 2.25MB, which exceeds the 2MB VRAM ceiling.

Gamma Adjustment

You would think the video card would convey the image to the monitor, the monitor would display the image, and that would be the end of it. But a monitor is ultimately an analog device, which means things get a bit convoluted in the translation from the video board to the screen. Rather than responding in a constant manner to each signal conveyed by the video board, the phosphors inside a CRT tend to diminish dark values and exaggerate light values. This means if you were to map the CRT response on a graph, the graph would appear as a sloping curve instead of a straight line.

For example, consider the simple gradient and photographic image included in Figure 7-17. If these images were conveyed to the monitor without compensation, the distortion inherent in the screen display would produce a washed out image, as illustrated in Figure 7-18. The solution is to distort the signal from the video board in the opposite direction, thus straightening out the response of the monitor, as shown in Figure 7-19.

Figure 7-17 To demonstrate the effects of gamma, we'll start with a white-to-black gradient and a digital snapshot.

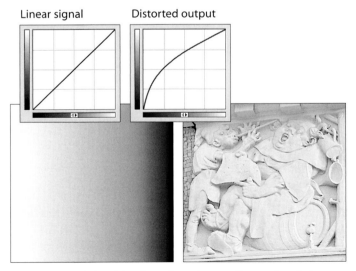

Figure 7-18 If the video board sends out a linear signal, the monitor distorts the signal (as illustrated in the graphs), resulting in an overly bright image.

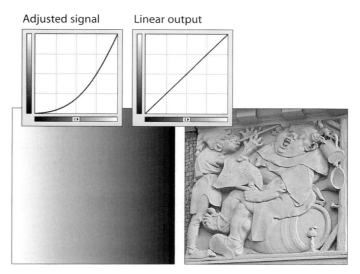

Figure 7-19 By adjusting the gamma, you instruct the video card to distort the signal in the opposite direction of the monitor's distortion, resulting in a linear output.

The monitor's brightness is proportional to the video board signal raised to an exponential power. The name assigned to this adjustable power is *gamma*. Hence, a correction made to the video signal is called a *gamma adjustment*. A gamma of 1.0—that is, the video signal raised to the power of 1—has no effect on the signal, leaving it linear and thus permitting the monitor to exaggerate the brightness, as in Figure 7-18. Higher values expand the shadows and compress the highlights.

The standard gamma setting for the Mac is 1.8. On the PC, the standard is 2.2, which equates to a few shades darker. But you don't have to accept these settings. If you're a Mac user who works with a lot of PC folks, you can change the gamma to 2.2. Similarly, Windows users can switch to a gamma of 1.8, or any other value for that matter.

Many video boards include software that lets you adjust the gamma setting applied to the monitor input signal. On the Mac, such software is probably supplied as a control panel. If you own an Apple monitor and you're running OS 8.5, choose the Monitors & Sound control panel and then click on the Color button. Under Windows, bring up the Display control panel. Then switch to the Settings tab and click on the Advanced button. Or look for a tab added by the video board, such as the Colorific tab featured in Figure 7-20.

If your video board does not include gamma controls, you might want to look into the cross-platform Adobe Gamma control panel, included with Photoshop 5. The advantage of Adobe Gamma is that it permits you to "eyeball" adjustments, as opposed to entering numbers into a bunch of cryptic options. The middle portion of the control panel features three visual tests, highlighted in Figure 7-21. Your task is to adjust the slider triangles until the middle of each square matches the border. As you do, Adobe Gamma adjusts the screen display to optimize the colors for a higher degree of accuracy. Any changes you make are saved to disk, ensuring that the adjustments will remain in effect from one session to the next.

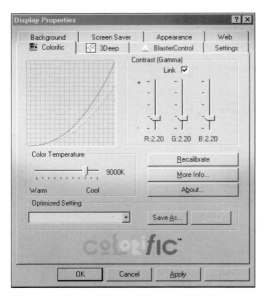

Figure 7-20 Included with some PC video boards, Colorific lets you adjust red, green, and blue gamma values independently from the Display control panel.

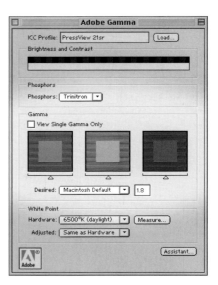

Figure 7-21 The Adobe Gamma control panel lets you adjust colors visually rather than rely entirely on complex numerical controls.

PRINTERS

The printer is at once the most and least important element of the darkroom. Clearly, you can't create prints without it. Some cameras go so far as to let you connect to a printer directly with no computer involved at all. However, many digital photographers will discover that they have little if any need for a printer. If you intend to distribute your photographs over the Internet, then the screen is your medium. If you're a designer who creates images and pages for professional print publications, then a desktop printer is unlikely to give you any better idea of what the final image will look like than your screen will. As a professional photographer, Katrin makes large-format prints of her photographs, but most are the products of remote printers owned and operated by commercial photo labs. Deke owns a few consumer printers, but he only occasionally makes use of them.

We cover the mechanics of preparing an image for output in Chapter 13, "Preparing Images for Print and the Web." For now, we'll concentrate on the two printer technologies that are most applicable to rendering continuous-tone images—ink-jet and dye-sublimation. Printers of either type can be had for less than $1,000, and some of them create terrific output that rivals professional devices costing $5,000 and up.

Ink-Jet Printers

The term *ink-jet* is associated with two very different kinds of printing technologies:

- **Solid ink** A solid ink printer relies on sticks of colored wax. During the print cycle, the sticks are melted into a liquid form and sprayed onto the page. The liquid then hardens to form solid, nearly opaque colors. Intended to compete with color laser printers, solid ink-jet devices are fast, they do a great job of printing overheads and other transparencies, and the colors look sharp and vibrant even on colored paper. The downside is that they tend to be big and expensive—the Tektronix Phaser 840 is a dainty bargain, weighing 80 pounds and starting at $2,500. Solid ink-jet printers are office workhorses, but they're probably a bit much for independent designers and photographers.

- **Liquid ink-jet** The more common variety of ink-jet printers uses liquid ink cartridges. The ink is forced onto the page through a roller containing tiny nozzles. A roller may contain only a few nozzles—say, 32 per color—but by keeping the rollers small and the nozzles tightly packed, the printers attain very high resolutions. Resolutions up to 1440 dpi are common among printers costing $500 and less. Most printers, including those in Epson's Stylus Color series, offer one cartridge for black ink and another for cyan, magenta, and yellow, as shown in Figure 7-22. Together, these primary colors mix to form several thousand color variations. Epson's Photo Stylus series adds two more inks— essentially lighter shades of cyan and magenta—to better simulate the colors in a continuous-tone photograph.

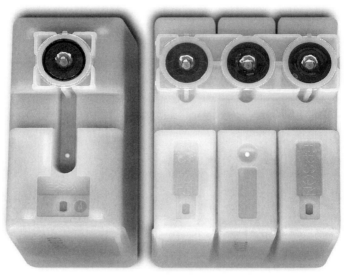

Figure 7-22 Cartridges for a typical liquid ink-jet printer, one for black (left) and the other for yellow, magenta, and cyan (right). The ink enters the printer through the black holes at top.

Like most printers, ink-jet devices are 1-bit printers. This means that they can either lay down a dot of color or not lay down a dot of color. Assuming the four inks, you have four different colors that can be laid down. This gives you just 4 x 4 = 16 color permutations. However, by packing different dot combinations very close to each other, ink-jet printers simulate thousands upon thousands of color variations.

By way of example, Color Plate 7-2 on page C12 shows a jellyfish that we then printed to an Epson Stylus Color 800 ink-jet printer. The first example in Color Plate 7-3 on page C13 shows a detail from the ink-jet printout, magnified so that you can see the individual dots of color. If you don't feel like flipping pages, Figure 7-23 shows a grayscale image with magnified ink-jet output. To simplify the figure, the printout was created using black ink only.

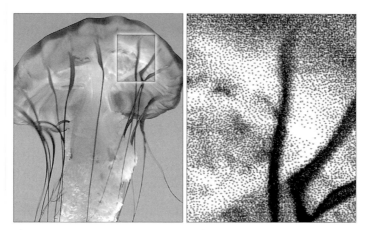

Figure 7-23 A grayscale jellyfish (left) and a magnified view from an ink-jet printout created using only the black ink (right).

Dye-Sublimation Printers

Another technology that's ideally suited to printing full-color digital photographs is *dye-sublimation*, or simply *dye-sub*. While dye-sub printers aren't nearly as popular as their ink-jets cousins, they are becoming more prevalent at the low end. And the quality of their output is absolutely amazing.

Sublimation means to convert a solid directly to a gas without having it pass through the liquid stage. So a dye-sublimation printer does exactly what its name implies—heating elements on the print head vaporize dyes, which then absorb into the surface of the paper. The printer makes separate passes at the page for each of the cyan, magenta, yellow, and black dyes. (Some prints forego black because they can generate excellent dark tones using just cyan, magenta, and yellow, as demonstrated in Color Plate 7-4 on page C14.) For each pass, the heating element burns the dye off a length of transfer ribbon, like the one shown in Figure 7-24. The heating element can range between any of 256 temperatures, each of which conveys a different amount of dye to the page. This means, if properly calibrated, the printer is able to convey every one of the 256 brightness values in an 8-bit color channel.

Figure 7-24 The transfer ribbon from a dye-sub printer provides a length of cyan followed by magenta, yellow, and in some cases black.

This means that a dye-sub printer can render a color image without using any sort of dot pattern whatsoever. Instead, each printer pixel conveys a premixed color, as demonstrated by the magnified detail shown in the second example of Color Plate 7-3 on page C13. Not only does this mean a dye-sub printer does the best job of matching what you see on screen, it also means it creates prints that look for all the world like they were developed from real film. Dye-sub output is truly photographic.

A couple of years ago, dye-sub printers cost $5,000 or more. But several devices can now be had for less than $1,000. The least expensive of these are the personal dye-sub printers, which print 3.5 by 5-inch snapshots at 300 picture-perfect pixels per inch. Our favorite is the P-300U from Olympus (recently updated to the P-330 Instant Photo Printer), featured in Figure 7-25. Casio, Canon, and other camera vendors offer similar dye-sub devices. The printers themselves cost less than $400, but the snapshots are bit expensive. A carton of 60 sheets of paper with transfer ribbon costs $35, putting the per photo fee at nearly 60 cents.

These personal devices also permit you to print directly from a compatible camera (usually one sold by the same vendor). In the case of the P-300U, you connect printer and camera with a serial cable, turn on the camera, use the camera's LCD screen to find the desired image, and press the printer's Direct Print button, labeled in Figure 7-25.

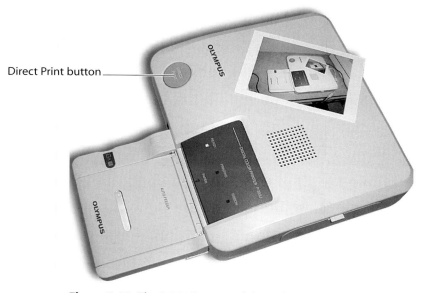

Direct Print button

Figure 7-25 The P-300U personal dye-sub printer from Olympus creates 3.5 by 5-inch snapshots, like the one resting on top of the printer.

Direct printing may be convenient, but it's hardly the best way to go. When printing directly from the camera, you sacrifice all options to balance the colors, correct the focus, crop the image, and perform all those other wonderful adjustments permitted by an image editor. In fact, you have so little control over the process, you might as well be using film.

CHAPTER EIGHT

The Desktop Studio

Setting up a studio for digital photography is not very different than setting up a studio for conventional film photography. Other than the fact that you don't need a darkroom or have to make trips to the photo lab for film processing, the basic elements are the same. There's a subject to photograph, a setting in which that subject is placed, light to illuminate the scene and a camera to capture the image. So if this is something you're familiar with, there will not be many surprises here.

Our focus in this chapter is the desktop studio. It is much like a full-size photo studio, but it costs a great deal less to establish and maintain. We will discuss what you will need to set up a small basic studio for still life photography on a limited budget. This kind of tabletop studio is great for photographing small objects for Web pages, on-line catalogues, or newsletters with deluxe point and shoot or professional lite digital cameras.

ESSENTIAL STUDIO REQUIREMENTS

Studio photography requires a lot more space than one might suppose and this is as true for tabletop work as it is for shooting furniture or fashion work. Not only do we need to build some kind of a set to work in, we need to place the lights (as well as whatever diffusers, reflectors, etc. we use with them) to create the *atmosphere* that marks the photograph as the work of a professional.

Camera position is another important factor creating the sense of space and scale in a photograph. We need room to move the camera around, up and down, and in and out to establish the perspective on the scene we want to the photograph to convey.

In a professional studio, even tabletop set-ups can be quite large—easily as big as eight feet square for large objects or groups of objects. We will limit our ambitions here to a studio suitable for photographing things smaller than a breadbasket. This way, we can get away with a table about three feet by four, and the total space we'll need for shooting can be kept to a minimum. Likewise, our lighting requirements will be a lot more modest.

The Set

The set is—quite literally—the basis of the studio. This is where we put the thing we're photographing. Sometimes we want the set to disappear so we can show the subject isolated or so we can cut it out and composite it into another environment entirely. Other times, we create a set to give a particular context to the subject of the photograph with the creative use of backgrounds, props, and lighting.

For most purposes, our set will be the size of a simple, sturdy wooden table. The table should be one you don't mind painting or putting nails into or using clamps on. Ideally, your shooting table should be one you don't need for anything else and don't have to move in and out of the way. It's a good idea to leave the shot set up until you're sure you have what you want; reconstructing a shot is nearly impossible.

Tripod

The tripod is an essential piece of equipment. It minimizes camera shake, maintains consistency between shots, and allows you to concentrate on the subject. Look for a solid tripod with legs that open and close smoothly as well as head rotation and tilt controls that are easily accessible when the camera is mounted. A tripod with rubber feet avoids slipping and scratching of floors.

It may sound odd, but working with a tripod requires practice. Learn to attach the camera securely without over-tightening. When extending the pripod, start at the top and work your way down. If you need still more height, use the center column of the tripod. This is your last resort, and if you find yourself working at full extension very often, you should consider buying a larger tripod. The more you extend the legs and raise the center column, the higher the center of gravity, and the less stable the camera.

TIP: When using a tripod have the "third" leg facing the set and not between your legs where you'll only stumble over it. Always point the third leg forward with the other two on either side of you.

Backdrops and Sweeps

Many photographers plan their photos from the back to the front—deciding on a background first and then working their way forward. It is a common convention in studio photography to avoid a sharp demarcation between the floor and the background to create the illusion of space. Photo supply stores sell rolls of seamless backdrop paper in a variety of widths and colors, and the usual way to use them is to hang the roll over the back of the set and pull down enough paper to cover the table and create a gentle curving transition between the vertical and the horizontal. When the set gets messed up, you just cut off the damaged portion and pull down some new paper. Another way to create this effect is to clamp a piece of posterboard onto the edge of your table and curve it up against the wall, as seen in Figure 8-1.

Figure 8-1 A typical small tabletop set with one light, a few light modifiers, and a small posterboard backdrop.

On occasion, you may want to have the objects in your photograph appear to be floating in space. For this effect, you will want to build a *sweep,* which you can rig up by forming a sheet of translucent plastic or Plexiglas into a curve like Figure 8-1. The plastic should extend beyond the back of the table so you can light it from below and behind. If you securely clamp the sheet to the front part of the table and force the other end up into the vertical plane, you'll have a pretty good approximation of what professional studios pay a lot of money for.

> **NOTE:** If you are using halogen lamps—or the less desirable photofloods—that generate a lot of heat, be very careful not to place the lights too close to the plastic.

Not-so-Nondescript Backgrounds

In some situations, you will want your photograph to convey a particular message by placing the subject in a context, either the expected or the surprising. You know, cologne bottles on old barn wood, wristwatches on steel plates, or esoteric tea on rice paper (as seen in Figure 8-2 and Color Plate 8-1 on page C14). Sometimes, you will want nothing more intrusive than a little texture, like velvet or satin or burlap, or even just a little wrinkling of the background paper. Inexpensive and effective backgrounds include hand-made artist paper (Figure 8-3) and marble-like floor covering as in Figure 8-4 that you buy in large hardware stores. These are aesthetic decisions you will have to make based on how the photograph will be used.

Figure 8-2 Using rice paper as a background adds interest to the shot of the box of tea without overpowering it.

Figure 8-3 Use handmade paper or rice paper as an inexpensive background.

Figure 8-4 These Formica tiles come in numerous colors and patterns and can serve as effective backgrounds.

Props

If you plan on *dropping out* the subject (floating it on white or transparency in a printed or Web catalog) then props are of no use. But when an image needs to stand on its own, the judicious use of props and creative lighting can help create a noteworthy photograph. As you can see from the sea of electronic and print work around you, the possibilities are endless.

The time invested in gathering your materials, setting up the shot, and fiddling around with it until it is exactly as you want it can seem endless, but in the end it is worth it if the image is a winner. How you use what you've got is at least as important as what props you use. In Color Plate 8-2 on page C15, adding a simple wineglass and changing the camera's point of view helps to create an interesting and interpretive image.

Chewing Gum and Baling Wire

Commercial and fine art photography is all about image and has very little to do with reality. Anyone can click a shutter, but what distinguishes a good photographer is the ability to craft a shot that creates a distinctive attitude for the subject. If you watch food photographers at work, you'll see that they spend an inordinate amount of time looking for the perfect subject and prop. For example, they sort through a five-pound basket of brussels sprouts to find just the right ones, glue each sprout into place, and arrange the leeks and the tarragon with wires, pins, and gaffer's tape to make the shot look like a home-cooked meal.

From behind, a well-crafted still life looks like a science experiment gone wrong resting on a clump of Silly Putty with pins sticking out of it and wires holding it just so. But through the camera it looks perfect—all the pins, wires, tape, and glue are hidden from view either behind the subject itself or blocked by a prop.

Clamps of all kinds and sizes are always useful in the studio (Figure 8-5). They can be used for everything from holding backdrops and reflectors to propping up otherwise recumbent objects in the photo. Spring clamps are essential; so are C-clamps and a variety of oddball styles. Finally, the ultimate weapon of photographic persuasion is the electric hot glue gun. Use it to defy gravity and guarantee that your subjects stay still.

Figure 8-5 Clamps, Silly Putty, wire, and a hot glue gun are essential to hold things together and in place.

LIGHT

Without light, photography doesn't exist, of course. The word *photography* means, after all, *light drawing.* Photographers work with light to make the subject more attractive or to create a mood.

Some light sources produce a broad spectrum of color; others produce only specific wavelengths. Human vision is remarkably adaptive and we are often not even aware of physical differences in the color of light illuminating a scene. Photography—both conventional and digital—records only the physical attributes of the light reflected into the lens, and we need to pay careful attention to the qualities of the light we use to make a photograph with.

In the early days of photography, the sun was the only practical source of illumination. It works as well as ever and provides a very broad spectrum of light, but it is notoriously difficult to control. When we set up a photograph under artificial lights, it is important to block out sunlight and other ambient sources.

Mixing lighting of different characteristics can produce unpredictable and unacceptable results.

The light entering the camera's lens is affected not only by the subject of the photograph and the spectrum emanating from the source, but by all the materials the light passes through and reflects off on its way to the camera. The light bouncing off a colored wall will give a particular cast to the image and whatever diffusers and reflectors you use may make their contributions too. This can be turned to your advantage (fashion photographers often use a gold reflector to warm up skin tones) but it can also create serious problems.

Matching the Camera to the Light

Most professional, some deluxe point-and-shoot, and many professional-lite cameras allow you to adjust the color balance in the camera. It is much better to set the camera for the type of light you'll be shooting under than to rely on the digital darkroom to correct the lighting balance in your pictures. Sometimes, color correction after the fact is impossible.

Color Plate 8-3 on page C15 shows how well the camera works when set correctly. In this case, the camera was set to daylight balance and the colors in the picture are natural. In the small inset in Color Plate 8-3, the photographer had the camera set for daylight at the dance presentation in the auditorium and, as you can see, the picture is an awful orange. The only thing the photographer could do to salvage this shot was to print it in black and white (see Figure 8-6).

Figure 8-6 Due to the low color temperature of the auditorium lights, the color of this image was so corrupted that its only salvation was to print it in black and white.

COLOR TEMPERATURE

Each type of light, be it sunlight, studio lighting equipment, or even your common house-hold light bulb, has a color temperature, which is measured in degrees Kelvin. As seen in Color Plate 8-4 on page C16, the lower the color temperature, the redder the light; the higher the temperature, the bluer. The odd thing about color temperature is that the human eye doesn't perceive it; our color vision automatically compensates for the temperature of the light. But digital cameras don't compensate, and that's why when you take pictures in a school auditorium (under incandescent bulbs) they look orange and why the shadows in your winter snowscape pictures (skylight without direct sun) are blue. Some film is balanced for daylight or tungsten light to help handle variations in color temperature. Many digital cameras allow you select light source settings to compensate for different color temperatures.

ARTIFICIAL LIGHTING

Artificial light allows you to exercise a high level of control. Working with studio lighting equipment and techniques is really the best way to create quality still life work. The term *artificial light* covers a wide variety of sources, ranging from the inexpensive photoflood to professional flash equipment.

Light can either be *continuous* or *flash*. Continuous light is on all the time, and flash or strobe light is emitted in short high-energy bursts just like the flash on a point and shoot camera. One-shot cameras from the deluxe point and shoot, professional lite, and professional camera categories can work with either continuous or flash equipment. Professional scanning cameras require a continuous light source and cannot be used with flash equipment.

Working with a continuous light source will seem very familiar. You position the light where you want to be, look at the subject, see where the shadows and reflections fall, and take the picture. On the other hand, working with flash equipment isn't as straightforward because the flash emits its light in a fraction of a second, and it is physically impossible to see how the light is affecting the picture that quickly. Working with flash equipment takes some practice and test shots, but it is something anyone can learn.

Continuous Light

Continuous light sources include photofloods, tungsten-halogen, HMI, and fluorescent lights.

- **Photofloods** are very similar to your standard household light bulb. They tend to be very warm in color and do not provide enough light in the blue region of the spectrum to give accurate color rendition. They have a very short lifespan of 3-5 hours, and their color shifts as they age. Although they are every inexpensive (costing little more than a good household lightbulb) we don't recommend them for any type of serious studio work.

- **Tungsten-halogen lamps** are much more useful for photographic purposes and are very common in professional still-life studios. They provide a broader color spectrum than photofloods and are more consistent in their output over their lifetimes. Halogen lamps can be used with a wide variety fixtures, including focusing spot lights and fiber optic illuminators to create special effects.

- **HMI** (hydrargyrum medium arc-length iodide) lights are the Rolls Royce of the continuous light source family. Normally used to light large movie sets, these lights give a very bright, cool light with the same color temperature as daylight (5000-5600°K). They are ideal for photographic applications, but they are *very* expensive. A 125-watt HMI light (which is equivalent to a 650-watt quartz light) costs $2400, and the replacement bulbs are about $250 apiece.

- **Fluorescent lights** work on a very different principle than the incandescent lights just described. Instead of heating a filament to a temperature high enough that it emits light, fluorescents have a small filament that emits electrons which strike the phosphor coating on the inside of the tube, which in turn kicks out photons of certain wavelengths. In the past, fluorescent lights were shunned in photo studios because they gave off a discontinuous color-spectrum light that could cause visible streaking of the image. Fluorescent technology is improving, and premium tubes are being manufactured for photographic use that generate a cool, broad light source ideal for flat copy work and fine art reproduction. One drawback to fluorescent lights is that they can't be directed or focused with light modifiers like the tungsten-halogen and HMI lights.

Type	Color Temperature	Cost	Life Span in Hours
Photoflood	3200–3400 °K	Low	3 Hours
Tungsten-halogen	3200–3400 °K	Moderate	300 hrs
HMI	5000–5600°K	Very High	350 hours
Fluorescent	Varies	Moderate	10,000 hours

Table 8-1 Continuous Lighting Equipment

> *WARNING: if you are working with photofloods or tungsten-halogen lamps, please be careful as they get very hot and can burn unsuspecting fingers and melt or even ignite props or light modifiers.*

Flash Equipment

Flash equipment or *studio strobes* emit very brief, high intensity bursts of light, which allow for short exposures to freeze even the fastest motion. The advantages to using flash equipment are: the light is close to the color temperature of daylight, and strobes don't produce a lot of heat, which can be very important when working with heat-sensitive subjects such as food, flowers, and children. The disadvantages of working with flash are that it is difficult to see exactly what you are going to shoot, and they are more expensive than tungsten or fluorescent light.

In the studio, on-camera flash units are of little value as they are too small and harsh. Furthermore, they cannot be moved relative to the camera to allow you the control you need to produce professional quality work.

- **Synching the flash** When using flash equipment, you need to have the studio flash fire exactly when the shutter is opened; this is called *synching* the flash to the camera. Many professional lite cameras such as the Nikon CoolPix 900s, Olympus D-620, Kodak DC260, and Agfa ePhoto 1680 have flash cord ports that allow you to plug in a cord that goes to the studio flash or to a handheld flash, as described in Chapter 9.

- **IR remote** Even better than this solution is to use an IR remote, which is a little 1 1/2 square plastic box that attaches to either the camera's flash hot shoe or to the flash sync port with a short cable. When you push the shutter, the IR slave triggers the studio flash. Bingo! A hot shoe IR remote costs about $100 and is well worth the freedom of not having yet another cable to trip over.

WHERE TO BUY LIGHTS

We recommend researching or buying your lighting equipment in a professional camera store such as the ones listed here. You don't need to buy everything at once, and remember to look at lighting kits that come complete with lights, stands, and reflectors, or softboxes.

B&H Photo
1-800-606-6969
www.bhphotovideo.com

Calumet Photo
1-800-Calumet
www.calumetphoto.com

Photoflex
www.photoflex.com

Bogen Photo
www.bogenphoto.com

How Much Light

The three variables that determine how strong a light is: the light's strength in watts, the distance between the subject and the light, and whether you have used any light modifiers such as softboxes (as discussed later in this chapter). Table 8-2 offers general recommendations as to how much light you will need for three typical photographic scenarios.

Subject	Watt-seconds (for strobe)	Watts (for constant sources)
Small objects	250–500	500
Head & Shoulders Portraits	1000–2000	1500
Full-length people shots	5000	5000

Table 8-2 Recommendations for Amounts of Light

How Many Lights

In most situations, you'll need more than one light to get the job done. Working with a single light source limits your ability to finesse the light to accentuate the subject. If you can, buy two lights, one to serve as a main light and one as a fill light to soften the shadows.

If you are considering buying flash equipment, we recommend working with monolights in which the capacitor and controls for the flash are built right into the flash head. Professional photographers usually use flash equipment with a separate power supply which offers more power and shorter cycling times, but until you start shooting cavorting fashion models, working with monolights will do the job just fine.

Many resellers sell lighting kits that come complete with lights, light stands, light modifiers, and all the required cables. This is our favorite solution because those kits usually come with good boxes or bags that can also be used to store the lights when not in use.

If you choose not to buy your lighting as part of a kit, you will need to get some light stands. The stands you select should be sturdy and should be capable of extending high enough to allow you to place your lights well above your head. You may also want to consider getting a boom that will put the light directly over your set or forward of the camera without obstructing the shot. As always, there will be trade-offs among cost and quality and sturdiness and portability that you'll have to weigh in your decision.

Critical Lighting Variables

When you need a light bulb for your home, you buy it, go home, screw it in and that's that; you don't care what its color temperature is. Buying and working with photo-quality lights isn't as straightforward, where even brand-new lamps may have different color temperatures. As tungsten lamps age, they shift away from blue toward yellow. If you are doing very color-critical work, tracking the age of the bulbs and working with a color temperature meter are essential to insure that unwanted color shifts don't creep into the image. And remember to check that none of your modifiers is making unwanted contributions to the color of the light.

Variations in the electric voltage also affect a light's performance, and when working with three-shot or scanning cameras, voltage variations create uncorrectable artifacts in the captured images. With a scanning camera, subtle jumps or drops in voltage for only a few seconds will cause noticeable lines in the image. In the case of the three-shot cameras, differences in the power of the flash among the three exposures will cause the red, green, or blue channels to be more or less exposed, causing troublesome color shifts.

Sometimes, fluctuations in your lighting output can be taken care of by making sure you don't have other heavy loads (an electric heater or the coffee maker) switching on and off on the same circuit. If that doesn't work, consider having your line tested for voltage fluctuations by a professional electrician.

Modifying the Light

Once a shot is set up and the basic lighting plan is established, it is time to work on the subtleties of the light. Softboxes as seen in Figure 8-7 are one common way to diffuse and soften the light illuminating your subject. The basic principle is that the light is mounted inside the unit and shines on a large screen on the front, which then acts like a very large and soft source. Umbrellas work in much the same way; the light is reflected off the inside of the umbrella, which acts like a large diffuse source. Either way, the effect is to light the subject with a broad light which give soft shadows. Umbrellas are quite inexpensive and easy to work with. Softboxes are a little more expensive and a little more cumbersome, but provide a superior quality of light.

Figure 8-7 The softbox provides a large light surface which creates a soft practically shadowless light.

Use white fill cards made out of standard foamcore to fill the shadows and silver reflectors to kick in light where needed. Figure 8-8 shows how the photographer used a large piece of white foamcore to lighten the left-hand side of the bottle, and 8-9 reveals the silver reflector that kicked light through the red wine, which gives the wine an attractive color. In Color Plate 8-5 on page C16 you can compare the effect that working with a single light and fill cards and silver reflectors makes on bringing the bottle of wine to life. These light modifiers can be used with either continuous light or flash equipment to create a mood in a photograph or to accentuate the subject of the photograph.

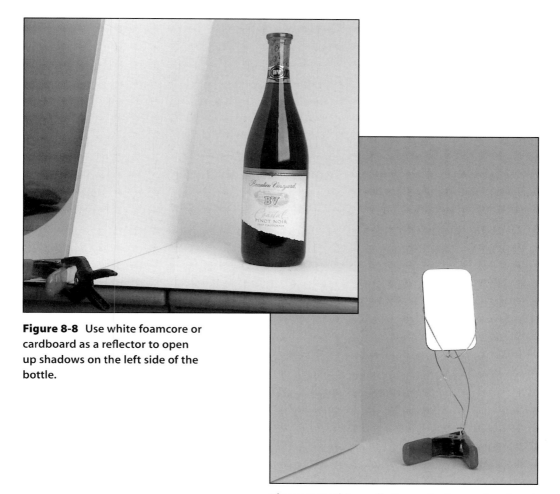

Figure 8-8 Use white foamcore or cardboard as a reflector to open up shadows on the left side of the bottle.

Figure 8-9 This small silver reflector can be placed behind the wine bottle to bounce light through the red wine, giving it an attractive color.

ESSENTIAL ACCESSORIES

Photographers work with a wide variety of tools and techniques to get the picture just right. Additional accessories that a self-respecting photographer would never be caught without include: a sturdy tripod, a light meter, test targets, and a good camera bag. Now we're not saying that you have to run out and buy all of this stuff right away—but we do think it is important to know what the tools of the trade are and what they're used for.

Light Meters

Photographers use light meters when they light their shots to measure the relative illumination of the various parts of the image. Meters come in a number of types. Incident light meters measure the light striking the subject and reflective light meters measure the light coming off of the subject. Spot meters are reflective light meters designed to measure a small area of the subject. Flash meters are incident light meters capable of recording the amount of light striking the subject for the few milliseconds of the strobe burst. Each has its use, and some meters combine several functions. For studio work, an incident light meter (with flash capability if you're using strobes) is probably your best bet.

Making test shots for lighting and composition is so easy with a digital camera that many photographers are using their light meters less and less. Make your test exposure and bring the image into an image-editing program like Photoshop to measure the highlights, midtones, and shadows. Make sure that the highlights aren't blown out and that the shadows aren't pure black. A safe range to work in is to keep the image between 15 for the shadows and 245 for the highlights on the RGB scale. Keeping an eye on the highlights and shadows is essential—especially when working with the cameras which have a low dynamic range or when you are going out to newsprint—where the reproducible tonal range is very narrow.

Test Targets

Photographers and printers use one or more of the following test targets to see how well their total imaging system (including cameras, lighting, separation software, proofers, and printers) is working. By including a standardized element in a picture, you can see and judge your camera's performance. The two most widely used targets are the 18% gray card and the Macbeth color checker. Targets can be bought in professional camera stores or graphic supply shops.

• **Gray card** A grey card serves a valuable role in determining exposure, how well the camera's light meter is working, and whether there are any color casts in either the capture or print. Including a gray card in an image is a simple yet effective method of defining a neutral balance. Figure 8-10 shows how the photographer shot one image with the gray card in the image (on the left), removed the graycard, and then without changing anything took the photograph on the right. After bringing both images into Photoshop, she created a Levels Image Adjustment layer, used the graycard to define a neutral gray, and then dragged the neutral reference Image Adjustment layer over to the final shot to balance out the shot perfectly.

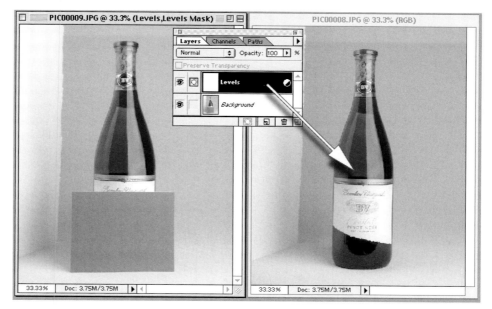

Figure 8-10 Using a gray card can make a big difference in how your shots come out.

• **Gray value balls** Developed by MegaVision, this three-dimensional target with gray, white, and black Ping-Pong-sized wooden balls mounted on flexible wires allows you to measure light falloff and color temperature. See Figure 8-11.

• **21-step wedge** Developed and distributed by Kodak, this target shows how the camera performs in the shadows, midtones, and highlights. If the dark areas of the target lack separation, add a light fill or card to open up the shadows. If the highlights are blown out, block some of the light with a gobo or flag to tone them down. In Figure 8-12 the photographer used the step wedge to control the midtones and to have a neutral gray reference in the image.

Figure 8-11 The flexibility and dimension of these tone balls makes them a valuable target to measure and judge light and color temperature.

Figure 8-12 Placing a 21-step wedge in a photo is useful to see how your camera and lighting are performing.

Color Plate 5-1
Digital video cameras
capture 30 images per
second, each measuring
720 pixels wide by 480
pixels tall. As a result,
this 70-second clip of a
sheepshead fish consumes
254MB when recorded to
a hard disk. (See page 107
for more information.)

C9

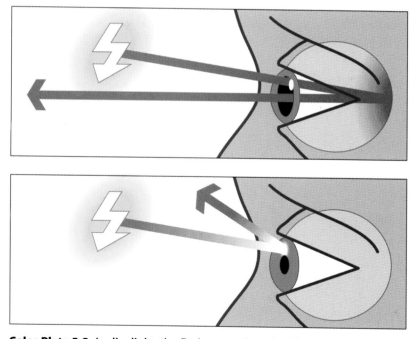

Color Plate 5-2 In dim light, the flash passes into the dilated eye of your
subject and reflects back to the camera as red (top). If you turn on the
camera's red-eye reduction feature, the camera emits a "preflash" to reduce
the size of the subject's pupils. Then the real flash bounces off the iris (bottom).
(See page 113 for more information.)

Color Plate 6-1 You can see color fringing or chromatic aberration on the edges between dark and light, such as on the edge of this sign. (See page 127 for more information.)

Color Plate 6-2 The inset shows the effect of compression damage. (See page 131 for more information.)

Color Plate 6-3 Oversaturation and image contrast can be an attempt to cover up the performance of a noisy sensor, as seen in this close-up of a Christmas bow. (See page 133 for more information.)

Color Plate 6-4 This image is less saturated than Color Plate 6-3 and reveals much better tonal detail and less noise. (See page 133 for more information.)

Color Plate 7-1 You know a medium has become popular when it's available in an array of designer colors. But besides looking spiffy in a drawer, these colorful Zips serve as a visual reference for organizing your photographs and other documents. In this case, blue signifies a book of some merit. (See page 154 for more information.)

Color Plate 7-2 A few aquarium-bound jellyfish captured with a Nikon CoolPix 900. A rectangle surrounds the area, enlarged in Color Plate 7-3. (See page 166 for more information.)

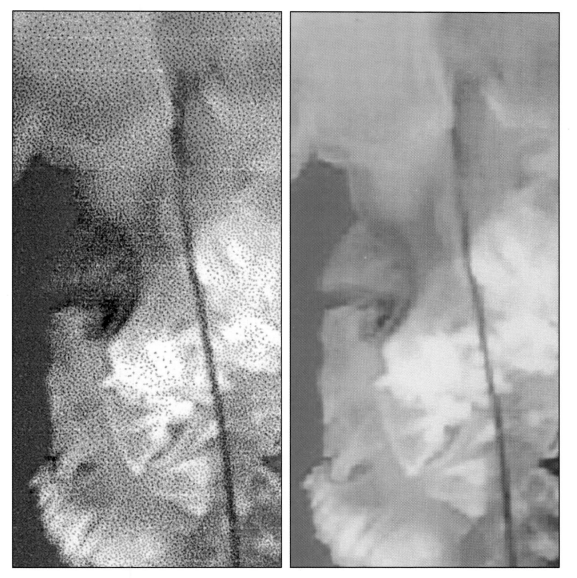

C 13

Color Plate 7-3 Magnified details from Color Plate 7-2 printed on an Epson Stylus Color 800 ink-jet printer (left) and an Olympus P-300U dye-sublimation device (right). While the printer dots are obvious in the ink-jet print, the dye-sub image is as smooth as the original photograph. (See page 166 for more information.)

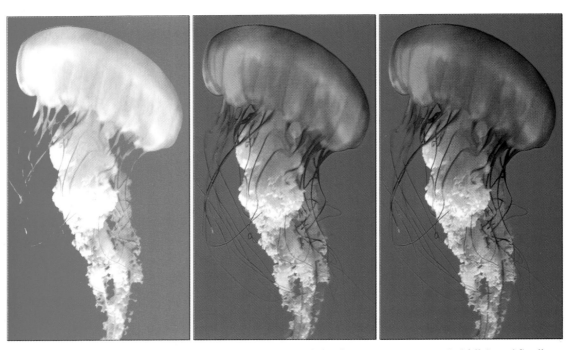

Color Plate 7-4 A dye-sub printer first makes a cyan pass (left), then a magenta pass (middle), and finally a yellow pass (right). Some devices also print a layer of black. (See page 167 for more information.)

Color Plate 8-1 Working with creative backgrounds in the studio can add a subtle atmosphere to an image. (See page 174 for more information.)

Color Plate 8-2 Working in the studio allows you to control the light, props, and the camera's point of view to create intriguing images such as this. Image was captured with the Kodak DC260 Zoom. (See page 176 for more information.)

C15

Color Plate 8-3 Shooting with the wrong color balance setting ruins the picture's color rendition. In this situation, the photographer should have set the camera for tungsten light to get a neutral image. (See page 178 for more information.)

18,000°Kelvin	High-altitude skylight
11,000°Kelvin	Skylight w/o direct sun
6,000°Kelvin	Flash/Strobe
5,000°Kelvin	Daylight
4,000°Kelvin	Flash bulb
3,400°Kelvin 3,200°Kelvin	Tungsten-halogen Photoflood
2,800°Kelvin	Household Lightbulb
1,900°Kelvin	Candle
200°Kelvin	Sunset

Color Plate 8-4 As the color temperature of the light increases, the color of the light gets bluer. (See page 179 for more information.)

Color Plate 8-6 Including a Macbeth color checker in location and studio photos adds standardized color references to the shoot. (See page 189 for more information.)

C16

Color Plate 8-5
From left to right: Photo taken with one light source; photo taken with the same light source plus a white foamcore fill card near the left side of the bottle; final image taken with light, fill card, and silver reflector placed behind the bottle to kick light through the red wine. (See page 185 for more information.)

- **Macbeth color checker** A standardized 24-color checker (as seen in Color Plate 8-6 on page C16) mimics many real world colors including various skin tones and hard to reproduce colors. Use the Macbeth checker in combination with profiling software such as Kodak ColorFlow ICC Profile to build an ICC profile.

- **IT-8 or Kodak Q-60 test target** A 264-color checker with a 22-step wedge commonly used to calibrate scanners and monitors. The Linocolor DCam software uses this target to build ICC profiles for professional digital cameras.

- **Build your own** Before starting any critical any job, many photographers build their own test targets that reflect the colors, dye sets, and materials of the job at hand. If you're going to be shooting running shoes, it makes sense to build a test target with the materials of the shoes and use that to test your imaging workflow from start to finish.

THE BOTTOM LINE

The initial cost of your desktop studio with a table, tripod, lights, and light modifiers should be between $500 – $2000. Professional photographers often spend more than this on a camera stand alone. Table 8-3 runs down the essential list.

Item	Price	Where to Buy
Table	$0–100	Thrift Store
Tripod	100–250	Camera Store
Lights	250–1000	Camera Store
IR Remote	100	Camera Store
Light stands per piece	50–150	Camera Store
Softboxes per piece	50–200	Camera Store
Reflectors per piece	50–100	Camera Store
Homemade Light modifiers	50	Crafts & Hardware store
Accessories	50	Crafts & Toy store
TOTAL	$500–$2,000	

Table 8-3 Cost of the Desktop Studio

YOUR CAMERA BAG

A camera bag is an essential piece of equipment whenever you are shooting on location, traveling, or transporting equipment. Protecting the equipment is the most important function of the camera bag, but don't forget to consider how efficient and comfortable the bag is.

- **Protection of equipment** The bag should hold the camera and accessories without letting them get banged around. Look for a sturdy bag with good padding. Bags with customizable interiors that hold your stuff securely and that you can reconfigure to meet you changing needs are definitely desirable.

- **Efficiency** You need to be able to get into and out of the bag quickly and easily. Choose one with a large flap that protects the equipment even when it isn't clipped shut and large exterior pockets for the items you'll need a lot like the extra batteries and disks. Cheap bags that look like thermal coolers with a zipper all the way around are to be avoided since you have to close the bag all the way to protect the equipment from rain, falling out, or pick pockets.

- **Comfort** Look for a wide, non-slip adjustable strap. Try the bag on with and without camera gear in it. If the bag doesn't feel right, don't buy it. Not only does the bag have to be comfortable loaded with equipment, it also has to fit just right when you're shooting and it is half empty.

Looking for the perfect camera bag can be a long but enjoyable quest as it gives you an excuse to visit professional photo stores and trade shows. For many photographers the perfect camera bag is as elusive as the Holy Grail, and their closets are full of discarded bags.

> **TIP:** Many bag manufacturers such as Lightware, Domke, Temba, and Lowepro have booths at regional and national photo shows and will often sell the show floor models for a reduced price on the last day of the show.

Although the camera bag is the most popular approach to carrying camera equipment, there are other possibilities:

- **Pouches** Your camera probably came with a pouch, and it's a good place to keep it safe from dust and scratches. Many have shoulder straps or belt loops. Ideally, they also hold a few accessories such as an extra set of batteries and memory card.

- **Fanny packs** Some people swear by these; others avoid the instant tourist look at all costs. If the fanny pack keeps everything you need in place and offers adequate protection (and you like it), then go for it. With a fanny pack, you don't have to worry about balancing the bag on your shoulder while shooting because it is securely cinched around your waist.

- **Backpacks** A photo backpack is more than a day pack with a photo label—it is made up of adjustable partitions and Velcro straps that allow you to place cameras, lenses, and accessories into separate compartments. If you're planning on traveling extensively or carrying a portable computer with you, a photo-specific backpack can be a wise investment. For the photo-journalist on the move, Lowepro has developed the jet-black Stealth digital backpack designed to hold a PowerBook G3-size laptop, Kodak DCS 520/D2000-size camera, plus a variety of lenses, a mobile phone, flash equipment, and other accessories in one airline-friendly package.

- **Cases** Use Lightware and Haliburton hard cases to transport and store large professional digital camera equipment. Any equipment that travels as checked luggage needs the level of security only a case can provide.

After you've bought the bag (or whatever form of camera luggage you've chosen), take a few minutes to get oriented with it and plan where the essential accessories should go. Getting to know your bag allows you to concentrate on the shoot rather than fumble around in your camera bag. Don't forget to attach a nametag and put an extra business card inside the bag.

One unsolved mystery remains: if cameras both digital and film cameras should be protected from heat, then why are most camera bags and cases black? We just don't know.

What's in Your Bag?

When packing your camera bag, the first temptation is to try to fit the entire studio in it—this is fine if you have an assistant or small donkey who will carry the bag. Keep the bag light and close-by and you'll be more likely to go out and shoot. In addition to obvious items such as the camera and extra batteries and memory cards, take a look at the following list to see what else you may want to pack to insure a happy photo shoot.

- **Flash and sync cord** Use an external flash to control the light and fill the shadows. See Chapter 9 for directions on when and how to use an external flash with a digital camera.

- **Filters** The most important filter to carry with you on location is a polarizing filter. Use it to control reflections as seen in Figure 8-13 and to cut through haze. If you are planning on taking pictures of buildings, use a wide-angle adapter to get the big picture and a telephoto adapter to move in on the details. Special effects filters are best left in the camera store—you can always add star effects or soften the picture later in the digital darkroom.

Figure 8-13
Using a polarizing filter
(bottom) allows you
to control and place
reflections.

- **Gray card** Having a neutral reference in an image is a tremendous help when doing critical color balance work. Take a 4 by 5-inch gray card with you.

- **Lens-cleaning cloth or tissue** Don't even *think* of using a paper tissue or shirtsleeve to clean your camera lens or LCD panel. The wood fibers in the tissue or dirt on your shirtsleeve can scratch the lens and ruin it permanently. Use only dedicated lens cleaning clothes, wipes, or papers to clean your equipment.

- **Small reflector** Photoflex makes collapsible reflectors that twist up to practically nothing. For example the 22-inch reflector seen in Figure 8-14 collapses into an 8-inch pouch and weights less than 8 ounces. You can buy white, silver, or gray reflectors to bounce in light just where you need it—besides being very functional, these reflectors also show that you are really cool.

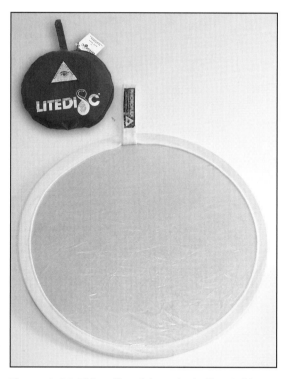

Figure 8-14 This collapsible 22-inch silver/white reflector collapses to fit into an 8-inch pouch.

CHAPTER NINE

Essentials of Photography

Photography combines physics and passion. The physics comes into play when the camera makes an exposure, and the passion comes from your interest in the photographic subject. A point and shoot camera can almost always be relied on to produce a recognizable picture, but making a *good* photograph requires an understanding of the principles of photography, as well as the enthusiasm to experiment, learn from your pictures, and try again.

The most important skill a photographer needs to develop is that of *previsualizing* the photograph—of seeing the picture in your mind's eye and understanding how the camera will see and capture it. Beginners see what they *know* is there and are often surprised that the picture doesn't convey the meaning they thought it had when they took it; photographers learn to see what the camera sees and to work with the image as it falls on the film (or sensor) plane. Previsualization pertains not only to composition (a subject we'll deal with in the next chapter), but also to light and the peculiarities of camera optics.

The difference between an ordinary picture and a good photograph is the difference between just pointing and shooting and consciously composing a shot and working with the light and the camera to capture a memorable image. Digital cameras are a great way (without wasting time or film) to learn the mechanics of photography and hone your aesthetic sensibilities.

SEEING THE LIGHT

Photographers use light to create images. The "quality" of light is determined by the following variables:

- **Brightness** How much light you have affects the mood and clarity of the photograph. Working with a lot of light allows the viewer to see your subject clearly; working with a minimum of light can add mystery and intrigue to an image.

- **Size** How large is the light source in relationship to the subject? A large light source produces a soft light and soft shadows. The smaller the light source, the harsher the light becomes, and the more distinct the shadows are.

- **Color** can add to the mood and expression of a photograph but it also can ruin an image by discoloring the subject or background. The color of light is controlled by the time of day, the color temperature of the source, the hues of surfaces from which it is reflected, and in the studio by the use of transparent gels to color the light. Please note: we recommend working with the professional heat-resistant colored gels found in photography stores.

- **Number of light sources** Working with multiple sources allows you to sculpt your subject. Start with one light source and then add fill, reflectors, and bounce lights as needed to accentuate.

- **Distance** The distance from the source to the subject controls both the relative strength of the light and its relative size. Moving a light away diminishes the intensity of the light but makes it act like a smaller (and harsher) source.

- **Direction** The direction the light comes from, above, below, beside, or even behind the subject, allows you to interpret the subject in many different ways. It determines where the shadows fall and influences how the edges of an object are separated from the background. The angle that the light hits the subject can either accentuate texture detail or flatten out details. Sweeping the subject with light from the side is a classic method to bring out texture as seen in this macro shot of coins in Figure 9-1.

Figure 9-1 Having the light come in at a low side angle helped to accentuate the texture of the coins. Image shot with the Nikon CoolPix 900s.

Study the light as it changes over the course of a day and through the changing seasons and learn to see how a body of water, the weather, unwanted pollution, or even a distant volcanic eruption modifies it. Get up early to see the soft and mysterious light that appears on the pre-dawn horizon. Notice how simple textures come alive as the first rays strike them in the early morning and how the harsh shadows of the midday sun can add a sense of drama to a seemingly uninteresting scene. Resist the urge to take a lot of happy snaps of Technicolor sunsets; instead, turn around and see how the light brings the surroundings to life, as seen in Color Plate 9-1 on page C17. In the city, watch how light is reflected from glass buildings and how a white wall can serve as a reflector to soften the shadows in an outdoor portrait.

> **TIP:** Observing the light as it changes, you can learn a lot about professional studio lighting. If you want to flatter a portrait subject, mimic the early morning light by using a soft, diffuse light source. To create sharp shadows, place a small light source above the subject like the noonday sun. You can even gel your lights to modify their colors.

MEASURING THE LIGHT

Exposure is determined by a light meter, either in the camera or by using an external light meter. Every meter assumes that the entire world is a gray card, the photographic standard that reflects 18% of the light hitting it, as illustrated in Figure 9-2. This is referred to as *middle gray* because it is roughly the average value in an average photo-graph; it works pretty well most of the time. Handheld meters used to be the norm, but internal light meters now offer considerable flexibility and convenience.

Figure 9-2 You might be seeing your cat's dinner (top), but all the meter sees is middle gray (bottom).

Metering Patterns

As digital cameras become more sophisticated, many models offer more than one light metering pattern. The three common patterns are *center-weighted, spot,* and *multi-segment* (or *matrix*), as illustrated in Figure 9-3. Working with the appropriate metering pattern allows you to get the best exposure in a variety of situations. Center-weighted metering is an older method and, because it assumes that the most important part of the picture is in the center, it often doesn't give great results. Of the three patterns, spot and multi-segment are the most useful.

- **Center-weighted** This meter pattern is the most basic and most entry level cameras use it. The meter measures the entire scene but gives greater weight to the center of the frame. Choose this option when the subject is centered in the frame and represents a reasonable approximation of medium gray.

- **Spot meter** A camera's spot mode measures the light in a 3° to 10° circle in the center of the frame (degree refers to angle of view—3° is about as large as a dime looks on the sidewalk between your feet). Use spot metering to measure a specific part of the picture you want the camera to expose for, such as a section approximating 18% reflectance somewhere in the frame. Handheld spot meters can measure spots as small as 0.5 degrees.

- **Multi-segment** The best pattern for most situations, multi-segment metering looks at the entire picture (the Nikon CoolPix 900s measures 64 areas, and the Nikon CoolPix 950 measures 256 areas) and compensates for overly bright and dark areas. This is a good metering pattern to use in contrasty situations such as landscapes where the sky and land are of equal importance. It is the metering pattern we use most often.

Figure 9-3 From top to bottom: Spot, center-weighted, and multi-segment meter modes.

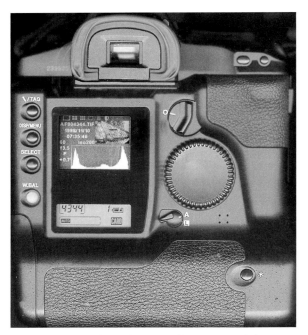

Figure 9-4 Checking the image histogram while shooting is a great way to double-check image exposure (the LCD screen of a Kodak DCS 520).

USING THE LCD SCREEN

If you work with your camera under a lot of different lighting conditions, you know how the LCD screen looks different in your office than outside in the bright sunlight. Whenever you come into a new lighting situation, take a picture of a neutral reference such as a gray card, the sidewalk, or some faded jeans and adjust your LCD brightness to match the review image to the reference target. This will help you to judge the images and exposure better. (Calibrating the LCD does not affect the exposure of the picture).

The image on the LCD screen is only a guide and cannot be used to judge critical exposure details. Some cameras also present the image's histogram, a graphic representation of the spread of its of tonal values. Setting the exposure from the histogram requires experienced judgment (different subjects will obviously have very different distributions), but it allows very precise control of the image. Being able to see the exposure histogram as shown in Figure 9-4 is one of the best features of the Kodak 520, 560, and 620 cameras.

Working with the Light Meter

The exposure meters in the newest digital cameras are so highly evolved you can rely on them to calculate the best exposure in most situations. Sometimes, though, it is necessary to outwit the meter. If the average tone of your scene is quite different from a medium gray, such as would be the case with a snow scene or sunny day at the beach, there are several strategies you can adopt to override the meter and get great results.

One approach is to meter a gray target and use that light meter reading to calculate the best exposure. This technique works with any type of metering pattern. Note: This assumes that you're using a digital camera that employs the technique of pressing the shutter button down halfway to lock in on exposure. Please refer to your camera manual.

1. Fill the viewfinder with an 18% gray area. Ideally this would be the standard gray card, but since many of us don't carry one, you can use a pair of faded jeans, a gray sidewalk, or a concrete wall. The reference has to be in the same light as your subject.

2. Push the shutter button halfway down and hold it to lock the exposure.

3. Frame the scene as desired and carefully push the shutter the rest of the way down to take the picture.

Overriding the Light Meter

On many cameras, you can use *exposure compensation* to override the light meter and make what the camera thinks should be gray come out lighter or darker. Exposure compensation is usually accessed through the camera's software control menu. By dialing in *minus* exposure compensation, you will underexpose the image and force the darks to be darker. *Plus* compensation increases the exposure to make the whites white rather than the muddy gray seen in the normal exposure in Figure 9-5.

Sunny beach and snowy winter scenes are the classic picture situations calling for +1/2 or +1 exposure compensation. Darker subjects usually require less compensation than when working with film, but try setting the exposure compensation to -1/2 or -1 to force the dark areas of the image to be really dark.

Figure 9-5 The camera does not know that the snow should be white and with normal exposure (at top) the snow looks dingy and gray. Using exposure compensation to increase exposure by 1/2 stop helps, but at 1 full stop, the snow is exposed correctly and looks as white as the day it fell.

Beating Backlight

In extremely high-contrast lighting situations, it is impossible to expose correctly for both the dark and light areas of the image. Backlit conditions are very difficult for even the "smartest" cameras. In the top example in Figure 9-6, the camera failed to read the person by the window correctly in multi-segment mode and exposed for the scene outside, which ended up silhouetting the intended subject. Using the spot mode to meter for the person allowed the photographer to take the center image of Figure 9-6, but the detail outside was lost. The only way to deal with such extreme lighting is to add light with a reflector or fill-flash as described later in this chapter or to use the digital darkroom to merge the two exposures (bottom photo in Figure 9-6).

Figure 9-6 Top: The meter was fooled by the strong window light and calculated an exposure that was correct for the outside scene but made the person a dark silhouette. Center: Using the spot meter helped the camera calculate the correct exposure for the person standing at the window. Bottom: Photoshop wizardry merged the two exposures; thankfully the photographer used a tripod and the model did not move between exposures.

The Digital Zone System

Ansel Adams, Edward Weston, and Minor White popularized the photographic *Zone System* based on previsualizing where the tones of an image will fall along an eleven-step scale. Adjusting the exposure to place the important values in a specific zone and processing the film accordingly, they were able to produce images with extended tonal ranges and strong emotional impact. Figure 9-7 shows the zone range from Zone 0 (pure black without detail) to Zone X (pure white without detail). Zone V is the 18% gray that the meter is calibrated to.

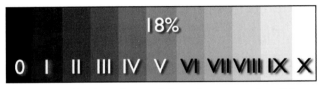

Figure 9-7 The Zone System is based upon previsualizing where the tones of an image should fall on the gray scale.

Richard Chang of MegaVision has developed a *Digital Zone System* to describe exposure in Photoshop. Photoshop will display a dot percentage in the Info palette from which you can derive a digital Roman number 0-X. To get the Zone value, subtract the dot percentage from 100 (the Zone System's 0 is no light—on the printer's gray scale it is no ink) and move the decimal one place to the left. Thus, 35% translates to a Zone value of $6^{1}/_{2}$ (VI $^{1}/_{2}$). See Table 9-1 for complete 1-100 and 256 value equivalents of the Digital Zone System.

Zone	Gray scale	8-bit Value	Visual Equivalent
Zone 0	100%	0	Pure Black
Zone I	90%	30	Near black, slight tonality
Zone II	80%	55	Dark with a hint of texture
Zone III	70%	80	Dark shadow with full texture
Zone IV	60%	105	Dark gray areas with full detail

Table 9-1 The Digital Zone System

continued

Table 9-1 *continued*

Zone	Gray scale	8-bit Value	Visual Equivalent
Zone V	50%	128	18% reflectance
Zone VI	40%	155	Medium-light gray
Zone VII	30%	180	Light values with full texture
Zone VIII	20%	205	High values with delicate texture
Zone IX	10%	230	Near white, slight tonality
Zone X	0%	256	Paper-base white

EXPOSURE PARTNERS—ISO, APERTURE, AND SHUTTER SPEED

Lighting decisions are aesthetic, but the time comes when you have to deal with the mechanics of capturing that image on the sensor. Relative to the human eye, the dynamic range of a CCD is very limited, and it is the photographer's job (plus the camera's automatic features, if any) to expose it with light it can record.

Three factors define the correct exposure: the sensitivity of the CCD, the strength of the light striking the CCD, and the length of time the CCD is exposed. The importance of making the right exposure cannot be underestimated, especially with a camera with limited dynamic range or when your final output (newspaper is a good example) can reproduce only a few middle tones. The shorter the range of tones you have to work with, the more important it is to get the exposure right—to not overexpose the highlights or let the shadows block up.

ISO Ratings

The CCD's sensitivity is usually expressed an as ISO (International Standards Organization) rating. Most entry-level and professional lite cameras have ISO ratings between 50-100, meaning that the camera needs quite a bit of light to take a good picture. As the ISO rating doubles, let's say from 50 to 100, the CCD's light sensitivity is also doubled, or can be considered twice as fast. For reference, standard films range from 25 up to 3200 ISO, and speeds of 200 or 400 are very ordinary.

The low ISO ratings of most digital cameras means that they do not perform very well in low-light situations, where long exposure of a CCD produces an unacceptably noisy result. Specialized digital cameras, such as the Kodak DCS 520 and 620 that were developed for photojournalists, have ISO ratings variable from 200-1600 and we have taken lots of pictures at 800 ISO without visible deterioration of the image (see Figure 9-8). The image becomes a bit noisier when the cameras are pushed to 1600, but sometimes getting a shot is worth a small sacrifice of image quality.

Figure 9-8 Shot with the Kodak DCS 520 in the available light of a dim mausoleum. Even the inset (enlarged 200%) does not reveal any bothersome noise from shooting at 800 ISO.

Aperture and Shutter Speed

Aperture and shutter speed work together to control the exposure by determining how much light falls onto the CCD to make the picture. As we explained in Chapter 3, *aperture* refers to the opening of the iris or diaphragm in the camera that adjusts to let more or less light hit the CCD, whereas the shutter (or its electronic equivalent) controls how long light is allowed to expose the image.

Think of the lens/aperture combination as a funnel, in which the big end is the lens (it gathers the light) and the small end is the aperture that controls how much light gets to the CCD in a given period of time. In this analogy, the shutter is the valve that controls how long the light flows into the CCD. The smaller the aperture, the longer it will take a given amount light to flow through the funnel, and the longer the required exposure will be. You can use a larger spout for a shorter period of time or a smaller spout for a longer period to admit equivalent amounts of light.

Aperture is measured in f-stops (the ratio between the focal length of the lens and the diameter of the opening in the diaphragm) and each stop in the standard series of stops represents a factor of two in the amount of light admitted. Thus, "opening up" from $f5.6$ to $f4$ admits twice as much light, and "stopping down" from $f11$ to $f16$ cuts the amount of light in half. Shutter speeds are measured in fractions of seconds, typically $1/2$, $1/4$, $1/8 \ldots 1/125$, $1/250$, etc. Doubling the exposure, say from $1/60$ to $1/30$, doubles the amount of light entering the camera. In this way, an exposure of $1/60$ at $f4$ is the same as one of $1/30$ at $f5.6$ as far as the amount of light is concerned.

Creative Exposure Techniques

Unfortunately, only a few deluxe point and shoot and professional lite cameras give *you* any significant control of the aperture or shutter speed. When you take pictures in low-light situations, a camera with automatic exposure control will choose a long shutter speed (use your tripod to avoid blurry pictures) and a wide aperture to allow enough light to strike the CCD. In bright situations the camera will use a fast shutter speed and a small aperture. Understanding how the camera adjusts the exposure, you can achieve greater creative control of your images despite the limitations of your equipment. Furthermore, manufacturers are introducing new models almost daily, and some include manual selection of aperture and shutter speed. And there are other ways around this "lack of control" problem.

Slow Shutter Speed Effects

Even if you don't have manual control over aperture and shutter speed, shooting in low-light situations will force the camera to make a long exposure and can produce some interesting and unexpected effects. Leaving the shutter open for longer periods of time changes how we see time and allows you to photograph swirled nighttime pictures such as Figure 9-10.

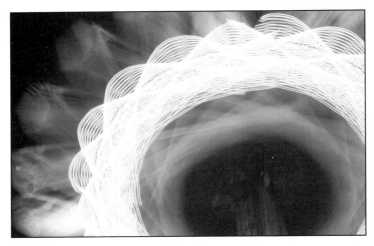

Figure 9-9 Shot with the Kodak DCS 520 and a long shutter speed makes this amusement park ride to come to life.

Slow Flash Synch

Another method of getting creative effects is to combine the slow shutter speed with a slow flash sync (see Color Plate 9-2 on page C17. Set the camera to slow flash sync (sometimes fill-flash mode does the trick) and a slow shutter speed. Then go to where the dimly lit action is: a bustling train station, a busy street during the holiday season, or a lively concert—anywhere there is not a lot of light but a lot of motion. Then experiment with the following settings:

• Without flash, keep the camera still and let the entire scene blur into a madness of color, as seen in Color Plate 9-2.

• With a slow synch flash: Take the picture and keep the camera still. This will freeze everything that is still and let the moving areas blur as in Figure 9-10.

- Take the picture and pan the camera with the motion of your subject. This will keep the subject in focus and blur the background as in Figure 9-11. Try to pan from your torso in one smooth movement.

- Take the picture and move in the same direction as the motion of your subject.

> **TIP:** *It is very difficult to predict how the light trails will turn out; shoot a lot to increase your chances of getting a good shot.*

Figure 9-10 Using a slow-sync flash speed allows you to freeze some of the action and let the rest be blurred. The image was shot with a Nikon CoolPix 900s.

Figure 9-11 Using a slow flash sync and panning with the subject keeps the main subject sharper than the blurred background. Who would have thought that commuting could be this exciting?

Aperture and Depth of Field

Aperture does more than control the amount of light. Most notably, it affects the *depth of field*. The lens focuses only light from a certain distance onto the sensor, and depth of field is the measure of how much nearer or farther than that distance an object can be and still be acceptably sharp. The smaller the aperture, the greater the depth of field and the more of the photograph is in focus. The distance from the camera to the subject also plays an important role; close-ups have much more limited depth of field than landscapes do.

Some entry-level point and shoot cameras (such as the Olympus D-400 Zoom) work with three *f*-stops (2.8, 5.6, and 11), and the Kodak DC265 allows you to select apertures ranging from 3 to 16, making it an interesting professional lite camera for studio work. More often, the user has no control over which *f*-stop the camera is using, but Table 9-2 shows how the camera selects the largest aperture in low light and closes down the aperture in bright light.

Light Conditions	Aperture	Relative Depth of Field
Low light	*f* 2.8	Very Shallow
Heavy Overcast	*f* 4	Shallow
Cloudy Bright (No Shadows)	*f* 5.6	Below average
Hazy Sun (Soft shadows)	*f* 8	Average
Bright Day (Distinct Shadows)	*f* 11	Above average
Very Sunny Day	*f* 16	Deep
Very Sunny Day (Snow or Beach Scenes)	*f* 22	Very Deep

Table 9-2 Apertures and Depth of Field

Understanding how aperture works gives photographers a wonderful creative tool. As long as there is enough light, we can open or close the aperture (while we shorten or lengthen the exposure) to control what in our image is sharp and what falls off into a miasma of softness. This, literally, gives focus to our photographs.

If you want the background to be indistinct, focus on the foreground and work with a large aperture to let the background go soft as in Figure 9-12. Wide-angle lenses have greater depth of field than do long focal length lenses, so it is often easier to achieve this effect by using a telephoto lens and a wide aperture.

Figure 9-12 By focusing on the water lilies in the foreground and using a large aperture, the photographer threw the background out of focus—drawing the viewer's attention to the flowers. The image was shot with a Kodak DCS 520.

In the top image in Figure 9-13, the photographer manually focused on the center duck at f4.5, a large aperture with short depth of field. In the middle one, without changing focus, the photographer stopped the lens down to f11, increasing the depth of field to make the other ducks sharper. At f32 in the bottom photo all ducks are sharp.

Depth of field is a function not only of aperture and distance from camera to subject, but of the focal length of the lens and CCD size as well. The wider the lens, and the smaller the CCD, the greater the inherent depth of field the camera will produce.

A 17mm lens, the typical "normal" lens on a consumer camera, has a depth of field from about 7 to 40 feet when focused at 8 feet, even opened up to f2.8. Although this presents a problem for artistic composition, it is great for snapshots; most of the stuff in your pictures (particularly in the background) will be more or less in focus.

Only with professional digital cameras whose CCDs are close to the size of 35 mm (or even medium format) film, do you have much creative freedom to work with depth of field.

Figure 9-13 In this image, the photographer focused on the middle duck and shot at ƒ4.5 (top), ƒ11 (middle), and ƒ32 (bottom) to increase depth of field.

LENSES

Light enters the camera through the lens, which focuses the light onto the sensor. Lens selection offers the photographer a range of points of view on the subject. The effect of changing lenses is very striking because the focal length of the lens establishes the space within the image.

A normal lens has an angle of view more or less like what you see with your eyes. A wide angle lens has the effect of extending the field of vision into the periphery and exaggerating the sense of depth. Telephoto lenses have a narrow field and give the impression of compressing distance. Many cameras have zoom lenses that allow a choice of working focal length.

Because the CCDs in digital cameras come in a variety of sizes, manufacturers usually translate the focal lengths of their lenses into the 35mm camera equivalent for the field of view: the normal lens is 50mm; longer lenses are telephotos and shorter ones are wide angle. Table 9-3 gives the angles of view for 35mm camera lenses.

Focal length	Angle of view
17mm (wide-angle)	104°
28mm	75°
50mm (Normal)	47°
135mm (Telephoto)	18°
300mm	8°

Table 9-3 Focal lengths and Angle of View for 35mm Cameras

Most deluxe point and shoot and professional lite digital cameras have zoom lenses that can capture a wider point of view or a narrower one. For example, taking pictures of the interior of a home, you'd probably want to work with a widest-angle zoom setting possible. The Kodak DC210 Plus offers a 29-59 mm zoom lens, whose wide-angle setting works very well for real estate interiors.

Avoid taking a portrait of anyone you like or want to flatter with a wide-angle lens. The wide-angle lens will distort the person's face and give them a big nose, as seen in Figure 9-14. The same picture with the lens zoomed to its longest setting created a much more flattering portrait as seen in the right photo.

Figure 9-14 Making a portrait with a wide-angle lens or the widest setting of your zoom lens will distort subjects close to the camera, as seen on the left. Using a telephoto zoom setting minimizes distortion. Both images were captured with the Kodak DC210 Plus.

Some digital cameras (including the Olympus D-400 Zoom, Kodak DC 210+, Nikon CoolPix 950, Fuji MX-2700, and Ricoh RDC-4300) offer *macro* settings for extreme close-ups. You usually push the "flower" button (it looks like a flower) and the camera will focus between 8 inches and approximately 2 feet.

> *TIP:* The two most important tips to remember when doing macro work are to turn-off the flash and use a tripod.

MODIFYING THE LIGHT

When we have seen and measured the light, the next step to making better photographs is modifying the light with fills and diffusion or by using on-camera and off-camera flash equipment.

Natural Light

In Chapter 8 we used a piece of white foamcore and some silver foil to make a wine bottle come alive. Outside the studio, fill and diffusion can be as simple as finding a light-colored wall to bounce in a little extra light, or having a person sit under a tree, or a light picnic umbrella to soften the light. Sometimes photographers carry collapsible reflectors to bounce light into the shadows. Softer light has lower contrast, the shadows aren't so harsh, and portraits in these conditions are much more flattering.

Another classic photographic technique is called "Waiting for the Light." Watch how a building façade comes to life at a certain time of day and plan to be there to take the picture. Go out after a storm when the streets are wet, the air is clean, and the light is popping through the last clouds. Get up early to catch the sunrise or take a walk in the evening to photograph with the slanting rays of the sunset and see how the final light illuminates the world with subtle mystery and intrigue, as in Color Plate 9-3 on page C18.

> **TIP:** When working in low-light situations such as early morning or late evening, don't forget your tripod.

Adding Light with Flash

Flash photography is tricky business. You can't see what you're doing before you do it. It has many virtues both in the studio and on location, but on-camera flash is of very limited utility.

Most cameras offer some of the following five flash settings:

- **Off** is off and is a very useful setting.
- **On** fires the flash at full-power when you push the shutter.

- **Fill** will pop in a little bit of light to open up the shadows a bit.

- **Auto** measures the light of the scene and fires the flash if the camera thinks the picture needs some light.

- **Red-eye reduction** either prefires a small flash or emits a ray of light to get the pupils of the subject's eyes to contract.

With on-camera flash, abstinence is a virtue. Avoid using it at all and try to work with the available light to capture the atmosphere of the scene at hand. If you are taking someone's portrait, try moving the person closer to the window as seen in Figure 9-15 or turning up the room lights. Photographing a room interior, open the drapes to illuminate the room or wait for a better time of day to take the picture. Other than off, the most valuable flash setting is fill.

Figure 9-15 Not every portrait needs to have direct eye contact. Experiment with different poses, moods, and expressions. Image captured with the Agfa 1680 in soft window light.

Using Flash on a Sunny Day

On-camera flashes are not much use as a main light source; you cannot do much about their position and they create harsh shadows. They are, however, useful tools on sunny days to lessen lighting contrast. In their absence, we are faced with the choice of exposing for the subject in the foreground and letting the background bleach out or getting the background right and silhouetting the figure. Flash, used judiciously, will bring the brightness of the figure up enough to make the contrast between it and the background manageable as seen in Figure 9-16.

Figure 9-16 When the sun is very bright or directly behind your subject, turn on your flash. This image was captured with the Fuji MX-700 in the late afternoon on the open water—a sure recipe for failure. Using the flash, the photographer was able to decrease the contrast and open up the shadows on the figure. In this instance the flash also improved the model's posture.

Use fill flash on bright sunny days to lighten up harsh shadows under a person's nose, open up the eye sockets, or to reach under the brim of a hat, as seen in Figure 9-17. When we work outside on bright days, we just leave fill flash on. In addition to opening up shadows, it adds tiny "catchlights" in a person's eyes, giving them a lively sparkle.

Figure 9-17 Using fill flash on bright sunny day helps open up harsh shadows and lighten up the areas under the hat.

HOW STRONG IS YOUR FLASH?

Every flash has a guide number that allows you to calculate how far the flash will reach with a given aperture setting. Because most entry-level point and shoot and professional lite cameras don't allow a fine control over the flash strength or aperture setting, you need to look in the camera manual to see how far the flash will reach.

Most on-camera flashes have a range from 1-12 feet, so using it to illuminate Manhattan when you are on the Empire State Building just won't work. Being too close to the subject will over-expose the image, and being too far away will under-expose the image. When using your flash, experiment with using a light-colored ceiling or wall to bounce some of the light back into the picture to act as a fill light.

Off-Camera Flash

Many professional lite cameras like the Kodak DC265, Olympus D-620L, Agfa 1680, and Nikon CoolPix 900s (shown below) have flash sync ports that allow you connect an external flash to the camera. While most manufacturers offer dedicated off-camera flashes, pretty much the same effect can be achieved with third-party equipment.

Figure 9-18 Connecting a digital camera to an off-camera flash unit allows for greater flexibility and control than just relying on the small on-camera flash.

Working with an off-camera flash takes a little bit of practice. You can hand hold the camera and flash in the so-called "Hail Mary" position with the flash at arm's length, above and to the side of the camera, as illustrated in Figure 9-19. Alternatively, you can buy a bracket that mounts the flash onto the camera, as seen in Figure 9-20.

Figure 9-19 Holding the flash high and to the side will make the shadows fall more naturally.

Figure 9-20
Mounting the camera and
the flash onto a bracket simplifies
shooting with off-camera flash.

Softening the flash with a third-party softbox or bounce system helps avoid blowing out the light areas of the image. The left side of Figure 9-21 shows a third-party softbox made by LumiQuest. If you don't want to invest any money in a bounce system, the tried and true photojournalist method of attaching a piece of paper or a white index card to the flash with a rubber band, as seen on the right side of Figure 9-20. Point the flash straight up, and the piece of paper will enlarge the light source, making it softer and less direct.

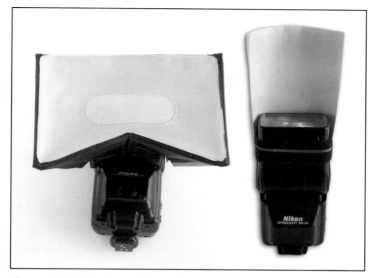

Figure 9-21 Hi-tech and low-tech methods to modify and soften a third-party flash include on the left a softbox made by LumiQuest and on the right a piece of paper and rubber band.

Working with an off-camera flash will give you more control over your lighting and where the shadows fall, but it is definitely something that you have to practice before showing up at a wedding to take pictures. There is nothing worse than ruining an entire shoot, especially when you don't have the option of reshooting the job.

Some in-camera light meters may not take off-camera flash into account when controlling the exposure—read your camera manual for recommendations. One great advantage of digital cameras is that you can see your capture right away. If the pictures are too dark, increase the flash power, move the flash nearer the subject, or open the aperture; if they are too light, do the opposite.

> **TIP:** Look for light ceilings and white walls to bounce your flash. Avoid colored surfaces that will give a cast to the picture or are so far away the reflected light will be dissipated. Keep the off-camera flash as high as possible. This will mimic the position of the sun and the shadows will fall more naturally.

Figure 9-22 The top image was taken without flash, and the bottom image was taken with a Nikon CoolPix 900s with an off-camera flash and LumiQuest softbox. Notice how well-lit the person is, and behold the lack of harsh shadows.

Figure 9-23 Modifying the on-camera flash with translucent paper softens the flash and can help reduce red-eye and harsh shadows.

THE DEVIL MADE ME DO IT

Since on-camera flashes are so close to the lens, subjects can look like candidates for exorcism when the light reflects of their retinas (see Chapter 5 for additional information). Here are a few tricks you can use to avoid red-eye:

- *Turn up the room light to contract the subject's pupils.*

- *Use the red-eye reduction flash mode on the camera. The drawback to this is that the first flash (designed to contract the pupils) makes many subjects think you just took the picture and they turn away before the real picture is shot.*

- *Tape a small piece of translucent tracing paper over the flash to diffuse the light, as we did in Figure 9-23. This softens the sharp point source of the flash and will cut down on harsh shadows and the possibility of red-eye.*

- *Not every portrait needs to have the person look straight into the camera. Pictures in which the person is looking away from the camera capture a different side of the subject.*

- *As a last resort, use an image-editing program to take the red out as shown in Color Plate 9-4 on page C18.*

To paraphrase the photographer and teacher Minor White, "We can teach you 95 percent of everything we know about photography in a week—the rest will take a lifetime." The 95 percent includes the essentials and mechanics of digital photography—the more important 5 percent is up to you. So go out with your camera, experiment, break the rules, and learn from your successes and failures. Thanks to digital photography you can easily erase the bloopers and try again.

CHAPTER TEN

Framing for Success

The most common mistake people make when shooting photographs—whether digital or film—is believing that the camera is impartial. If you look around and see a pretty scene, then you naturally think the camera will see a pretty scene as well. But in fact, the camera's eye operates very differently than your eyes do. And where photography is concerned, the camera's eye is the only view that counts.

When you look at the world, you see a panorama that extends across your field of vision and fades away at the edges. Trace the outer edges of your field of vision with your hands, and you'll see that it's roughly elliptical and considerably wider than it is tall. Although attempting to represent your field of vision in a figure is impossible, Figure 10-1 comes fairly close. If you were to enlarge the figure and wrap it around your head, you'd get an imitation of how your eyes work.

Figure 10-1 Our eyes perceive the world as a wide panorama, the focus and visibility of which fade along an approximately elliptical perimeter.

A camera sees a rectangle—not an approximate rectangle with fuzzy edges, but an absolute, hard-edged rectangle. This convention grew up out of some of the earliest film cameras and continues in force today—in print, on the Web, and in digital photography. As demonstrated by the stock image in Figure 10-2, the rectangle produces a very different picture than the view you see on a daily basis. It's like a static glimpse of the world with blinders on.

Figure 10-2 The camera sees life as a flat image inside the confines of a strictly rectangular frame.

The boundary of the camera's view is called the frame. Your job as a photographer is to get the image you hope to convey inside that frame. Don't try to take in the entire scene—you can't. Don't expect a beautiful scene to make a beautiful photo—it doesn't. Photography is a highly subjective process in which you show people only what you want them to see. Show them the wrong view, and the photo fails; show them the right view, and the photo succeeds.

Figures 10-3 and 10-4 feature exaggerated examples. If the camera were objective, Figure 10-3 would be hands down the better picture. It features a pretty bridge over a pleasant stream surrounded by foliage in full bloom. But where the scene in real life looked dreamy, the framed photo appears cluttered and unremarkable. It's the kind of picture that someone might see and say, "Oh, I'll bet that bridge is really pretty." If we had shot it properly, there wouldn't be any doubt.

Though shot with the same camera—Nikon's CoolPix 900—Figure 10-4 is the exact opposite. Captured on one of those dismal winter days when the sun comes out for ten minutes and the snow is old and thin, the purpose of the photo was merely to record a bridge under construction. Yet none of these conditions prevented the photo from being a success—and, in fact, the bleakness of the image contributed to it. The image includes sharp contrast, balanced composition, good use of geometry, and an almost perfect symmetry. No one's going to say, "I'll bet that bridge is pretty"; you may even think it's ugly. But it gets a long look and it delivers a subjective perspective that only a photograph can convey.

Figure 10-3 This small bridge makes a great subject for a photograph, but the composition of bank and brush intrudes on the scene.

Figure 10-4 This rigid frame is several times less graceful than the bridge from Figure 10-3, but the geometric form contrasts almost eerily with its bleak background, imparting tension and a point of view.

This chapter examines ways to exploit the limitations of the frame to create pictures that go beyond simply capturing a subject to actually invoking a mood and a point of view. Clearly, there are no right or wrong answers. We're often caught completely by surprise when a picture we thought would look great turns out awful or a picture we shot on the spur of the moment looks terrific. So think of this chapter as a source of ideas. Some you'll want to begin using immediately, some you might save for later. But all will help you frame your shots better—whether your goals are personal or professional, artistic, or purely bottom-line.

GET CLOSE, REALLY CLOSE

If we had to sum up our number-one tip for better framing in just two words, it would be, "Get closer!" Not just sort of close, but *really* close. Think like a hunter, and go in for the shot.

The first examples in Figure 10-5 and Color Plate 10-1 on page C19 show some typical snapshots taken inside the Tower of London. At first glance, these photos might look fine. They're relatively well balanced, the focus is sharp, and the lighting is even. As an added bonus, there are no chopped off heads or elbows (though we're missing some feet in the color plate). In fact, these are just the sort of pictures that litter virtually every photo album in the civilized world. But what's the one problem they share in common? At least half the space in each picture is taken up by background—and boring background at that. Lots of brick and mortar, windows and railings. There's far too little of the people, which are after all the reasons these photographs were taken in the first place.

Fortunately, there's a very easy way to make the subject larger and the background smaller. Use your feet to propel yourself toward the subject of your photograph. Most cameras include macro features for close-ups, but even those that don't— like Kodak's DC220—let you shoot as close as one or two feet, which is plenty close for a great picture. The second images in Figure 10-5 and Color Plate 10-1 were captured at a distance of about three to four feet apiece.

NOTE: *You can, of course, crop an image to get rid of excess background. But given the nature of digital photography—that you only have so many pixels to work with—cropping is a better method for fine-tuning a composition than for radically modifying it. Also, shooting close resolves problems that cropping can't. In Figure 10-5, the first image includes a railing at the guard's feet. Cropping that image would leave the railing intact. But shooting close, as in the second image, gets rid of the railing. Naturally, it's far easier not to shoot the railing than to erase it away in an image editor.*

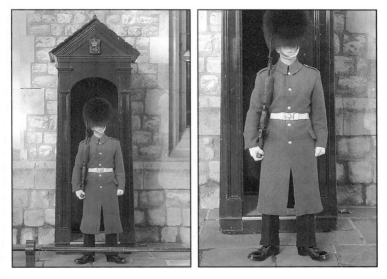

Figure 10-5 As far as models go, this immobile guard couldn't be easier to work with. But do we really need to see five feet to his left and right and seven feet above his head (left)? Three paces forward get you a better shot (right).

Getting close is absolutely imperative when the camera doesn't give you many pixels to work with. The images in Figure 10-6, for example, measure a scant 756 by 504 pixels—not even half megapixel. It's a crying shame to waste what few pixels we have, as in the first photograph. Only by getting about 18 inches from our furry friend, as in the second photo, can we make every pixel count.

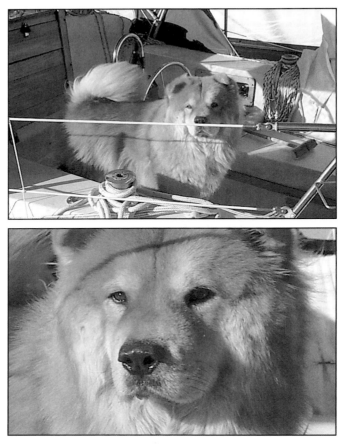

Figure 10-6 Captured with a Kodak DC50, these images measure just 768 by 504 pixels apiece. With such low resolution, you have to make every pixel count (bottom).

Is there a limit to how chummy you should get with your subject? Isn't it possible to poke your camera too far into someone's personal space? Theoretically, yes, but you have to get awfully close before that's a problem. Figure 10-7 shows a relatively distant shot of a horse in a stable. Color Plate 10-2 on page C19 shows this same animal from a distance of a few inches. If this were a human being, we'd caution you against such an up-the-nostril shot. But given that this is a horse, we're inclined to think the jutting nose and mouth add drama. In our opinion, as long as you can keep it in focus, there's no such thing as too close. And too close is always preferable to too far away.

Figure 10-7 This photo provides a good view of the subject surrounded by the right amount of background. But it lacks the drama of an in-your-face close-up, like the one in Color Plate 10-2.

LOOK FOR DETAILS

A photograph captures a fragment of the world as it appears at an exact instant in time. Some of the best photographs manage to capture fragments that cross your field of vision every day but somehow go virtually unnoticed. The trick to finding these fragments is to pay close attention to details. Plainly, this means getting near to your subject, as discussed in the previous section. But it also requires you to develop an eye for the little things that get lost in the crowd, that one particular tree that says more than the forest.

The graveyard in Figure 10-8 is fine as graveyards go. If you have loved ones buried there, it means a lot to you. If not, it's like a million other small-town cemeteries in the world. But inspect the headstones a little closer, and the grave-yard takes on a life of its own, so to speak. Figure 10-9 shows a couple of the more distinctive members of the cemetery staff that conjure up very different pictures of life after death than the pastoral Figure 10-8. And unlike a machine-cut slab of marble, these curious pieces tell us something about the people, both those below and above the ground.

Figure 10-8 For the Little family, this gravestone provides a reminder of a special life. For the rest of us, it's just another head-stone—albeit, an uncommonly shaped one.

Figure 10-9 These details from private graves provide some insight into the lives of the people who are buried here—as well as their survivors.

Details can also help to bring out the character of a time or place. Katrin discovered Figure 10-10's mermaid riding a flying fish in the dining room of the vintage luxury liner *Queen Mary*. Hand-carved and cast in metal, this unique ornament speaks of a time when traditional craftsmanship was giving way to Industrial Age automation. In contrast, Figure 10-11's picture of dining room looks like just another ocean-going dining room. By shooting small, Katrin has eliminated any hint of the modern world so that all we see is a fragment from an instant in time a century old.

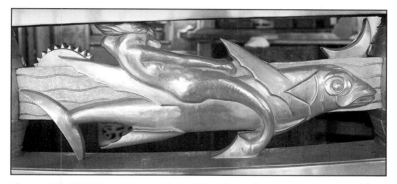

Figure 10-10 This ornamental detailing from the *Queen Mary* provides a glimpse into a time when an overseas excursion meant a ride on the ocean.

Figure 10-11 By drawing the camera back to take in the entire dining room, we lose much of the sense of where we are and what this place is about.

If Figure 10-10 is about a time, Color Plate 10-3 on page C20 is about a place. In the first photograph, we see a grimy fish market scale. But a closer examination reveals the life of a business, with inspection stickers, scratches, and occasional colonies of rust consistent with repeated exposure to salt water and humidity. The close-up reveals an object that's reached its half-life—as much a function of nature as a work of man. It's not disgusting; it's organic, random, and complex.

ROTATE THE FRAME

We're not sure why this is, but new photographers have a tendency to keep the camera level, as it appears when resting on a table. This means every shot is oriented horizontally, so it's wider than it is tall. But you can—and should—feel free to rotate the camera, either 90 degrees to take a vertical shot or whatever orientation is necessary to make the image better fill the frame.

> **TIP:** The manuals for many point-and-shoot cameras will suggest that you hold the camera a certain way to take a vertical shot. If the flash is on the left side of the lens you rotate the camera clockwise so the flash is above the lens. If the flash is to the right of the lens, you rotate the camera counterclockwise. This is important when using the flash, so it's a good habit to get into. But feel free to violate this rule on occasion. When shooting under some amount of natural light, the framing is more important than the angle of the flash.

As we've mentioned several times, we always take several pictures of every subject we deem worthy of converting to pixels. (We mention it again because it's so important: shoot often, shoot a lot.) We experiment with different distances, as outlined in the previous sections. We also mix it up between horizontal and vertical orientations. Sometimes one works better than the other, sometimes both yield interesting results. In Color Plate 10-4 on page C20, for example, the horizontal shot provides a nice overview of the starboard deck of the ship. The vertical shot makes for a better photo of the brightly painted air-intake vent.

Whether you favor a horizontal or vertical orientation—that is, whether you take more horizontal or vertical pictures of a subject—depends on the subject itself. The tortoise in Figures 10-12 and 10-13 is a shifting target. It doesn't move fast, but it does move. When the tortoise pointed to the left or right, the reptile fit better inside a horizontal frame, as in Figure 10-12. When the tortoise went vertical, however, we went vertical, too (Figure 10-13). Ours is not to question the ways of such beasts, but only to rotate the camera to accommodate them.

Figure 10-12 A tortoise angling to the left fits snugly inside a horizontal frame, with a bit of room to spare.

Figure 10-13 A head-on shot of the tortoise works better inside a vertical frame. We have some extra room above and below, but if we shot any closer, we'd cut off the legs and shadow.

Horizontal and vertical aren't your only options. In attempting to capture his brother working a puzzle, Deke tried horizontal and vertical shots without great success, examples of which appear in Figure 10-14. The horizontal shot is especially messy, with far too much table, hot lighting, and general clutter. But when his brother obliged the frame by hunching over, Deke rotated the camera to match the angle of his shoulders. The resulting shot is more vertical than horizontal, but it works when printed in either orientation, as in Figure 10-15.

Figure 10-14 Perhaps it's the light, perhaps it's the clutter. But neither a horizontal nor a vertical shot proves all that successful in capturing this scene.

Figure 10-15 But when the subject bent his head, we were able to achieve a picture that works equally well when oriented either vertically or horizontally.

VIOLATE SYMMETRY

Throughout the ages, various schools of art and design have sung the praises of symmetry. Even in photography, there's a lot to be said for a standard symmetrical shot like the one in Figure 10-16. It ensures a balanced composition, in which the left and right halves are blessed with equal amounts of visual information. It's safe, it's practical, and it's what viewers expect.

Figure 10-16 There's nothing in the world wrong with a symmetrical image, in which the left and right halves convey equal amounts of visual information.

But any rule worth observing is worth violating as well. Precisely because viewers expect a centered subject, shooting out of center may add drama and tension to an otherwise run-of-the-mill photograph. But it's important to impart that you *mean* for the picture to look this way, lest it your viewer mistakes the effect for a clumsy accident. The first image in Figure 10-17, for example, is only slightly out of symmetry. It looks not so much dramatic as just plain sloppy. By removing ourselves from the track entirely—so that even the right rail angles to the left—we create the effect of an image with a decisive and intentional skew.

Figure 10-17 Both of these image are out of plumb, but where the first image looks like it might have been an accident, the second is obviously quite intentional.

Notice we say it's important that off-center photographs *look* intentional—even if they are in truth happy accidents. Deke shot the first image in Color Plate 10-5 on page C21 using a Kodak DC40 with a close-up lens. This early model lacked an LCD preview and its optical viewfinder didn't account for the close-up. So he had no idea what he was shooting. He thought he had the bee roughly centered; fortunately, the insect just so happens to look better way over to the side. The silos in the color plate were shot out a car window with a Konica Q-M100. Most of the time, shooting out a car window is a great way to waste memory and batteries. But this time, what was intended to be a centered shot turned out wonderfully off kilter.

The asymmetrical approach works as well for portraits as for other subjects. Figure 10-18 compares two candid portraits, one centered and one not. Both are dynamic photographs, but the second one seems all the more candid for its off-the-cuff framing. It seems more representative of the kinds of glimpses of events we get in real life—spontaneous, unrehearsed, utterly lacking in any pretension of planning or preparation whatsoever.

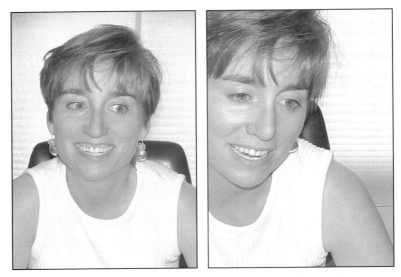

Figure 10-18 We always prefer candid portraits over rehearsed ones (left). Somehow, an asymmetrical composition can make the portrait feel that much more casual and spontaneous (right).

TAKE THE SHOT LESS TAKEN

Another great way to frame a shot is to point the camera in a completely different direction. While everyone else is trying to snap a picture of a home run at a baseball game, for example, turn around and shoot a picture of the jubilant spectators. Everyone in the audience will think you're nuts, of course, but who do you think will get the better photograph?

Another example: You're on a tour of a famous cultural attraction. The place has been photographed to death, so you're unlikely to get a shot that's never been captured before. As in Figure 10-19, you could take a picture of the festively garbed tour guide—into the sun, no less—or the fascinating but fairly boring-looking item that the tour guide is talking about. Or you could take a picture of the large crowd amassed around the tour guide, as in Color Plate 10-6 on page C21. The latter gives you a better idea of what it was like to be there, bumping elbows with members of the general public, all craning their necks to see or wandering away bored to snap their own photographs.

Figure 10-19 When shuffling along with a tour, the most obvious things to shoot—the tour guide (left) and the attraction (right)—are the things that have been shot before.

Sometimes pointing the camera in a different direction means getting a different shot of the same subject. For example, Figure 10-20 shows a photograph taken in Las Vegas. This image departs from your typical picture postcard views of Vegas in that this particular fountain isn't functioning. Otherwise, it's a pretty run-of-the-mill view of your gambling dollars at work. However, immediately in back of this fountain is a mirrored window. By shooting into the window, we not only see Katrin the photographer at Caesar's feet, we're also treated to a singular take on the fountain that you're not

Figure 10-20 A snapshot from the conspicuously opulent Caesar's hotel.

likely to find anywhere else. See Color Plate 10-7 on page C22.

Katrin has a penchant for shooting into and through glass. Figure 10-21 shows a series of cars and taxi cabs that she captured by shooting reflections from the highly polished surface of a pedestrian overpass. In Color Plate 10-8 on page C23, Katrin shot a series of silvery "lookdown" fish through the glass of a giant, ring-shaped aquarium. Because the fish were swimming, Katrin had to match their motion to maintain focus. This meant moving the camera with the fish. It's a chancy technique, and many of the pictures came out blurry. But Katrin took dozens of photos knowing that only a few would be successful.

Be forewarned that people will stare at you when you take these kinds of pictures because you're doing something out of the ordinary. And if you're taking a particularly interesting shot, the passers-by may even shake their heads and mutter. But as every artist is well aware, you're only doing your job when you're at least partially misunderstood.

Figure 10-21 These cars were captured with the help of the mirrored surface of a cylindrical pedestrian overpass.

CHAPTER ELEVEN

Immersive Imaging and QuickTime VR

As you might imagine, we take a lot of pictures—of our travels, family, friends, and the things and places that just catch our eye. And there are times when a single picture just doesn't show enough of what we experienced. Wouldn't it be great if the viewer of the photo could look left and right, up and down, and move from one spot in the scene to another, almost as if he or she were actually there? Amazingly, that is not so remote a fantasy.

Since the advent of Apple Computer's QuickTime VR technology (also known as QTVR—the VR stands for Virtual Reality), the viewer has been able to move from scene to scene and look at objects from different points of view by clicking and dragging the mouse. The term *QTVR* has largely been replaced by the more generic *immersive imaging* (and even more loosely by *movie*). Creating, distributing, and viewing QTVR images has been made completely cross-platform—that is, you can create and view QTVR images on a Mac or PC. The basic concept of QTVR is to take a series of source photographs and "stitch" them together so that they can be viewed as a continuous 3D image that simulates the experience of viewing the real world. This is significantly more sophisticated than simply cutting and pasting a set of images together in Photoshop or linking them in HTML; the result is seamless and the viewer can zoom in and out of any part of the image while panning around.

KINDS OF IMMERSIVE IMAGES

Immersive images are divided into two groups: *panoramic* and *object*. With panoramic images (also shortened to *panos*), the viewer can turn completely around (virtually, of course) to view the scene (see Figure 11-1). The viewer can zoom in and out and even direct their gaze upward and downward to a limited degree. A panorama that doesn't extend a full 360° is called a *partial*.

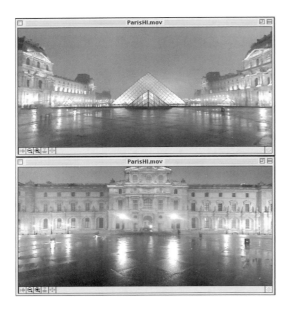

Figure 11-1 In a panoramic immersive image, the viewer can pan left or right and zoom in to see details. In this image, the viewer can look all around the Louvre Museum Courtyard. *Image by eVox Productions.*

In object images, the viewer can turn the object (the subject of the photo) to see it from different sides (see Figure 11-2). *Multi-row object movies* allow the object to be tilted to show top and bottom surfaces as well. The most sophisticated object movies include animation in which not only can the object be spun but it can be changed or moved as well. For example, as you look around a convertible you can open and close the roof.

Both panoramic and object images can be augmented with *hotspots*, graphic hyper-links that allow the viewer to move to another immersive image, a higher resolution image, a sound, a text, or any other kind of file. (These are good hotspots, as opposed to bad hotspots known as "blown out highlights" in regular photography.)

Figure 11-2 Object immersive images allow the viewer to turn the object to view it from many sides. *Image by eVox Productions.*

There are many commercial applications for immersive images. Museum curators use object movies to document pieces in their collections; police professionals use panos to present complete views of a crime scene; and, of course, the idea of having a customer see a product from many different sides is an exciting idea with positive implications for electronic commerce. Immersive images are used by scientists, educators, artists, sales organizations, and insurance agencies to add new information and dimensions to Web sites and can be even be printed—as seen in Color Plate 11-1 on pages C22 and C23. A popular Web site is the online seed catalogue at *www.burpee.com*, where you can "walk" through the gardens (see Color Plate 11-2 on page C24), learn about, and (Burpee hopes) buy the seeds and plants they offer.

MAKING PANORAMIC MOVIES

Making and showing immersive images is fun. You probably already have most of the tools you need to make panos. All you need is a camera (preferably with a wide-angle lens), a tripod, and a $50-100 stitching software package.

Planning and Shooting the Panorama

Start planning your panoramic image by looking all the way around. The next time you're in an interesting environment—a beautiful landscape, a quiet park, an uncommon building—think about the best point of view from which to shoot your source images. Observe how the quality of light influences the scene and estimate when the light will be best for the shoot. But don't shoot at a time of day when you'll have to shoot directly into the sun to complete the 360°. In Figure 11-3 Katrin shot right into the sun, causing terrible lens flare problems and demonstating that there are limits to what Photoshop can fix.

Figure 11-3 Avoid shooting straight into the sun as it can cause flare problems.

Image Composition

When you set up your camera, think about how you want to convey a sense of the place and the space. The viewer will be looking at the panoramic scene from wherever you put the camera. Work with foreground and background relationships by placing the camera near to an object in the scene. In Figure 11-4, Katrin the placed the camera near the bamboo bench and the tree to give the viewer a sense of the temple environment. Panoramic movies in which everything is exactly the same distance away are just plain boring.

Figure 11-4 By placing the bench and the tree in the foreground of this immersive image (as seen on the right and left sides), the photographer gave the movie a sense of space and place.

Placement refers not only to the location of your tripod, but also to the height at which you set it. Discover the world from a different point of view by raising or lowering the camera. The world looks a lot different from a bug's point of view (Figure 11-5) than it does from above the town (Figure 11-6). Don't be afraid to change your point of view and keep your photography and panoramic images fresh and interesting.

Figure 11-5 Shooting down low and close to these plants gives the pano an interesting twist.

Figure 11-6 Shooting panoramics from high scenic viewpoints is a great way to convey a grand sense of space.

Avoiding Ghosts

If people are in the image, ask them to hold still for at least two exposures. If they don't, you might have a spiritual experience after stitching the images (see Figure 11-7). *Ghosting* occurs when the person (or other object) falls on the edge of one exposure and moves out for the frame for the second. When the software stitches the image, it tries to blend the person into the scene and creates a ghosted effect.

Figure 11-7 The person circled was in the scene for one exposure and not for the second, which caused ghosting when the images were stitched together.

The Camera

You can use practically any digital camera to shoot the source files for a panoramic movie. We've used digital cameras ranging from the bare bones Kodak DC-50 to the high-resolution Kodak DCS 520 to shoot the source files for both panos and objects; others have used professional scanning cameras to shoot extraordinary immersive images. It is even possible to scan in film photographs, though very laborious; a digital camera is the best way to go.

A wide-angle lens captures more of the subject and gives greater drama to your movie, emphasizing the differences in distance from the viewer. Longer lenses create narrow panos that can be rather annoying to look at. Orienting the camera vertically (in portrait mode) requires more shots to cover 360°, but it gives the viewer more headroom to tilt up and down within the image.

If you are using a zoom lens, set it to the very widest setting possible. Cameras such as the Agfa 1680 and Nikon CoolPix 900/900s/950 can be outfitted with wide-angle filters made by Tiffen and sold by Digital Camera (*www.dcprodirect.com*). If you have the opportunity to work with a professional digital camera that has interchangeable lenses, try to use a *rectilinear flat field* lens to minimize the distortion. Having said that, the Nikon CoolPix 900/900s/950 and the Olympus D-320 support a $650 fisheye lens (as pictured in Figure 11-8) that can be used with specialized IPIX software to create a 180° bubble view of the world.

An LCD screen is useful to check image alignment, overlap, and to see if you have covered the complete 360° view. Large in-camera image storage is an advantage as well—the more pictures you can shoot without having to switch disks or download, the better.

Figure 11-8 Adding a super wide-angle lens to the Nikon 950 allows you to capture a full 180° in one shot.

Setting up the Camera on a Tripod

It is possible to shoot the source files for a panoramic movie without a tripod, but the results are generally disappointing. A tripod guarantees that the horizon line will stay level so that the tops and bottoms of the images don't get cropped, chopped, or lost due to inconsistent alignment of the camera, as seen on the top of Figure 11-9. Because this is a tripod that you'll be walking around with, try to balance out the sturdiness versus weight issues in your purchasing equation. A heavy tripod is the tripod you may leave in the car.

Figure 11-9 Working without a tripod and panoramic head can cause misalignment and cropping, as seen in the black area at top.

To ensure the optimal performance of the software, it is important to set up the camera so that it rotates parallel to the horizon around the *nodal* point of the lens. The nodal point is the optical center of the lens where the rays of light converge and the image flips. To avoid nodal point error, the optical center should be on the camera's axis of rotation. If the optical center is offset from the center of rotation, objects in the foreground look as if they are sliding in space in relationship to the background. But don't worry about it too much. In most landscape panoramas, where most subjects are rather far away, you'll never notice this effect.

While a standard tripod head generally does not place the lens's nodal point on the axis of rotation, a panoramic tripod head (Figure 11-10) is designed specifically to optimize the camera's position for panoramic photography. On many panoramic heads, the settings for a variety of lenses are marked. Kaidan, Bogen Photo, and Peace River Studios all make very good panoramic heads. Some manufacturers offer panoramic tripod heads for specific cameras; Kaidan makes the Interactive Imaging System for the Kodak DC 220 Pro Edition and the KiWi 900 for the Nikon CoolPix 900 and 950.

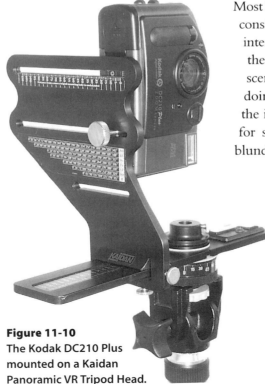

Most heads have *protractors* to help maintain consistent frame overlap, with indexing intents that click into place as you rotate the camera around to photograph the scene. Either way, if you are going to be doing a lot of panoramic photography, the investment (between $100 and $200 for smaller cameras) is well worth the blunders you will be spared.

Figure 11-10
The Kodak DC210 Plus
mounted on a Kaidan
Panoramic VR Tripod Head.

FINDING THE NODAL POINT

Hold your finger out at arm's length and align your finger with a door, window frame, or picture on the wall. Keeping your head still, close one eye and sweep from left to right with the other eye. Notice that the position of your finger stays still in relationship to the background. Next, move your entire head from left to right. The perceived motion of your finger relative to the background is the result of parallax error; the optical center of your eye is not on the axis of rotation (your neck).

Set the tripod up so that the rotation of the head is horizontal. Then mount the camera and line up its optical center on the axis of rotation by following these steps.

1. *Mount the camera on the panoramic tripod head with the axis of the lens perpendicular to the axis of rotation and over the pivot.*

2. *Place a light stand or another tripod about 3 feet away from the camera.*

3. *Pan the camera from left to right. If the object "moves" in relationship to the background, you're not on the optical nodal point.*

4. *Slide the camera back to front until you find the nodal point.*

Number of Images

The number of shots you take depends on the focal length of the lens, lighting conditions, and your final image quality requirements. The wider the lens, the greater the image coverage, and the fewer images are required. When the lighting differences in the scene are distinct, allow more frame overlap to avoid *banding*, as illustrated only too well in Figure 11-11. For optimal results, the image overlap should be no less than 20 percent and no more than 50 percent.

Figure 11-11 Banding can be caused by not shooting enough images or when the original scene has a lot of exposure difference.

In Table 11-1, we offer guidelines for the number of pictures you should take in *vertical* (also known as *portrait*) orientation to make good panoramic movies. By the time you read this, other cameras will undoubtedly be available. To find out how many exposures to take with your camera, find a focal length in Table 11-1 that matches the focal length of your camera (see your documentation.)

Camera	Focal Length (Equivalent to 35mm)	# of Exposures
Agfa ePhoto 1280 & 1680	38 mm	18
Apple QuickTake 200	38 mm	18
Canon PowerShot 600N	28 mm	12
Casio QV-5000SX	35 mm	16
Epson PhotoPC 550, 600, & 700	36mm	18
Fuji DC 300, MX-700, & MX-2700	35 mm	16
HP PhotoSmart C20	39 mm	18
Kodak DC-50 and DC-120	38 mm	18
Kodak DC210 Plus	29 mm	14
Kodak DC220	34.5 mm	16
Kodak DC260 & 265	38 mm	18
Minolta Dimage V	38 mm	18
Minolta Dimage EX 1500	28 mm	12
Nikon CoolPix 600	36 mm	16
Nikon CoolPix 900 & 950	38 mm	18
Olympus D-400 Zoom	35 mm	16
Olympus D-620L	36 mm	16
Ricoh RDC-4200	35 mm	16
Polaroid PCD-2000	38 mm	18
Sony Mavica FD7	40mm	20
Toshiba PDR-M1	35 mm	16
Vivitar Vivicam	38 mm	18
Yashica KC600	47 mm	20

Table 11-1 How Many Pictures to Take

TIP: When in doubt about how many frames to shoot, opt for too many frames versus too few, and for optimal results try to shoot an even number of frames such as 12, 14, or 16—not 13, 15, or 17.

Keeping Exposure and Depth of Field Consistent

When you look at a scene, your eyes are constantly adjusting to adjust for brightness and focus. A camera with automatic exposure and focus will do the same thing, and that may create problems for your panorama. Variations in f-stop will vary your depth of field and this may interfere with the stitching process. Variations in focus, in fact, can be so distracting that the illusion of "being there" that you're trying to create vanishes.

Point and shoot digital cameras give very little control over focus or aperture, but they are certainly good enough to learn about and enjoy making immersive images. Shooting source images for immersive imaging with a professional lite camera, on which you can control exposure and aperture, offers you much greater control over the final image quality.

When professional photographers shoot, they *bracket the exposure* by taking the same picture at different exposures to insure that they get the optimal exposure. This is a particularly good idea when shooting panoramic images in a contrasty light. Katrin shot the evening scene of Tivoli Gardens in Copenhagen shown in Figure 11-12 when the exposure difference between the foreground and the sky was greater than the CCD could handle. To compensate for the exposure spread, she captured a set of images based on the best exposure for the foreground and then, without moving the camera, a set of exposures for the sky. Later, she merged the images in Adobe Photoshop to create the ideal exposure for both the foreground and the sky, as seen in Figure 11-13.

Figure 11-12 Shooting the same scene twice to compensate for extreme brightness differences is a good method to insure optimal results. In this example, the top row was exposed for the sky, and the bottom row of images was exposed for the foreground.

Figure 11-13 After merging the two sets of exposures and restitching, this immersive image features the best of both exposures.

Mental Focus

Because of the repetitive nature of the process of shooting immersive images, it is important to develop a mental focus strategy to help you make sure that you come home with all the pictures you need. Believe us, returning from a fantastic shoot only to realize that you missed a shot is devastating. There is absolutely no way to return to a location to reshoot the missing image of a panoramic scene.

Develop a mantra to create a rhythm to block out distractions and keep you focused. We use "shutter, rotate, pause; shutter, rotate, pause," which translates to "click the shutter, rotate the camera to the next position, wait for the camera to write the file to disk, repeat." This simple incantation soon becomes second nature, and if by chance our concentration lapses, we can usually figure out where we were—of course the LCD screen is a big help, too. If you plan on doing a lot of immersive imaging, taking notes is also very helpful. In fact, we often shoot the actual note to mark where the pano starts.

STITCHING THE PANOS

After you've returned from the shoot, it's time to download and stitch the individual files into a panoramic immersive image. This is the step that still amazes us—taking a number of still photos and turning them into an interactive experience. This is definitely where digital photography is changing the experience and possibilities of photography. The steps in stitching a panoramic image are:

1. Download and organize.

2. Resize, rotate, and sharpen (if necessary).

3. Retouch.

4. Stitch.
    Optional: retouch and composite. Stitch again.
    Optional: add hotspots.

5. Display or print.

Software

In the old days (going back to 1994), stitching software was very difficult to use; now it is almost magically simple. Immersive imaging takes ordinary still photos and warps and stitches them around a virtual cylinder, as illustrated in Figure 11-14.

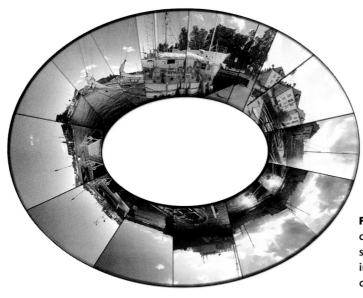

Figure 11-14 This illustration conceptualizes how stitching software wraps photographs into a cylinder that the viewer can pan around in.

Image recognition algorithms automatically control the overlap of the images, recognizing for example that the tree branch at the left side of the frame is the same one that appears on the right side of the last one. Most stitching software also smoothes out unevenness of the light to eliminate banding. And, when you enter the focal length of the lens used to capture the images, the software builds the correct curvature into the finished movie. Basically, you point the stitching software at your image files and it gives you a QTVR or IVR movie or a flat still file that you can print on your desktop inkjet printer. Epson offers 8 by 22.5-inch panoramic paper specifically designed to print immersive images.

Commercially available stitching software ranges from Visual Stitcher to the full-featured QuickTime VR Authoring Studio (Table 11-2). Some of the less expensive stitching applications may yield disappointing results (they tend to produce movies with distinct banding), but Live Picture PhotoVista and others like it are quite easy to use and give remarkable results. What you get for your money in the more expensive software packages is greater flexibility and control, including ability to create hotspots in your images. Apple's QuickTime VR Authoring Studio and Live Picture's Reality Studio also allow you to make object movies, as discussed later in this chapter.

Name	Manufacturer	Platform
Visual Stitcher	PanaVue	Windows
VR Toolbox	VR PanoWorx	Macintosh/Windows
COOL 360	Ulead	Windows
Spin Panorama	PictureWorks	Macintosh/Windows
PhotoVista	Live Picture	Macintosh/Windows
Nodester	Roundabout Logic	Macintosh
QuickStitch 360	EnRoute	Windows
PowerStitch	EnRoute	Windows
Reality Studio	Live Picture	Windows
QuickTime VR Authoring Studio	Apple Computer	Macintosh

Table 11-2 Stitching Software from Basic to Full-Featured

Download and Organize

Follow the directions that came with your camera to download the files to your computer's hard drive. The order that you shot the images is most likely the order in which they need to be stitched, so don't start renaming or rearranging the files. In fact, we don't change any of the original filenames but we do create separate folders for each pano (Figure 11-15). When it comes time to stitch the pano, we just point the stitching software at the folder and it accesses the images in the right order.

Although we don't rename the files, we still get confused sometimes about where each pano starts and stops. (If only we had listened to our own advice and taken a picture of a note saying "First Picture/Lakeside"). We use Extensis Portfolio software to create a visual database of all our files (Figure 11-16) so we can locate the start and end of each pano and then we move the required files into their own folder. The harbor panorama starts with frame number AH306124.pct and ends with frame number AH306137.pct.

TIP: *Most stitching software recognizes PICT and JPEG files. Because most digital cameras deliver JPEG files, keep the files as JPEGs to save hard drive space.*

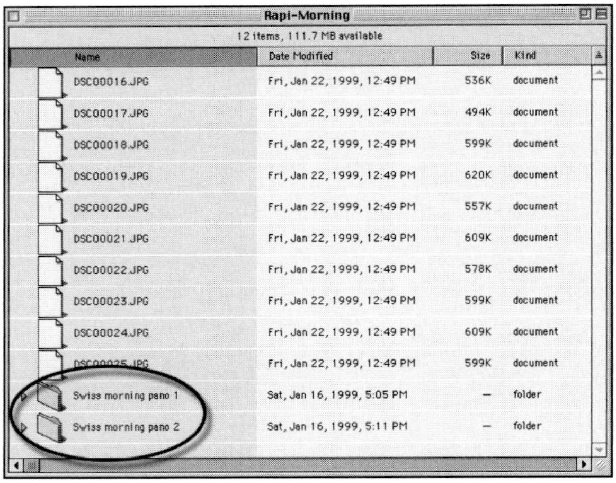

Figure 11-15 Copying or placing the files into folders that make up each panoramic image keeps them organized. When you stitch the files, point the stitching software at the right folder to access the source images in the correct order.

Figure 11-16 Using a visual database such as the one Extensis Portfolio creates is a great way to identify where source images begin and end.

Resize, Rotate, and Sharpen

It is often helpful to downsize your images before you stitch them. If your camera delivers files at or under 640 by 480 pixels, we don't recommend sizing down. But if your camera delivers larger files, you should consider sizing down to minimize the final movie file size. If you are planning on making large format prints, resizing down is a bad idea. Once you've thrown away the information, there is no amount of pixel magic that can recreate it. If you are displaying your panos on the Web, sizing down the source images will minimize the file size of the final immersive image.

> **TIP:** *Always size down in increments of 50 percent to maintain relative image quality. Keeping the interpolation in even increments allows your imaging software to throw out exactly every other pixel, which is faster and results in files with less anti-aliasing.*

An additional reason to size the source images down is that most stitching software loads all the source images into RAM, and if your computer is low on RAM, downsizing the source files will allow you to complete the stitching process. When Katrin is out on location with her Apple PowerBook 3400c (with its 80 MB of RAM), she has to size the files down by 50 percent for the stitching process to run. When she returns to her studio's main computer (with over well 400 MB of RAM), she accesses the original camera files and restitches the panos to create high-resolution files.

> **TIP:** *Never crop individual source images. Stitching software requires that all source images have an exactly identical pixel size and proportion. You may resize as long as all images are resized identically. You may not crop—cropping by hand may add inaccuracies that will cause the stitching process to trip up.*

Sharpening the source images with Unsharp Mask (described in Chapter 12) should be done judiciously. Professional stitching software packages like QuickTime VR Authoring Studio and Live Picture's Reality Studio allow you to control the amount and type of sharpening applied to an image during the stitch. When we have sized an image down, we use some Unsharp Mask sharpening to bring back the original crispness of the photo. We recommend that you experiment with sharpness to see what works best for you.

TIP: *Build a Photoshop action (Figure 11-17) to do all of the repetitive resize, rotate, and sharpening work and speed up your image production. DeBabelizer or Mainevent's PhotoScripter are two additional programs that automate image processing and cut down on tedious work.*

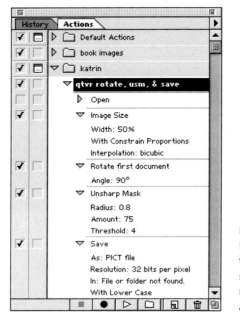

Figure 11-17 Use a Photoshop action to finish repetitive tasks such as image resizing, rotating, sharpening and saving.

After resizing, rotating, and sharpening never, *never* save over your original files. Always save the modified files into a new directory or folder. Keeping your original files intact allows you to return to the original source images to restitch or to make a high-resolution print.

Retouch

During the stitching process, you have two chances to retouch the image before you stitch the individual source images together and after the initial stitch.

The first retouch includes the following:

1. **Basic tonal and color correction** If all of your source images are flat, have a color cast, or lack good shadow detail, now is a good time to correct them. Use the techniques described in Chapter 12 to make the source images clear and crisp.

2. **Removing bothersome artifacts** Use the Clone Tool to retouch out dis-
    tracting elements such as lens flare, litter, or the occasional tripod leg. In
    Figure 11-18, Katrin removed her own camera bag and a garbage can from the
    scene before stitching.

Figure 11-18 Original file is on the left. Retouched version on the
right to remove the photographer's camera bag and a garbage can
in the background.

The second retouch takes place after the initial stitch:

1. **Finessing color and contrast** Work with Photoshop to open up shadows or
    to improve contrast as desired.

2. **Removing stitching artifacts** Use the Clone Tool to retouch out overlap
    mistakes, bothersome reflections, or the afore-mentioned ghosts.

3. **Compositing exposures or creative backgrounds** Now is the right time
    to composite two separate exposures together or to experiment with creative
    filtering to make abstract immersive movies as seen at *www.vrview.com*.

Stitch

Shooting and prepping your images well allows the next step—the actual stitching—to be the most fun and magical of the entire process. Every stitching program uses approximately the same work order to create the immersive image.

1. Load the source images.

2. Determine camera settings.

3. Build a preview stitch.

4. Adjust stitch alignment.

5. Build final panorama.
   Optional: Save the file for printing (PICT or JPEG). Retouch and/or composite. Print.

6. Create the file for interactive viewing.
   Optional: Embed into Web page.

7. Add hotspots.

This is how to stitch a panoramic image with Live Picture's PhotoVista. We selected this package to illustrate the process because it is a cross-platform application and its interface is refreshingly straightforward (Figure 11-19).

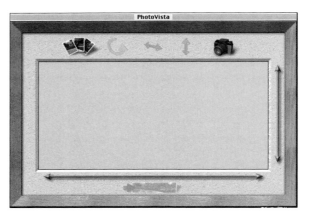

Figure 11-19 That's all there is to the Live Picture
PhotoVista interface. Simple, yet effective.

- **Load the source images** Point the application to the directory with the files and click Add All to import all source files into the picture frame analogy. Rotate the files if necessary.

- **Determine camera settings** Click on the picture of the camera and select the camera and/or lens you used to take the source images (Figure 11-20). This gives the software the information to calculate the percentage of warp and overlap to use when stitching the files. Some software packages such as EnRoute's QuickStitch 360 calculate the warp needed by analyzing the images themselves.

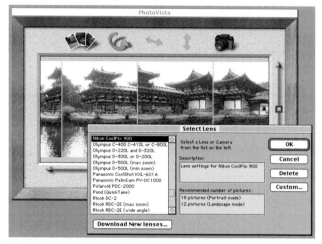

Figure 11-20 Telling PhotoVista which camera you used to take the source images tells it how much to warp and overlap to give the images.

- **Build a preview stitch** Click on the panoramic button underneath the frame and select Preview Stitch. Take the time to build the low-resolution preview because it will reveal any stitching or alignment problems the scene may have before you invest the time to render a high-resolution file.

- **Adjust stitch alignment** Inspect the preview stitch. If you notice some alignment problems (Figure 11-21), return to the picture frame window and use the mouse to manually align the images. If you're satisfied, return to the stitch interface and stitch the high-res version.

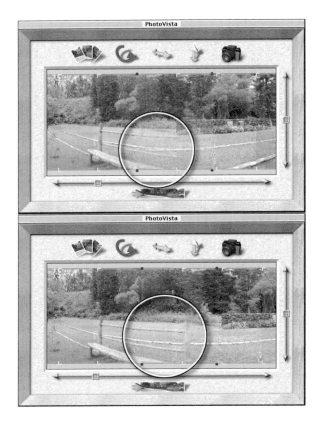

Figure 11-21 Inspecting the preview stitch revealed some alignment problems with the bamboo in the top image. PhotoVista allows you to drag individual frames to correct for these types of alignment errors, as seen in the lower image.

- **Build final panorama** After aligning the images to your liking, build the final high-resolution image.

- **Display option 1: Create the file for interactive viewing** Convert the file into a cylinder which will enable you to select .mov from the file format options. The Macintosh version of PhotoVista will save the panoramic image as a QTVR file into your hard drive; the PC version will save it as an IVR (Image-based Virtual Reality) file. On the Mac, PhotoVista will also automatically create an IVR file in the Live Picture format that is optimized for use on the Web. IVR files are really JPEG files with the additional cylinder and playback information and are typically three to four times smaller than files saved as QTVR. (For additional information, go to *www.livepicture.com*.)

- **Display option 2: Save the file for printing** If you plan on printing, compositing, or doing additional retouching, save the file as either a JPEG or PICT file. Note: The horizontal pixel dimension limitation of the PICT file format is 4095 pixels wide. Rotate the panoramic file by 90° to overcome this horizontal limitation. Open the file in Photoshop 4.0 or 5.0 and rotate it back by 90°. Save the file as a Photoshop file where the horizontal pixel limitation is a generous 30,000 pixels.

- **Retouch and composite** Open the panoramic image in your image-editing program and use the clone tool to retouch any unsightly seams. Experiment with compositing in new skies or balancing out exposure. If you desire, you can also modify the image by applying filters or even painting on the image.

- **Restitch** To restitch the retouched or composited image, use Roundabout Logic's Nodester (Mac $59), Apple QuickTime VR Authoring Studio ($395), or QTVR Make Panorama 2 (free–download it from *www.apple.com/quicktime/developers/tools.html*).

Adding Interactivity and Hotspots

Hotspots allow you to connect immersive images with one another and to embed additional movies, sounds, images, or links to other Web pages. The possibilities are endless: imagine that your viewers are in the scene, and as they pan they click on a hotspot and that takes them to another immersive image or opens up a text file with additional information.

Place your hotspots so that they will be intuitively understood by your viewer. For example, if you are designing a tour of a museum, keeping the hotspots consistent from room to room will help the viewers feel comfortable and teach them to navigate quickly. In the museum example, try making all the doors hotspots for the next room or make the works of art the hotspots for higher resolution images or explanatory text.

To create hotspots, you need more sophisticated software packages such as Roundabout Logic's Nodester and Widgetizer (Mac), Sumware's PanoMAGIC (Mac) (*www.vrtools.com*), Apple QuickTime VR Authoring Studio (Mac), or Live Picture's Reality Studio (Windows/NT).

The Technology Behind the Magic

There are several systems of *codec* (*compression-dec*ompression) that make immersive images work. When using the more sophisticated stitching software, you can select which one you use to optimize your image for either image quality or speed of download.

Here are the four primary compression codecs for immersive images:

1. **Cinepak** offers fast decompression for playback, but compression in production is slow. Fast decompression is good for CD-ROM playback but this codec often adds artifacts that can ruin the viewer's experience.

2. **Sorenson Video** is similar to Cinepak, but maintains image quality in playback. Sorenson is reaching the mainstream as we write and to view Sorenson compressed movies, your target audience must have QuickTime 3.0 installed. If you are producing immersive images professionally, we recommend you buy the full codec from Terran Interactive or Sorenson.

3. **JPEG** (Joint Photographic Experts Group) codec is well designed for photographically based panoramic images. Viewers with QuickTime 3.0 installed will be able to see a low-resolution version of a JPEG immersive image rather quickly.

4. **Graphics** 3D artists, graphic designers, and industrial designers who create immersive images with graphic files or with 3D software—as opposed to photographic source material—should look into using the Graphics settings for their compression needs.

The second piece of the panoramic magic is the tiling technology. In a nutshell, only that part of the image actually on the screen is decompressed and loaded into RAM, while the tiles to the left and right of the image viewing area are only partially decompressed to allow for a speedier viewing. To sidestep the 4095-pixel limitation of the PICT file format, the panoramic images are rotated by 90° and them tiled into 24 even tiles (Figure 11-22). On playback, they are rotated back and placed edge to edge for a seamless image.

Figure 11-22 Chopping the immersive image into 24 tiles allows for faster playback, panning and zooming.

INTERACTIVE OBJECT MOVIES

As we mentioned at the beginning of this chapter, the second type of immersive imaging is the interactive object movie in which the viewer sees an object and can examine it from different points of view (Figures 11-23 and 24) using the mouse to spin the object. The object can be as small as a single rose or as large as a Toyota van, and the movie can have hotspots that trigger other movies, sounds, or links just like a panoramic movie. To create simple object movies, you can use the same camera and tripod but you will need to add a turntable and some object maker software (starting at $60).

Figure 11-23 Object movies allow the viewer to turn the image and see different sides of the subject. *Image by eVox Productions.*

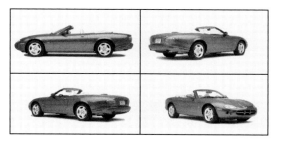

Figure 11-24 eVox Productions, the premier interactive image production company, has worked with more than 45 automobile manufacturers and produces high quality object movies. Visit *www.evox.com* to see numerous examples first-hand. *Image by eVox Productions.*

Object movies range from single-row spins in which the object turns on a single axis to multi-row movies that allow the viewer to turn the object to see the top and bottom as well. Think of the single-row movie as if the object were the earth and the camera a satellite flying above the equator taking pictures at regular intervals. In a multi-row movie, the object is still in the earth, but now the camera is also taking pictures from additional latitudes north and south of the equator. Shooting a frame every 10° creates very smooth motion; shooting in increments of 20° produces a jerkier movie but a smaller final file.

The decision to make a single-row or multi-row object movie depends on how much information you want to give the viewer. The Cocteau flower vase (Figure 11-25) doesn't need to be seen from the bottom or top, so using a single-row spin is very efficient and gives the viewer plenty of information. The movie of the angel (Figure 11-26) shows the viewer the sides, the bottom, and the top of the figure, which add to the total experience.

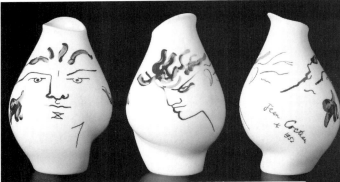

Figure 11-25 Three views of the same vase from a single-row object movie.

Figure 11-26 In a multi-row object movie, the viewer can look at the subject from more points of view. *Image by eVox Productions.*

The Equipment You Need

Object movies are a hybrid between motion pictures and photography, and interestingly enough the motion of the object covers up any lack of image quality. Given the number of source frames required (from 18 all the way to 684, depending on how many shots per row and how many rows you take), a digital camera is the obvious choice to speed up image production. You can use practically any type of single-shot digital camera and many professional scanning cameras to shoot the source images. For object movies, a longer lens is usually a good choice to avoid the distortion associated with wide-angle lenses.

> **TIP:** Try to have enough removable camera memory to get you through the shoot without having to download the files to your computer. Shooting all the files without moving the camera will cut down on potential image alignment problems later in the stitching process.

Turntables

The object is placed on the turntable (a kitchen Lazy Susan will do) which has been marked with increments so you can take a picture every 10° or 20° degrees as required. The shooting mantra, like that for panoramas, is "shutter, turn, wait; shutter, turn, wait." This translates into "click the shutter, turn the turntable to the next position, wait for the camera to write the file to the disk, repeat."

You can learn about object movies with the Lazy Susan or Lazy Bob, but if you are planning on doing any of this work professionally, you will want a motorized turntable. Unlike panoramas which allow considerable latitude in the overlap of the source images, object movies are quite jumpy if the increments of rotation are not precise. The Kaidan Magellan Desktop Turntable (Figure 11-27, $975) is a motorized computer-controlled turntable that works in sync with Roundabout Logic Widgetizer and Apple's QuickTime VR Authoring Studio software. PhaseOne also offers a motorized turntable that works with its high-end scanning cameras for the most demanding high-resolution applications. Turntables range in size from a large dinner plate all the way up to 30-foot motorized platters that can support full-size cars and trucks.

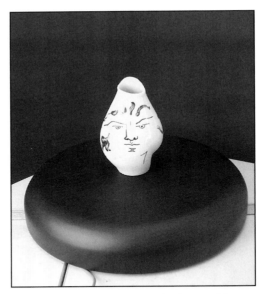

Figure 11-27 Using a motorized turntable simplifies and automates making object movies.

Object Rigs

For multi-row movies, an object rig is required. Instead of the object turning, the camera moves around it. Kaidan, Peace River, and PhaseOne make object rigs that look like medieval torture devices but guarantee precise angles of movement both around the object and up and down. The rigs alone can range in price from a few hundred dollars up to $15,000, but if you are doing a lot of production in a catalog or museum setting, the automation that these devices allow will amortize the initial outlay very quickly.

Lighting

For single-row object movies shot with a turntable, keeping the light in one place is a straightforward approach and works especially well with non-reflective subjects. For multi-row movies (or single-row movies shot with an object rig), you can either keep the light fixed so that areas of light and shadow remain the same as the movie progresses or you can mount the light to the camera's position so that the light tracks over the object as the viewer spins it. The second option is usually the most practical for lighting cars or other large objects. In either case, the more even your lighting, the less it matters whether the light is fixed or moving, and the simpler the process of stitching the frames together will be.

The primary challenge in lighting objects is controlling the reflections. Working with a diffuse light source and reflectors (Figure 11-28) helps minimize reflection. Of course, you could retouch the reflections in Photoshop, but doing that to 18 to 684 images is a tedious if not impossible task.

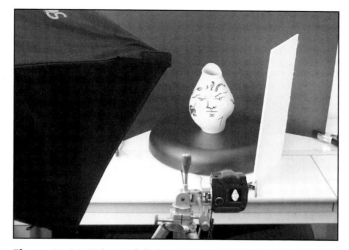

Figure 11-28 Using soft lighting and large reflectors helps to even out lighting.

SHOOTING THE MOVIE

Shooting the source images for object movies requires more effort and concentration than shooting a pano does. Start by deciding whether you want to make a single-row movie or a multi-row movie in which the viewer has more control of the view. If this is your first experience shooting objects, we suggest that you get comfortable doing single-row movies before graduating to multi-row productions. Follow these steps to shoot the source images for your first object movie:

1. Sketch out the pictures you'll need, include the starting and ending points of the shoot. Make a shooting checklist that includes how many frames you need and in what increments you'll be shooting. See Table 11-3 for guidelines.

2.   Set-up the scene. Attach the object to the turntable with tape or modeling clay to minimize movement, which would cause image alignment problems later on in the stitching process. Planning ahead at this stage will save you hours of digital retouching later on. Most likely, you'll want to drop out the object from the background, so using contrasting colors between your object and your set will speed up the digital silhouetting process.

3.   Focus mentally, concentrate, and cut out all distractions.

4.   Make a test frame, download it to your computer, and check it for exposure and focus. Few things are more aggravating than spending a lot of time shooting source images for object movies only to see that the exposure or focus was off.

5.   Photograph the object. Rotate the object in a clockwise direction. If the camera is moving relative to the object, move the camera in a counter-clockwise direction.

6.   For a multi-row object start the shoot at the highest vertical point, shoot around the object, lower the camera to the next vertical point and shoot around the object again. Shoot the same number of frames in each pass around the object from top to bottom. Although Table 11-3 below shows up to 19 rows, generally far fewer—usually only three—rows are used.

7.   Save the files to the computer's hard drive and move into the digital darkroom for a serious masking and retouching session.

Type of Object Movie	High-quality (10°)	Good-quality (15°)	Adequate (20°)
Single-row	36	24	18
Multi-Row 3 heights	108	72	54
Multi-Row 5 heights	180	120	90
Multi-Row 7 heights	252	168	126
Multi-Row 9 heights	324	216	162
Multi-Row 11 heights	396	264	198
Multi-Row 13 heights	468	312	234
Multi-Row 15 heights	540	432	270
Multi-Row Full 360°	684	456	342

Table 11-3 Number of Source Frames Required

TIP: Deciding how many frames to shoot depends on the final playback medium. Use high-quality settings for playback from a hard drive or CD-ROM and use the lower quality recommendation for Web distribution. Higher quality files require more images, which will increase the file size.

PUTTING THE MOVIE TOGETHER

Once you have amassed the source file—and this obviously can be quite a few images—it is time to put them together. Object movies are more labor-intensive than panoramas are; normally we do a fair amount of retouching and masking to create the illusion of viewing an object floating in space.

Software

The software options for making object movies are definitely Apple-centric (see Table 11-4). Thankfully, playback is platform independent, and anyone will be able to see and interact with your object movies as long as they have QuickTime 3.0 or higher loaded.

Name	Manufacturer	Platform
QTVR Object VR	Apple (shareware)	Macintosh
Spin PhotoObject	PictureWorks	Macintosh/Windows
VR Toolbox	VR ObjectWorx	Macintosh
Widgetizer	Roundabout Logic	Macintosh
Reality Studio	Live Picture	Windows
QuickTime VR Authoring Studio	Apple Computer	Macintosh

Table 11-4 Object Software from Basic to Full-Featured

Prepping the Files

After shooting and downloading all the files to your computer's hard drive, it's time for some serious digital darkroom work. Your primary objectives will be silhouetting and retouching, after which the files will be consistently resized and resaved in a new directory or folder.

Silhouette your images using Photoshop's Quick Mask. To make your work more efficient, after you have completed one mask, drag the selection over to the next file and use Transform Selection and the painting tools to fine-tune the second mask. After completing the mask for each file, fill the background with a uniform color that complements your object. Solid backgrounds compress very efficiently.

Retouching the files includes removing undesired reflections, dirt, and studio aids such as the wire, tape, or modeling clay used to hold the object. As you can imagine, this post-production often takes longer than the actual shoot, and many professional immersive imaging studios such as eVox Productions have a highly skilled and dedicated team of Photoshoppers for the silhouetting and retouching production.

After silhouetting and retouching, resize the files (most likely down) to the desired proportions, keeping in mind that all files must be exactly the same size. Once again, we recommend that you do not rename the files so that the stitching software will access them in the same order in which you took them.

Stitching

Use object-stitching software to make your individual files into an interactive object movie. We used Spin PhotoObject by PictureWorks (it's cross-platform—Mac and Windows) to stitch the single-row movie of the horse model. PhotoSpin walks you through a four-step process of bringing the images into the application, to aligning, cropping, and creating the final object movie (see Figures 11-29 through 11-31). Spin PhotoObject is highly regarded for the compression algorithms it employs to minimize file size.

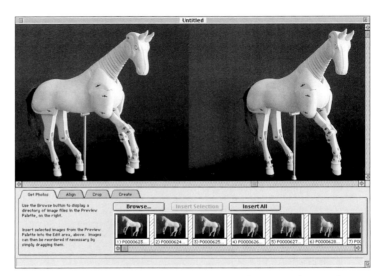

Figure 11-29 Step 1: bringing the prepped files into PhotoSpin.

Figure 11-30 Step 2: aligning the frames. The best aspect of PhotoSpin is that it allows you to see through the frames to check for any alignment or registration errors.

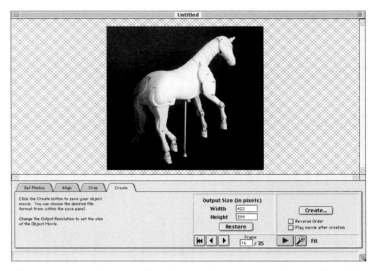

Figure 11-31 After cropping the movie, you create the movie and within a few minutes you're ready to play and spin the object.

Animating the Objects

If making multi-row object movies isn't enough of a challenge for you, try adding animation to your objects. So far we discussed still objects that the viewer can spin in any direction and see from different points of view. Animating the object requires that you think in both the horizontal (the spin) and the vertical (the animation) levels. Imagine spinning a convertible and as you turn the car the roof opens and then closes, as seen in Color Plate 11-3 on page C24.

EMBEDDING IMMERSIVE IMAGES IN A WEB PAGE

Adding immersive images to a Web site is straightforward. The simplest and crudest method is to use the <A> tag, which will open the movie onto an empty gray window. To display the movie in context, use the embed tag, as follows: <EMBED SRC="yourqtvr.mov" HEIGHT=320 WIDTH=240>. Replace the name "yourqtvr.mov" with the name of your movie and the values for width and height attributes with your movie window dimensions.

The QuickTime plug-in displays QTVR movies with the controller off by default. In order to show it, add the CONTROLLER parameter to your EMBED tag. For example:

```
<EMBED  SRC="yourqtvr.mov"  HEIGHT=320  WIDTH=240  CON-
TROLLER=TRUE>
```

If you use values for WIDTH and HEIGHT other than those of the movie, the plug-in will scale the movie. If the controller is showing, it can appear cropped. To avoid this, use the SCALE parameter with the value "ToFit."

There are several parameters to control the appearance of the QTVR movie when it is displayed for the first time, including PAN, TILT, and FOV.

- **Pan** The default setting for when a VR photograph opens is centered on the left side of the original image. If you would like to specify a specific starting point, use the PAN tag "PAN=*xxx*" where *xxx* is the number of pixels that you want the opening image moved to the left.

- **Tilt** The default setting for when a VR photograph opens is centered, on the middle (of left side) of the original image. You can have the viewer looking up or down by using the TILT tag "TILT=*xxx*" where the *xxx* is any number between -42.5 and 42.5. Negative numbers look down, positive numbers look up.

- **FOV** The FOV (field of view) attribute is where you can define how zoomed in or out the initial opening scene is, as in "FOV=*xxx*" where *xxx* is 5.0 (zoomed in all the way) to 85.0 (zoomed all the way out).

As QuickTime movie files tend to be large, they are not cached by default. In a case where caching is desired, you can set CACHE=TRUE.

> **TIP:** *Additional information regarding playback options can be found at Apple's Web site dedicated to immersive imaging:* www.apple.com/quicktime/authors/webmas.html#tags

It is polite (read: imperative) to let viewers know that they are about to look at a VR photograph, because time and plug-ins will be required to see it. Most Macintosh computers and Netscape Navigator 3.0 and later have the required QuickTime system extensions loaded; Windows users can download the extensions from Apple's QTVR site: *www.apple.com/quicktime/qtvr/index.html*

ADDITIONAL TYPES OF IMMERSIVE IMAGES

In addition to the panoramic and objects movies, there are a number of other immersive image possibilities which require creative image enhancement, specialized camera equipment, or additional software, as listed below.

- **Creative immersive imaging** Who says you have to shoot the individual original source images? Many artists featured at *www.vrview.com* have created fantastic images by enhancing Photoshop files and 3D images and stitching them into panoramic and object movies. The most important thing to remember when creating single original source files for immersive imaging, or when resizing existing files, is to make sure that the file's pixel width is divisible by 24 and its height divisible by 96. Because the stitching process slices the image into 24 tiles, making sure that the file's width and height follows the 24/96 rule will prevent any problems in the final wrapping and stitching process.

- **IPIX** Developed by Interactive Pictures, these interactive scenes are made by shooting just two source images with an extreme fisheye lens. Using special software, the two files are stitched together to form a sphere in which the viewer is in the middle and can look up and down all around. These images are especially effective for interiors where the environment, floor, and ceiling are of interest. Both the Nikon 900/950 and Olympus D-340 support IPIX ready fisheye lenses.

- **MetaFlash** The MetaFlash system uses a Minolta Dimage 1500EX (see Figure 11-32) with a modified flash that projects a grid onto the object. The object is transformed into a wireframe with the MetaStream software. By combining images taken from different angles, the software is able to create a 3D photograph that the viewer can move at will.

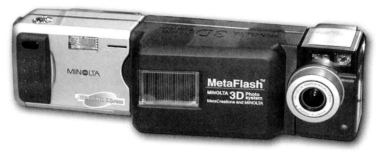

Figure 11-32 The Minolta MetaFlash uses a modified Minolta Dimage 1500 to produce photographs with three-dimensional depth.

- **BeHere** BeHere uses a mirrored parabolic dome that reflects an entire panoramic scene into its specialized optics that focus the image onto a 35mm-film camera. Not an inexpensive solution but an intriguing one.

- **Smooth Move** Kaidan recently announced the $1500 SmoothMove Spherical PhotoSolution, which allows you to create spherical panoramas. It includes a spherical tripod head from Kaidan and SmoothMove software from Infinite Pictures, which can stitch together multiple rows of photos to allow the viewer 360° of freedom—both horizontal and vertical—to move through the scene.

- **RoundAbout Video System** This is a collaborative project combining Immersive Media Company hardware and EnRoute's software expertise to create fantastic immersive video images through which the viewer can walk, stop, and turn around at will inside the live action video. It all starts with the cameraperson shooting the scene with eleven video cameras that are mounted onto an eleven-sided frame, and then the software stitches the eleven signals together to create immersive video.

A WORLD OF RESOURCES AND INSPIRATION

To see fantastic immersive imaging, visit www.evox.com, www.vrview.com, *and* www.iqtvra.org. *Many of the examples seen in this chapter can also be seen at* www.photoshopdiva.com. *Also check out:*

- http://www.apple.com/quicktime/qtvr/index.html
- http://www.worldserver.com/turk/QTVRAuthoringTricks.html
- http://www.QuickTimeFAQ.org/qtvr/
- *The QuickTime VR Book by Susan A. Kitchens, published by Peachpit Press.*

Now go out, spin in circles, look around you, have a blast with immersive imaging, and help create the future of photography.

CHAPTER TWELVE

Correcting Your Photographs

The number one attraction of digital imaging is that you are permitted absolute control over your photographs, starting the moment you shoot them and continuing well after you print the photos or post them on the Web. Some folks call this the digital development process, but that doesn't really tell the story. After all, the image is already developed when you download it to your computer. You don't have to dip the photo in a chemical bath or run the print through fixatives to see the colors as the camera captured them. The notion of development is dependent on film; without film, development has no meaning.

But just because digital photographs arrive fully developed doesn't mean they're developed to their fullest potential. The image may be dark, the colors may be inaccurate, and the focus may be soft. These and other problems are not unique to digital—film photos may likewise suffer darkness, color drift, and blur. The difference is that even an inexpensive image editor provides as many ways to fix a problem photo as a fully stocked traditional darkroom. And at least one image editor, industry standard Adobe Photoshop, leaves the darkroom in the dust.

To give you an idea of just how miraculous digital image restoration can be, take a look at Figure 12-1. Deke captured this winner a few years ago inside a dimly lit museum without the aid of a flash. The camera used to shoot this particular image, Kodak's DC50, was incapable of long exposures, so the image simply came out dark. And not just a little dark—so dark that you'd swear the image was beyond hope. The lightest color is about 50 percent black—which is to say, the gray precisely midway between black and white. This means that fully half the 256 brightness values permitted to a grayscale image go unused. The remaining half are poorly used, with the image tending in no uncertain terms toward black.

But 100 or so brightness values are better than none. By setting the lightest color in the image to white and stretching out the rest of the grays to fill in the gaps, Deke was able to arrive at the first example in Figure 12-2. The image looks several times better, yet it's the result of a single command. More subtle adjustments—enhancing the contrast, smoothing out defects, sharpening the focus, filling in the background —require more effort, but they have a pronounced effect on the final appearance of the image. The second example of Figure 12-2 may not be high art—and one might could argue that you might may as well paint the image from scratch if you're going to expend this much effort—but it's a heck of an improvement over the original.

Figure 12-1 Shot indoors without a flash using a low-resolution Kodak DC50, this image appears to be a candidate for the trashcan.

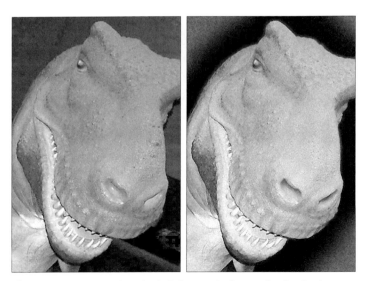

Figure 12-2 Correcting the brightness is the work of a single command (left). Toss in a few more edits, and you arrive at a remarkably serviceable image (right).

The left photo in Color Plate 12-1 on page C25 shows an example of an image in a grave condition having nothing to do with a misuse of the camera. Despite (or perhaps because of) plenty of direct light, the image suffers from a shocking amount of color drift and excessive contrast between lights and darks. (For the record, the photograph is the work of the Ricoh RDC-2, a contemporary of the DC50 better known for its gadgetry than its ability to capture a decent image.) Though it may seem counterintuitive, this image presents more of a challenge than the no-flash dinosaur. You have to lighten the dark colors, darken the light ones, restore the skin tones, remove the green cast from the clothing and hair, cover up the white hot spots on the faces, and sharpen the focus without drawing out the deluge of JPEG compression artifacts. Even so, it can be done, as the right photo in Color Plate 12-1 shows.

The moral is, no matter how bad off a digital image is, there's a very good chance it can be corrected. We're not saying it's always worth the effort—in some cases, reshooting the photo is still the most efficient solution—but image editing is an option.

In this chapter, we explore a few methods for fixing digital photographs. Naturally, we can't explain every image editing technique. There are literally hundreds of books available on the topic of image editing, some of which we're told reach 1,000 pages in length. (A few of Deke's own books come to mind.) Nor can we explore every image editing program on the market, of which there may be 50 or more. Instead, we concentrate on the techniques you'll need most often. And we focus on just one program, Photoshop, the most popular image editor among designers, photographers, and other imaging professionals. Fortunately, many competing image editors take their cues from Photoshop, so the techniques we describe in this chapter are applicable to a wide range of software, including Adobe PhotoDeluxe, Ulead PhotoImpact, CorelPhoto-Paint, Micrografx Picture Publisher, and Jasc Paint Shop Pro, just to name a few.

STRAIGHTENING AND CROPPING

Editing an image is like tearing down a brick wall and rebuilding it. Done properly, the new wall will look better and last longer, even though a few bricks inevitably get damaged in the process. Handled improperly, you can end up with a weakened wall that looks worse than it did when you started.

For better or worse, the original pixels in a digital snapshot represent what the camera saw. Any change made to those pixels amounts to a distortion of reality. Approached deliberately and skillfully, the image continues to look photographic, even after editing. But if you just jump in and start tearing things apart without a plan, you can destroy the image with very little effort.

One key to successful image editing is to work through problems in order of priority. Start with the changes that are likely to have the most dramatic effect on the image and end by finessing the details.

For example, suppose your image is crooked, like the one in Figure 12-3. Because an image editor always draws pixels in perpendicular rows and columns, you can't physically rotate a pixel; the program has to redraw the pixels to represent the straightened version of the image. This is tantamount to knocking the wall down and assembling the bricks in a new order. That's a big change, one that should be handled early on.

Figure 12-3 Even when armed with a good LCD preview, like the one built into Agfa's ePhoto 1680, it's easy to shoot a slanting picture.

Color Plate 9-1 Rather than watching the sunset, this photographer worked quickly and saw how the warmth of the sunset light was bringing the simplest forms to life. Shot with the Kodak DCS 460c. (See page 197 for more information.) *Image by John McIntosh.*

Color Plate 9-2 Working with a long shutter speed with the Kodak DC 260 Zoom allows you to create abstract images of everyday scenes, as this frenzied commute shows. Image was shot with a Kodak DC 260 Zoom. (See page 208 for more information.)

C17

Color Plate 9-3 Taking pictures in the early morning or evening allows you to capture uncommon moods and scenes, like these summer chairs at dusk that look like they're ready for a warm vacation. (See page 215 for more information.)

Color Plate 9-4 Red-eye is caused by the flash reflecting off of the subject's retina. In the top image it almost ruins the image of father and son; the digitally retouched version below it is much more attractive. (See page 223 for more information.) *Photo by Margo Seymour.*

Color Plate 10-1 In addition to the main subjects of the photograph, the first image contains lots of extraneous brick, railing, and window, none of which adds anything to the image. The second shot is much tighter, giving us a better view of the smiling faces. (See page 228 for more information.)

Color Plate 10-2
Can you get too near your subject? As long as the focus holds out, we're not sure such a thing as too near exists. There's no denying that this photograph captures a horse as you rarely see it—which is a good thing, in more ways than one. (See page 230 for more information.)

C19

Color Plate 10-3 After looking at the top image, our first thought is, "We're supposed to eat something that's been weighed on this scale?" But get closer (bottom), and the function of the object falls away, revealing a complex network of glass, stickers, metal, paint, and rust. (See page 234 for more information.)

Color Plate 10-4 Shot aboard the *Queen Mary* with a Kodak DCS520, these horizontal and vertical shots better display different elements of the ship. The horizontal shot (left) provides a better overview, whereas the vertical picture (right) better displays the vent. (See page 234 for more information.)

Color Plate 10-5 These two off-center photos may look intentional but were anything but. The bee was shot using a close-up lens that wasn't accounted for by the viewfinder. The silos were shot out the window of a slowly moving car. Both were supposed to be centered shots, but through chance or folly ended up wonderfully lopsided. (See page 239 for more information.)

Color Plate 10-6 The best pictures of an event are often those that turn the camera on the spectators. In this case, we get a better sense for the experience of touring the Tower of London than we do from the pictures in Figure 10-19. (See pages 240–241 for more information.)

Color Plate 10-7 A reflective surface provides an alternative view of your subject. It also permits you the rare chance to include yourself in the photo. (See page 242 for more information.)

Color Plate 10-8 When shooting a moving subject, try moving the camera with the subject as you press the shutter release. In these images, moving the camera has resulted in sharply defined fish set against moving backgrounds. You can be sure many of your shots won't turn out, so take lots of pictures. (See page 242 for more information.)

Color Plate 11-1 Printing panoramic images such as this Swedish harbor scene reveal an abstract yet familiar world. (See page 245 for more information.)

Color Plate 11-2 Visiting the Burpee Test Garden on the Web, viewers can click and "stroll" through the garden to see the flowers in different areas. (See page 245 for more information.)

Color Plate 11-3 Animating the object as seen here where the convertible top opens and closes as the viewer spins the car requires planning and concentration. (See page 276 for more information.) *Image by eVox Productions.*

Using the Measure Tool

The easiest and most precise way to straighten an image in Photoshop 5 and later is to use the Measure tool, which appears labeled in Figure 12-4. Drag with the tool to create a line that matches the angle of an element in your photograph that should appear perpendicular—that is, exactly horizontal or vertical. In Figure 12-4, we've drawn the measure line along a horizontal ledge along the castle wall. You can adjust the line by dragging either endpoint. The angle of the line tells Photoshop how much the image veers from the horizontal mean.

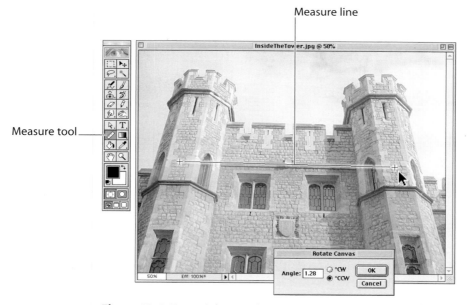

Figure 12-4 To straighten an image in Photoshop, draw a measure line along an element that should be perpendicular and, then choose Image » Rotate Canvas » Arbitrary.

After you get the line the way you want it, choose the Arbitrary command from the Rotate submenu under the Image menu. The Angle value in the Rotate dialog box automatically records the angle of the measure line. For example, the Angle value at the bottom of Figure 12-4 shows that the measure line is 1.28 degrees off horizontal. Press the Return or Enter key, and Photoshop automatically rights the image. As Figure 12-5 shows, one degree can make a lot of difference.

Figure 12-5 A modest 1.28-degree rotation puts the castle on an even plane.

Using the Crop Tool

The downside of rotating a photograph is that it leaves wedges of white along each of the four sides of the image. (By default, Photoshop's background color is white. If you set it to some other color, the wedges appear in that color.) To get rid of the wedges, you have to crop the image.

There are two ways to crop an image in Photoshop. One is to select a region with the rectangular marquee tool and choose Image » Crop. The other and more popular method is to use the crop tool, labeled in Figure 12-6.

The easiest way to select the crop tool is to press the C key on the keyboard. Then drag inside the image to specify the crop boundary. Drag a corner or side handle to resize the crop boundary, as illustrated in Figure 12-6. You can also drag inside the boundary to move it or drag outside the boundary to rotate it. (Rotating with the crop tool lets you perform two operations in one; however, it's less precise than the measure tool.)

> **TIP:** *One constraint of Photoshop is that while you use the crop tool, you can't access any other tool or command in the program. If this becomes a problem, you can cancel out of the crop mode by pressing the Escape key.*

Crop boundary

Crop tool

Figure 12-6 Use the crop tool to surround the portion of the image that you want to retain and, then press Enter to crop the image.

To apply the crop boundary to the image, press the Return or the Enter key. Photoshop deletes all pixels that fall outside the crop boundary and leaves the pixels inside the boundary intact. Figure 12-7 shows the result of rotating and cropping the crooked castle photograph. To look at the image, you'd never know an edit took place.

Figure 12-7
Thanks to the measure and crop tools, this image appears for all the world like it was shot straight in the first place.

Cropping One Image to Match Another

Photoshop's crop tool offers a few other handy options, including the ability to exactly match the size of one image to that of another. Double-click on the crop tool icon in the toolbox to display the Crop Options palette, shown in Figure 12-8. After that, you can crop one image, we'll call it Image A, to match the size of another, Image B, as follows:

1. Click inside Image B to make it the front image.

2. Click on the Front Image button in the Crop Options palette, highlighted in Figure 12-8. This copies the size and resolution information from the file.

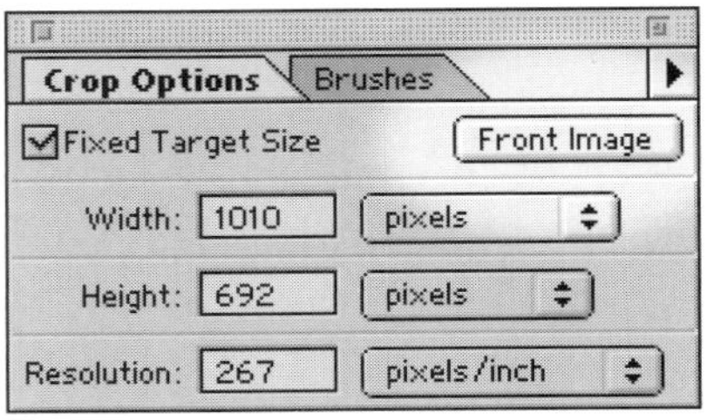

Figure 12-8 Click on the Front Image button to load the size and resolution settings from the image that you're currently working on.

3. Click inside Image A to make it the front image.

4. Drag with the crop tool inside Image A. Photoshop constrains the proportions of the crop boundary to the proportions of Image B.

5. Press the Return or Enter key. Photoshop automatically sizes Image A to match Image B.

Figure 12-9 shows an example of two images that we scaled to precisely the same size—pixel for pixel—using the Front Image button in the Crop Options palette. Obviously, this technique comes in handy when you need to match images to the same size on a page. But we also find it to be helpful when outputting to snapshot printers, like those mentioned in the "Dye-Sublimation Printers" section of Chapter 7. Once we figure out the maximum image size that the printer accommodates—say, 3.5 by 5 inches at 306 ppi—we can set up a dummy image and match other snapshots to that same size.

Figure 12-9 We cropped these two images to exactly the same size using the Front Image button.

BRIGHTNESS AND CONTRAST

The most common problems associated with digital photographs are brightness and contrast. The contrast—which is the difference between blacks and whites in an image—is often too low, giving which gives the photograph an ashen or muddy appearance. Meanwhile, the brightness is more often than not too dark, resulting in lackluster highlights and obscure details in the shadows.

Figure 12-10 is a fairly typical example. Shot in the shade of a roadway embankment in late afternoon, this image contains wonderful variety in texture and depth. But despite some help from a fill flash, the photo came out drab and dark. We can't go back and reshoot the photo—the snake long ago made a beeline for the brush—and, fortunately, there's really no need to. Everything we need is here; we just need an image editor to draw it out.

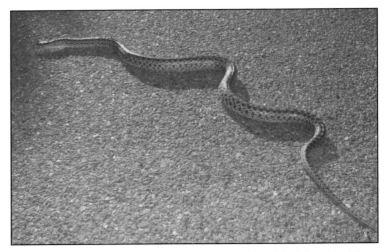

Figure 12-10 Shot in afternoon light with a Polaroid PDC-2000, this lucky shot of a moving reptile came out way too dark.

Reading a Histogram

You would think that the best way to correct problems with brightness and contrast would be to choose Photoshop's Brightness/Contrast command (under the Image » Adjust menu). But we urge you not to do this. The Brightness/Contrast dialog box is limited to two meager options, as we begrudgingly display in Figure 12-11. The Brightness and Contrast sliders work like the brightness and contrast knobs on a monitor—you drag the triangles until the image looks more or less the way you think it should on screen. But where eyeballing is an acceptable (if imperfect) solution for adjusting the colors on your monitor, it is far too vague a method for correcting digital images. Photoshop provides commands that offer greater control, so you might as well learn to use them.

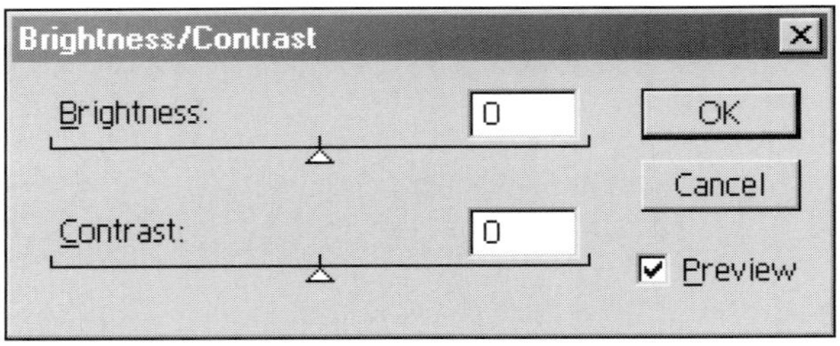

Figure 12-11 The imprecise Brightness/Contrast dialog box is limited to two vague slider controls.

The command that provides the best compromise between precision and ease of use is Image » Adjust » Levels, which you can choose from the keyboard by pressing ⌘-L on the Mac or Ctrl+L in Windows. Photoshop responds with the Levels dialog box, shown in Figure 12-12. Named for the 256 levels of brightness in an 8-bit color channel, the Levels dialog box may at first appear a bit intimidating, rife with some very foreign looking controls. But most of your work will center around a few options, labeled in Figure 12-13.

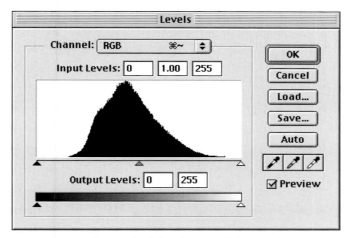

Figure 12-12 The Levels dialog is more elaborate than Brightness/Contrast, but it's several times more capable as well.

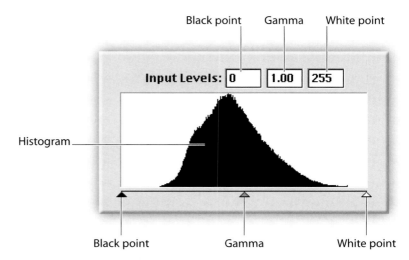

Figure 12-13 The most important area of the Levels dialog box is the histogram and surrounding options.

Pictured in Figure 12-13, the *histogram* is the central element in the Levels dialog box. It graphs the colors of the pixels in the image from black on the left to white on the right. If you were to measure the width of this histogram, you would discover it to be exactly 256 pixels wide, one pixel for each of the 256 levels. This means the histogram is actually a bar graph with a total of 256 bars running from left to right. The taller the bar, the more pixels in the image that are colored with that specific brightness value.

Although highly accurate, the real purpose of the histogram is to provide you with a general feel for how the colors in an image are distributed. The histogram in Figure 12-13 graphs the colors in the snake snapshot from Figure 12-10. The fact that the histogram peaks near the dark end of the brightness spectrum indicates that the image is predominantly dark. Generally speaking, if the histogram looks like it could balance on the gray gamma triangle (labeled in Figure 12-13), then the colors are well distributed. In the case of the snake, the histogram would flop over to the left; hence the image is overly dark.

The other problem with the snake histogram is that the bars drop off well short of the left and right edges of the graph. This means no pixel in the image is black or any of several dark shades of gray. The image is likewise bereft of white or very light gray pixels. Hence, the image is low on contrast.

Correcting the Levels

After reading the histogram, you can make changes based on it. Figures 12-14, 12-15, and 12-16 show the three simple steps we took to correct the snake image:

1. In Figure 12-14, we moved the white point slider to the left, to the point where the histogram appears to drop away. This sets the lightest color in the snake image to white, and stretches the other colors to lighter points in the spectrum. Note that when you move the slider, the third of the three Input Levels values updates to reflect the new white point. In the figure, the value is 230, meaning that any color with a brightness value of 230 of higher turns to white. (For reference, white is 255, and black is 0.)

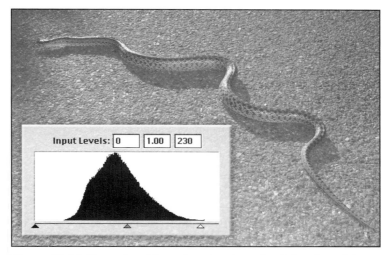

Figure 12-14 Move the white point triangle to the right edge of the histogram to turn the lightest colors in the image to white.

2. In Figure 12-15, the black point has moved to the point at which the first bars in the histogram begin. The first Input Levels value, 40, indicates that a brightness value of 40 or darker now becomes black. This ensures a desirable amount of contrast between lights and darks, but it also leaves the image darker than it was before we started. The next step will remedy this problem.

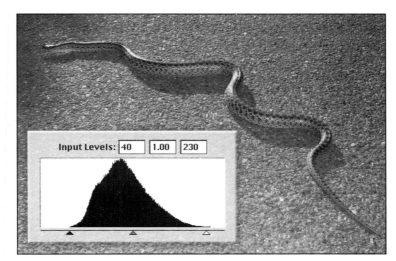

Figure 12-15 Move the black point triangle to the left edge of the histogram to make the darkest colors black.

3. The final step is to adjust the *gamma*, or middle slider triangle. As you may remember from Chapter 7, the gamma is an exponential power applied to the colors in the image. While this may sound very technical, the gamma triangle is actually quite easy to use. Move it to the left to lighten the image, move it to the right to darken the image. In Figure 12-16, we moved the gamma triangle to just below the histogram's peak, so the graph looks like it might balance on the triangle. This lightens the colors in the image without changing the black or white points, ensuring a gradual transition of brightness values evenly distributed between black and white.

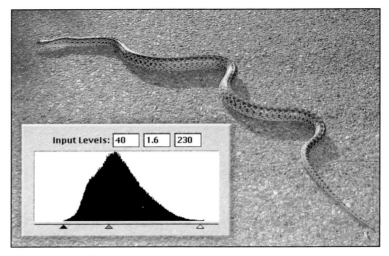

Figure 12-16 If the image remains dark after setting the black and white points, move the center gamma triangle to the left to balance the histogram.

NOTE: *In Figure 12-16, moving the gamma triangle has raised the middle Input Levels value to 1.6. This tells Photoshop to raise the colors in the image to the power of 1.6. If you know anything about math, this may seem odd. For example, if you raise white, which is 255, to 1.6, you get 7,087, which is completely off the spectrum. To account for this, Photoshop runs a separate gamma calculation where black is 0, white is 1, and the other brightness values are decimal values in between. This ensures that gamma lightens and darkens all values except black and white. We know, it's technical, but we're confident there are a couple of readers out there who just had to know.*

If you're feeling particularly on the ball today, you may notice a discrepancy between this discussion of Levels gamma and the monitor gamma discussion from Chapter 7. Here, a gamma value of 1.6 lightens the image. By contrast, higher monitor gammas darken the screen image (with the 2.2 PC gamma being darker than the 1.8 Mac gamma). Photoshop chose to reverse the gamma calculation in Levels so that it makes more sense.

Adjustment Layers

Photoshop offers a few additional methods for correcting the brightness and contrast of a digital image. Our favorite is the *adjustment layer*, which lets you apply a color correction as a separate layer, so that the original pixels in the image remain intact. The adjustment layer acts like a coating of correction that can be moved, modified, or deleted at any time in the future. Katrin goes so far as to suggest that you should *always* use adjustment layers because they ensure greater flexibility when applying other edits in the future. (Deke is forced to agree, but rarely follows this advice out of sheer laziness.)

To create an adjustment layer, you first need to bring up the Layers palette by pressing the F7 key. You'll notice a small page icon near the lower right corner of the palette. Press the ⌘ or Ctrl key and click on this icon. A dialog box appears, asking you what kind of adjustment layer you want to create, as in Figure 12-17. To apply a Levels adjustment, choose Levels from the Type pop-up menu. Then press Return or Enter.

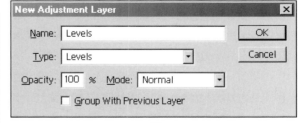

Figure 12-17 On the Mac, ⌘-click on the new layer icon to make an adjustment layer. On the PC, Ctrl-click on the icon.

⌘-click or
Ctrl-click here

Photoshop adds a new layer named Levels and displays the Levels dialog box. You use the histogram and Levels options exactly as described in the previous section. The difference is that after you apply your Levels adjustments, you can revisit and edit them by simply double-clicking on the Levels layer in the Layers palette. Photoshop offers up the settings you last applied to this layer so that you can further tweak them to get the precise effect you need.

Curves and Beyond

The Levels command is sufficiently capable to correct 90 percent of the brightness and contrast problems you're liable to encounter. But if it doesn't quite do the trick, Photoshop offers the even more capable Image » Adjust » Curves. Pictured in Figure 12-18, the Curves dialog box lets you create and adjust specific brightness values on a graph. So instead of limiting you to three brightness points—white, black, and gamma, as in the case of Levels—you can plot as many points as you like.

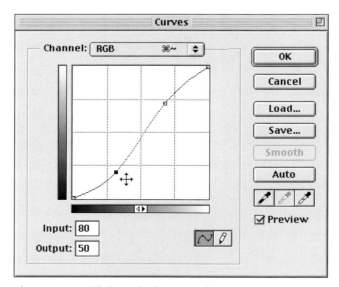

Figure 12-18 Click on the line to add a point to the Curves graph and, then drag the point to lighten or darken the color.

We're not suggesting for a moment that this is all you need to know on the topic of Curves. However, given the mandate of this book, this is all the discussion we can afford. If you're interested in exploring Photoshop's brightness correction capabilities in more detail, we can recommend three highly rated titles. The first is another entry in the *Real World* series from Peachpit Press, *Real World Photoshop 5* by David Blatner and Bruce Fraser, which devotes close to 100 pages to the topics of Levels, Curves, and adjustment layers. The other two are Deke's *Macworld Photoshop 5 Bible* and *Photoshop 5 For Windows Bible* (both published by IDG Books Worldwide), the bestselling guides to Photoshop so far published. We are told all three are required reading inside Adobe's own technical support department.

CORRECTING COLORS

When you add the element of color, correcting an image becomes more complicated. You have to consider not only brightness and contrast, but also color cast, saturation, and the occasional color mismatch. Luckily, most image editors provide a wealth of commands to fix these problems, and Photoshop is no exception.

Variations: the Intuitive Approach

Photoshop's most straightforward color correction feature is the Variations dialog box, pictured in Figure 12-19 and more accurately in Color Plate 12-2 on page C25. Displayed by choosing Image » Adjust » Variations, the Variations window includes postage stamp-sized thumbnails to show you how an image will look when subjected to different color adjustments. All you have to do is click on the thumbnail that looks better than the current state of the image.

For example, if an image is too dark, click on the thumbnail labeled Lighter. If an image appears too yellow—or, in trade parlance, it suffers from a yellow *cast*—click on the thumbnail opposite the one named More Yellow, which is labeled More Blue. Each correction thumbnail appears opposite its color compliment so More Blue removes a yellow cast, More Cyan removes a red cast, More Green removes a magenta cast, and so on.

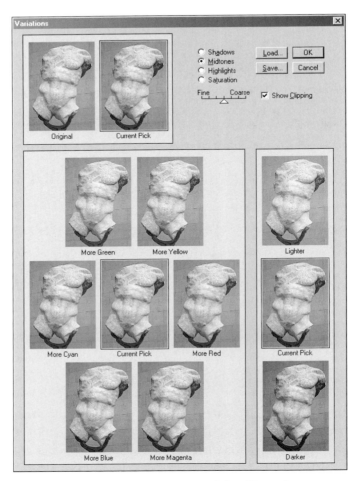

Figure 12-19 The Variations command simplifies color
correction by asking you to click on a thumbnail that looks
better than the current pick.

The Variations dialog box lets you modify the colors of highlights, midtones, or shadows independently by selecting the aptly named Highlights, Midtones, or Shadows buttons. You can likewise adjust the intensity of a single click on a thumbnail using the slider labeled Fine on one end and Coarse on the other. Fine adjustments are subtler.

The downside of working in the Variations window is that the thumbnails are too small to depict your corrections in much detail. Once you okay the correction and see it applied to the entire image, it may appear quite different than it did in the postage-stamp view. Fortunately, Photoshop provides a painless remedy. Assuming that you went a little overboard with the correction—which is the most common outcome—you can back off the effect by choosing the Fade Variations command from the Filter menu. This brings up the Fade dialog box shown in Figure 12-20. Lower the Opacity value to mix the corrected image with the original one.

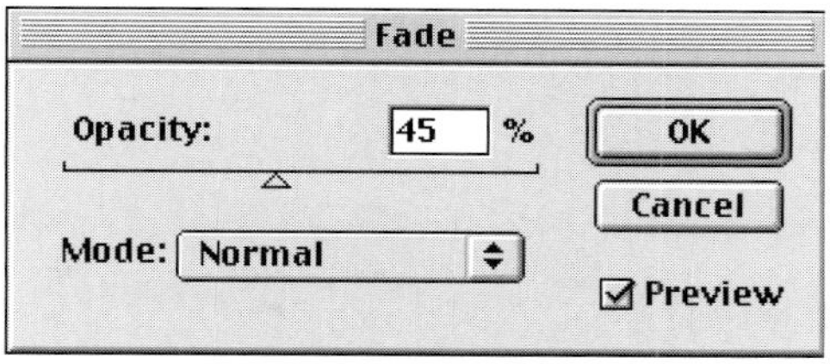

Figure 12-20 Immediately after invoking a color correction command, you can tone down the effect using the Fade command.

In Color Plate 12-3 on page C26, for example, we applied one click each of the More Blue, More Cyan, and Lighter buttons inside the Variations dialog box. Judging by the thumbnail, we thought the effect was a bit overstated, but basically essentially on target. After seeing it applied to the entire image, however, we knew we had gone too far. Choosing the Fade Variations command and knocking the Opacity value to 45 percent made for a more natural effect.

Adjusting Saturation

The Variations dialog box offers one additional option that we haven't yet mentioned—Saturation. Highlighted in Figure 12-21, the Saturation option replaces the color cast and brightness thumbnails with two adjustment options—Less Saturation and More Saturation—where *saturation* is merely another word for the intensity of a color. Highly saturated colors are vivid and garish. As you lower the saturation, the colors tend toward gray.

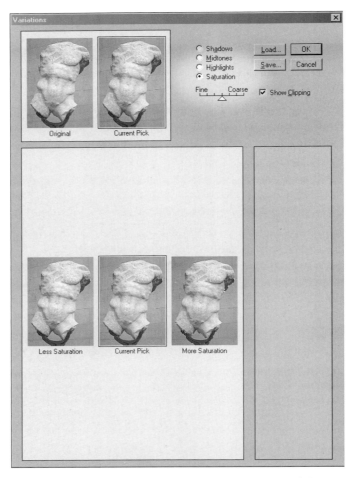

Figure 12-21 Select the Saturation button at the top of the Variations dialog box to leech the color from an image or make the color more vivid.

Highly saturated colors may sound desirable, and on occasion they are. But the practical purpose of correcting an image is to make it appear more natural, and oversaturation produces a distinctly unnatural effect. Consider the images in Color Plate 12-4 on page C26. Both images were shot in the same room unaided by a flash at the same time of day. But whereas the lower image appears more or less natural, the top image appears bathed in brilliant amber light, as if the building next to it were on fire. We solved some of the color problem by clicking on the familiar More Blue, More Cyan, and Lighter buttons, but as shown at the top of Color Plate 12-5 (page C27), that still left us with too much color.

To drain away some of this excessive brilliance, we selected the Saturation button at the top of the Variations window. Then we clicked three times on the Less Saturation button. The bottom image in Color Plate 12-5 on page C27 shows the result. Although the colors in the corrected Ricoh image still don't entirely measure up to those capture by the DC260, they bear a much stronger resemblance to the colors you would expect to see in real life.

Balancing Colors with Levels

The fact that Variations is so easy to use makes it a perfect choice for quick brightness corrections and cast removal. But there's no denying that its controls are somewhat vague. Though Variations is significantly better implemented than Brightness/Contrast, it likewise also requires you to eyeball your changes. If a job requires precision, Variations may not be the right tool.

The more reliable alternatives, once again, are Levels and Curves. Both commands permit you to either correct all colors in an image simultaneously, or to address the red, green, or blue color channel independently. Color Plate 12-6 on page C27 shows a gavial crocodile accompanied by its histogram in the Levels dialog box. Because the image was captured through glass, a flash could not be used. Reds and oranges from surface light are quickly absorbed by water, so not surprisingly, the image is predominantly yellow-green with a dark histogram.

By choosing an option from the Channel pop-up menu, you can examine the independent histograms for the red, green, and blue channels. Figure 12-22 shows each of the gavial's 8-bit channels along with its histogram. The red and green channels are low on contrast but relatively balanced in brightness. The blue channel is several shades darker, coming the closest of the three to offering true blacks.

To correct the image, we first matched the white and black points for each of the three channels, just as we would if they were separate grayscale images. Then we boosted the gamma values to taste. Figure 12-23 shows each of the channels subject to revised Levels settings. The result was to tip the color scales in favor of the reds and violets, as shown in the first example in Color Plate 12-7 on page C28.

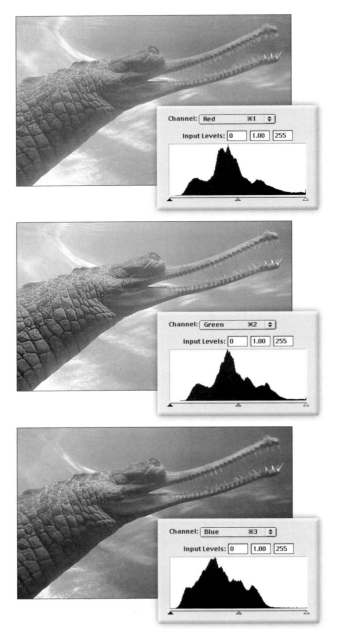

Figure 12-22 If we examine the channels for the gavial from Color Plate 12-6, we see that the yellow-green cast of the image is caused by low-contrast red and green channels and few bright values in the blue channel.

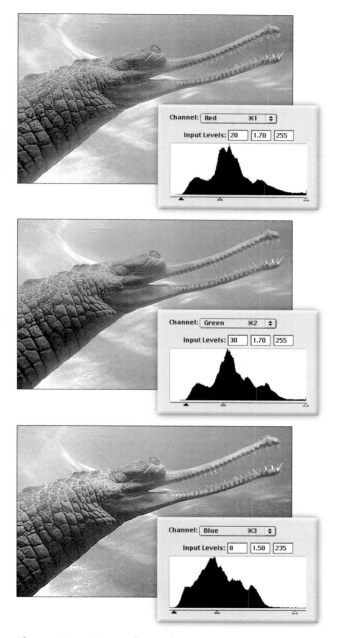

Figure 12-23 You apply Levels to a color image just as if you were applying the command to three separate grayscale images—that is, by responding to the histogram for each channel and previewing the changes as they're applied to the image.

Restoring Saturation

When you increase the gamma settings of a color image, the Levels command has a tendency to drain some of the saturation. You can restore this saturation using the Variations command, but we prefer the numerically precise Hue/Saturation. Choose Image » Adjust » Hue/Saturation to display the three slider bars shown in Figure 12-24:

- The first slider, Hue, controls the colors in the image, as measured on a rainbow color wheel. We'll discuss this option in the next section.

- The third slider, Lightness, raises and lowers the brightness of *all* colors in an image, much like the Brightness slider in the Brightness/Contrast dialog box. Because it affects all colors equally, you can easily shift large sections of color to black or white, which may ruin a photograph. Except in special cases, you should steer clear of this slider.

- The middle slider, Saturation, controls the saturation of the image. Raise the value to make the image more colorful, lower the value to drain the colors.

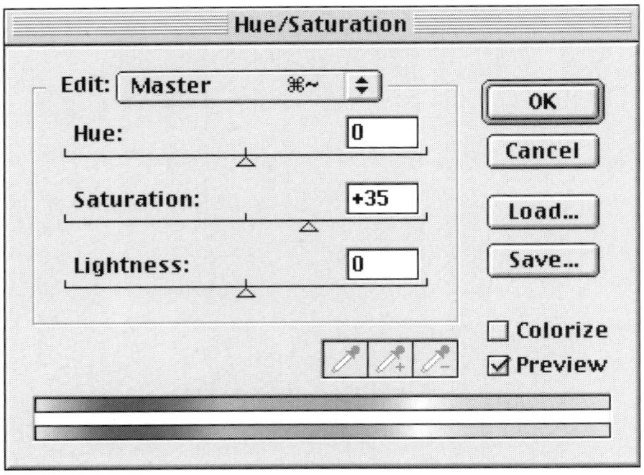

Figure 12-24 The Hue/Saturation dialog box lets you modify the hue, saturation, and lightness of an image by entering numerical values.

For our part, we wanted to boost the colors. So we raised the Saturation value to +35 percent, as in Figure 12-24, to produce the more colorful gavial shown in the bottom example of Color Plate 12-7 on page C28.

NOTE: *Use discretion when increasing the saturation of an image. JPEG compression artifacts are marked by slightly unrealistic shifts in color between one pixel and its neighbor. As you raise the saturation, those color differences become more pronounced. With very little effort, you can draw attention to artifacts that would have otherwise have been invisible. (For one way to work around this problem, read the "Suppressing Artifacts" section later in this chapter.)*

Changing a Specific Color

The Hue/Saturation command is also useful for selectively altering colors in an image. Suppose you've shot a model in a red dress, but then the client says the dress should appear orange. Photoshop 5 and later permits you to make such changes without reshooting or sacrificing believability.

Consider the first top image in Color Plate 12-8 on page C28. Deke shot this picture of an iMac with Kodak's DC200. It's a careless, cheesy image, but the remarkable thing is that, although the colors of the background elements came out fine, the purple detailing on this grape iMac photographed as indigo.

The best way to fix this lapse in color accuracy is to open the Hue/Saturation dialog box and choose Blues from the Edit pop-up menu, as shown in Figure 12-25. This limits the modifications to just blue pixels in the image. To make sure that the correct blues are selected, move the cursor outside the dialog box and click somewhere in the portion of the image you want to modify. Photoshop automatically selects the proper color spectrum. Then edit the Hue and Saturation values until the colors look the way you remember them.

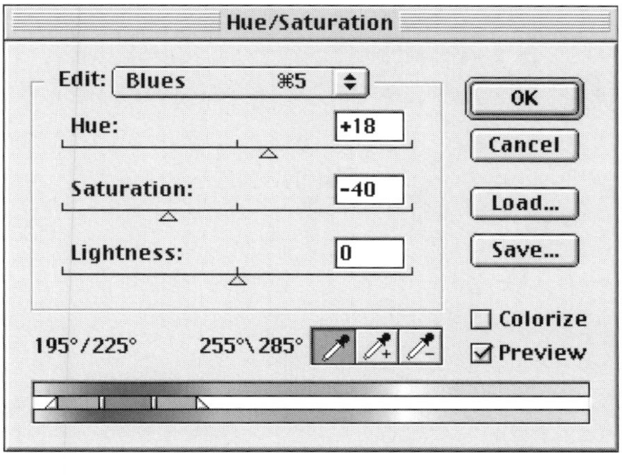

Figure 12-25 The Edit pop-up menu lets you call out a color in your image that you want to edit independently of other colors.

In Figure 12-25, the Hue value has been changed to +18 degrees. Hue is measured on a 360-degree circle, from red to orange, then yellow, green, blue, purple, and back to red again. Adding 18 degrees to the blues in the image shifted them to shades of purple. Deke also decreased the Saturation value by 40 percent, to better match the translucent purple of the iMac. The result of these changes appears in the bottom example of Color Plate 12-8. Considering that the change involved so little effort, it's frankly amazing that the new colors blend in seamlessly.

The wonderful thing about this technique is that it doesn't require you to fuss with Photoshop's selection and masking tools, which can be quite tedious at times. The only caveat is that Hue/Saturation changes *all* of the pixels of a certain color in the image. If something other than the iMac were colored blue in Color Plate 12-8, we would have had to select the region we wanted to modify before choosing Image » Adjust » Hue/Saturation.

SHARPENING FOCUS

Every image editor includes commands that sharpen the focus of an image. These commands are designed to take elements in a soft photograph and give them the appearance of greater clarity with more distinct edges. Figure 12-26 shows a prime example of the kind of photograph that image editors are capable of sharpening. Captured with a Polaroid PDC-2000—which employed a unique CCD design that required it always to interpolate images, regardless of image resolution—the photograph is soft on focus but otherwise in excellent shape. Figure 12-27 shows just how much sharper the image can be with the help of an image editor. In this case, we've oversharpened the picture to make our point; but if for some reason this isn't sharp enough, you can go much farther.

Figure 12-26 Shot with a Polaroid PDC-2000, this image is just right in terms of brightness and contrast, but a bit weak on focus.

Figure 12-27 Applying a single command in Photoshop makes the window frames, statues, and other ornaments stand out much more clearly.

Bear in mind, however, that sharpening is merely a digital parlor trick, not full-blown magic. An image editor cannot rescue focus where none exists. Consider the festive (but purely non-denominational) pine tree shown in the first example of Figure 12-28. The image is the product of an Olympus D-620L. Despite its many excellent qualities, the D-620L is all but incapable of autofocusing on dimly lit objects, so we had to experiment with manual focus overrides, which in this case quite obviously missed the mark. By sharpening the image in Photoshop, we were able to increase the contrast around the edges of the blurry dollops of light—as in the second example—but the details remain gummy and indistinct.

Figure 12-28 If a picture is shot out of focus (left), applying a sharpening command in an image editor results in hard-edged fuzziness (right).

Focus is ultimately a function of the camera. If an image comes out blurry, the only real solution is the traditional one—reshoot it. Fortunately for us, these trees have a habit of popping up every other solstice, so we'll probably get another shot at it next year.

Using Unsharp Mask

Like most image editors, Photoshop provides several commands for sharpening the focus of an image. But only one, Filter » Sharpen » Unsharp Mask, gives you any control over the process. The Unsharp Mask command is named after a traditional lab technique in which two negatives—one normally focused and one blurry—are laid one on top of the other and shot together using a prolonged exposure. If you're one of the few folks who is familiar with this technique, then you'll find that Photoshop's command operates along the same lines but with much greater control. For those of you who have never heard of unsharp masking, the command is unfortunately named—the word "unsharp" implies exactly the opposite of what it does—but it remains an essential ingredient in the process of correcting a digital image.

Displayed in Figure 12-29, the Unsharp Mask dialog box offers three numerical options—Amount, Radius, and Threshold. Of the three, Amount is the most obvious in function. Cranking up the Amount value—as high as 500 percent—increases the degree of sharpening applied. Reducing the value makes the sharpening effect more subtle. (There is no way to blur an image from Unsharp mask, so don't worry about taking the Amount value too low.)

The Radius option is less implicit but every bit as important to the functioning of the command. Unsharp Mask works by touring the image and comparing neighboring pixels. When it finds pixels that differ from each other, it considers these pixels to be an edge. The command

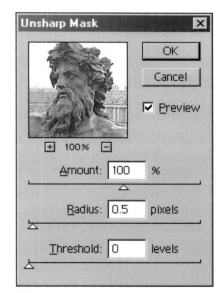

Figure 12-29 The Unsharp Mask command highlights areas of contrast in an image according to the values you enter into these options.

then increases the contrast along both sides of the edge, creating a halo effect. The thickness of this halo is determined by the Radius value, as measured in tenths of pixels.

The concept of Radius is sufficiently foreign to warrant a couple of examples, hence Figures 12-30 and 12-31. To keep things very simple, we've drawn a dark brushstroke against a textured background. Figure 12-30 shows the original version of this image, followed by three applications of Unsharp Mask with increasingly larger Amount values. In each case, the Radius is fixed at 2.0 pixels. You can see the 2-pixel halo emerge and become more pronounced as the Amount value increases. The halo appears black on the inside or darker side of the brushstroke and white along the outside or lighter edge. This fast transition between black and white is read by your eyes as an abrupt edge, hence the image appears sharply focused.

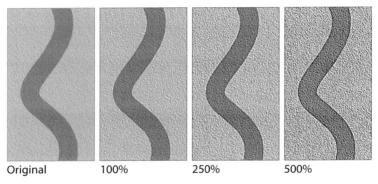

Original   100%   250%   500%

Figure 12-30 Starting with an original brushstroke on left, we applied a series of increasingly high Amount values. In each case, the Radius value is set to 2.0 pixels.

Figure 12-31 gives you a sense of what happens when you leave the Amount value fixed, in this case at 250 percent, and raise the Radius value instead. At a setting of 1.0 pixel, the halo is barely perceptible. But as it grows, it becomes increasingly obvious, eventually emerging as a full-fledged glow. Incidentally, the resolution of all these figures is 267 ppi. So a 1.0-pixel Radius amount to $1/267$ inch, while a 20.0-pixel Radius is about $1/13$ inch.

As you can see, the Unsharp Mask command affects brushstroke and background texture equally. If you want to sharpen only the brushstroke and avoid the texture, you can experiment with the Threshold value—for all the good it'll do you. The Threshold value is designed to rule out low-contrast edges in favor of high-contrast ones. It tells Photoshop that any two neighboring pixels have to be so many brightness levels different than each other to be considered an edge.

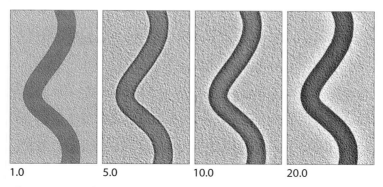

1.0   5.0   10.0   20.0

Figure 12-31 This time we left the Amount value set to 250 percent and applied increasingly high Radius values resulting in thicker halos.

For example, suppose one pixel in an image is dark gray with a brightness value of 80 and one of its neighbors is light gray with a brightness value of 140. That's a difference of $140 - 80 = 60$ levels. If you set the Threshold to 40, that's less than 60, so Photoshop would see the pixels as an edge. A Threshold of 80, on the other hand, is more than 60, so it rules out the pixels and tells Photoshop not to sharpen to them. This means, opposite of Amount and Radius, higher Threshold values result in *less* sharpening, as illustrated incrementally in Figure 12-32.

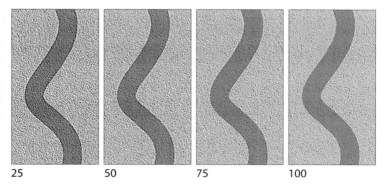

25   50   75   100

Figure 12-32 The results of incrementally increasing the Threshold value while the Amount and Radius are set to 500 percent and 2.0 pixels, respectively.

Our complaint with Threshold is that it turns Photoshop's sharpening all the way on or all the way off. There's no middle ground. As a result, you get speckling, as evident in the magnified views of the brushstrokes included in Figure 12-33. For our part, we prefer to leave Threshold set to its default setting of 0—as it was for Figures 12-30 and 12-31—which tells Photoshop to sharpen all portions of an image evenly. If you want to sharpen a specific portion of an image, select it using Photoshop's selection or masking tools.

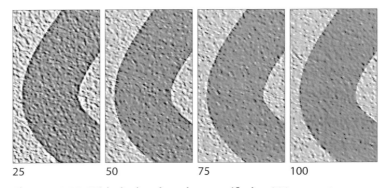

25   50   75   100

Figure 12-33 With the brushstroke magnified to 300 percent, you can see how higher Threshold values do less to avoid sharpening texture and more to increase random speckling.

Practical Applications of Unsharp Mask

While a simple brushstroke is a good subject for demonstrating how Unsharp Mask works, it isn't the least bit representative of the digital photographs that you'll be sharpening on a regular basis. So, before we close our discussion of sharpening, we'd like to demonstrate Unsharp Mask on an actual photograph, namely the one in Figure 12-34.

Figures 12-35, 12-36, and 12-37 show a variety of sharpening settings applied to the huskier of the two masks from the photo. In each figure, the Amount value varies from 50 to 500 percent. The ingredient that changes from one figure to the next is Radius, which is 0.5 pixel in Figure 12-35, 1.0 pixel in Figure 12-36, and 2.0 pixels in Figure 12-37. (The Threshold is always fixed at 0.) The resolution of all three figures is 267 ppi, just as it was for the brushstrokes.

Figure 12-34 Captured using an Epson PhotoPC 750Z, this image has been cropped and color corrected but not yet sharpened.

50%, Radius 0.5   100%   150%

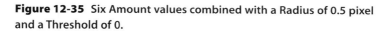

200%   350%   500%

Figure 12-35 Six Amount values combined with a Radius of 0.5 pixel and a Threshold of 0.

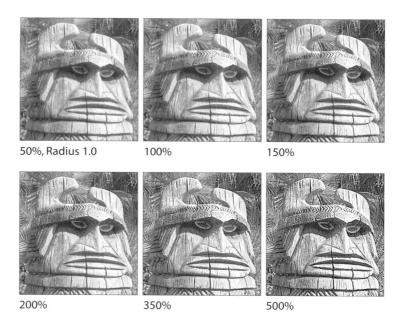

50%, Radius 1.0   100%   150%

200%   350%   500%

Figure 12-36 Here, we kept the Amount values the same but raised the Radius value to 1.0 pixel.

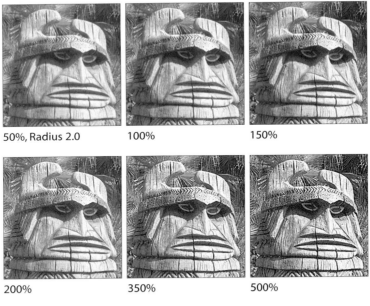

50%, Radius 2.0   100%   150%

200%   350%   500%

Figure 12-37 Again repeating the same six Amount values, we nudged the Radius value up to 2.0 pixels.

The figures help illustrate a few general rules that you'll want to keep in mind when sharpening:

- **Go easy on the gas** Amount values combined with higher Radius values produce more extreme effects. But extreme isn't necessarily good. In most cases, you want your image to appear crisp and clear, not deeply grooved. An Amount value of 200 percent is considered quite high, and should be used only with a low Radius value. If you want to take the Radius higher, lower the Amount value to compensate.

- **Keep the Radius tight** The best Radius value is one that goes unnoticed. If you can see a clearly defined halo, you've probably gone too far. The Radius values shown in Figures 12-35 through 12-37 represent a range of settings that are likely to accentuate the definition of an image without making the edges glow. Higher Radius values may boost the contrast of an image, but they rarely produce results that you would call sharp.

- **Radius changes with resolution** Because the Radius value is measured in pixels, it produces a different effect at different resolutions. If you're sharpening a low-resolution image for the Web or screen, keep the Radius low—about 0.5

usually does the trick. When printing an image at 200 ppi or more, you can raise the Radius to 1.5, 2.0, or even higher. The sharpened edges may look a little thick on screen, but they'll slim down as more pixels get packed into a smaller space.

If you go too far with Unsharp Mask, you can always back it off after applying the command by choosing Fade Unsharp Mask from the Fade menu. This brings up the same dialog box featured back in Figure 12-20. If you elect to undo the command and reapply it using different settings, press Ctrl+Z (or ⌘-Z on the Mac) to undo, then press Ctrl+Alt+F (or ⌘-Option-F on the Mac) to redisplay the Unsharp Mask filter. This technique works only when Unsharp Mask was the last command from the Filter menu that you used.

SUPPRESSING NOISE AND ARTIFACTS

Sharpening and color corrections are great for improving the appearance of a fundamentally sound image, but they have a nasty habit of bringing out the worst in grainy or heavily compressed photographs. Take Figure 12-38, for example. This typical picture postcard of Boulder, Colorado's Flatirons was shot with a Kodak DC120, which has a real problem with noise, as evident in the magnified view in the lower right corner. The problems grows even worse if we sharpen the image, as shown in Figure 12-39. Although this is a heavy-handed application of Unsharp Mask—an Amount of 200 percent and a Radius of 2.0 pixels—a decent image should be able to hold up to these settings without problem.

Obviously, one way to account for noise in an image is to ease up on the Unsharp Mask settings or just avoid the command entirely. But Photoshop offers a few additional functions that can downplay noise and artifacts while leaving most of the detail in the image intact.

Figure 12-38 This otherwise pleasant view of some scenery in Deke's home town is marred by some major noise, shown up close in the magnified inset.

Figure 12-39 Applying the Unsharp Mask command with an Amount of 200 percent and a Radius of 2.0 pixels makes a mess of the image.

Averaging Pixels

Noise and compression artifacts are ultimately a factor of a few thousand pixels gone bad. The majority of the pixels in the photograph are in good shape or the image wouldn't be identifiable, but many good pixels have bad pixels as neighbors. The best way to clean up the bad pixels is to average them with the good ones. This hurts the good pixels, of course, but assuming that there are more good pixels than bad, it tends to even out in the wash.

There are two ways to average pixels in Photoshop:

• **Downsampling** When you downsample an image, you throw away some pixels and interpolate (or average) the others. To downsample an image in Photoshop, choose the Image Size command from the Image menu. Be sure the Resample Image check box at the bottom of the Image Size window is checked, as in Figure 12-40. For best results, the pop-up menu directly to the right of this check box should read Bicubic (meaning that Photoshop blends each pixels with every one of its neighbors). Then reduce the Resolution value to dump a few thousand pixels. To create Figure 12-41, we lowered the resolution of the original Flatirons image (Figure 12-38) from 267 ppi to 200 ppi. Then we applied Unsharp Mask, again at 200 percent and 2.0 pixels. The noise isn't altogether gone, but it has certainly abated.

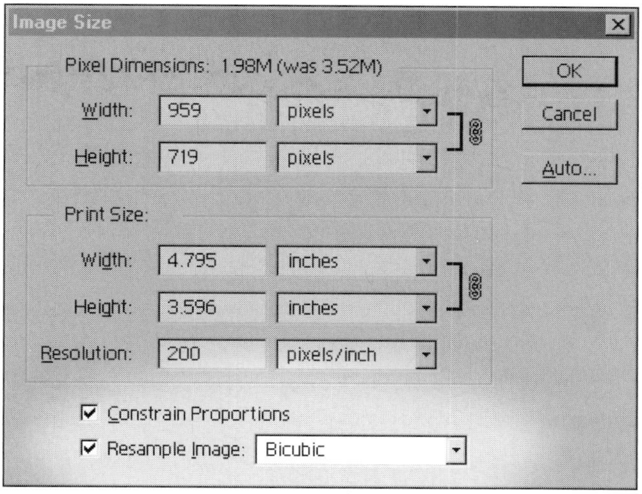

Figure 12-40 Select the Resample Image check box inside the Image Size dialog box to interpolate the pixels inside an image.

Figure 12-41 Starting from the original image, we used Image Size to downsample from 267 ppi to 200 ppi, and then we reapplied Unsharp Mask. The result is an improvement over Figure 12-39.

• If you're the least bit nervous about downsampling, Photoshop offers another way to average without losing a single pixel. Choose Filter » Noise » Median to bring up the Median dialog box featured in Figure 12-42. The lone numeric option, Radius, controls how many pixels Photoshop averages at a time. As the name Radius implies, Photoshop averages pixels in circles; the diameter of these circles is twice the Radius value. But the more important thing to remember is that higher values result in more averaging.

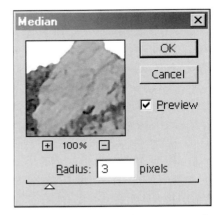

Figure 12-42 The Median command averages the colors of groups of neighboring pixels.

To achieve the effect in Figure 12-43, we began by applying the Median command to the original image from Figure 12-38 using a Radius value of 3 pixels. This produced an excessively soft effect, so we mixed the averaged image with the original by choosing the Fade Median command from the Filter menu and reducing the Opacity value to 50 percent. Finally, we again applied Unsharp Mask with an Amount of 200 percent and a Radius of 2.0 pixels. As a compromise between smoothness and sharpness, this wins our vote as the best view of the Flatirons in four figures.

Figure 12-43 After applying the Median command with a Radius of 3 pixels, we chose Fade Median and backed off the effect to 50 percent. Then we applied Unsharp mask as usual.

The best way to judge the benefits of averaging pixels would be to compare the raw sharpened image from Figure 12-39 with the version that had the help of the Median command from Figure 12-43. Because these figures are now separated by a few pages, we've chosen to show side-by-side views of the two images in color. To see these images, please turn to Color Plate 12-9 on page C29.

Median and Saturation

Another command that tends to emphasize the noise and compression artifacts in an image is Hue/Saturation—particularly when you use the command to boost saturation. The first example in Color Plate 12-10 on page C29 shows an image Deke shot a few years ago with a Kodak DC40, the only entry-level digital camera we've seen that includes an extreme wide-angle lens. The fish-eye view is dramatic, but the saturation is incredibly low, so the 24-bit image appears nearly gray. When we chose Hue/Saturation and raised the Saturation value to +80 percent, Photoshop restored all the original color and then some. But it also awoke a wealth of JPEG compression artifacts that had previously lied lain dormant, as witnessed in the second example of the color plate.

The solution to this problem takes advantage of Photoshop's layering capability, a function that we've discussed so far only in the context of color corrections. However, the following steps are sufficiently straightforward that you should be able to follow them even if you've never used layers before:

1. **Open the original, undersaturated image** In our case, we would open the first image in Color Plate 12-10.

2. **Copy the image to a separate layer** The easiest way to do this is to press Ctrl+A to select the entire image, and then press Ctrl+J to layer it. On the Mac, press ⌘-A then ⌘-J.

3. **Choose Image » Adjust » Hue/Saturation** Increase the Saturation value as high as you like. Don't worry if you enhance noise or compression artifacts. We'll address this issue in a moment. In the meantime, just concentrate on the colors and push them as high as you like.

4. **Choose Filter » Noise » Median** As before, the way to wash away noise and artifacts is to apply the Median command. Set the Radius to a sufficiently high value to merge the colors together and remove virtually all traces of compression. In the first example of Color Plate 12-11 on page C29, we set the Radius to 8 pixels. This wipes away most of the image detail—but that's okay because the detail still resides on the base layer.

5. **Display the Layers palette** The Layers palette is probably already up on screen. However, if it isn't, press F7 to open it.

6. **Select the Color blend mode** At the top of the Layers palette, you'll see an item labeled Normal. This shows that the active layer is opaque. Click on the

word Normal to bring up a pop-up menu, and then select the Color option, as highlighted in Figure 12-44. This blends the colors in the saturated layer with the details in the original layer below. Suddenly, both color and detail come together—free of compression artifacts—as in the bottom example of Color Plate 12-11.

7. **Merge the layers together** If you like, you can downplay the saturated colors by reducing the Opacity value, also at the top of the Layers palette. Then press Ctrl+E on the PC or ⌘-E on the Mac to merge the two layers into one.

Figure 12-44 Select the Color option at the top of the Layers palette to blend the saturated version of the image with the original image below.

Layers are an excellent way to experiment with different variations on an image and then mix them together to form a seamless whole. Alas, we regret that we don't have more space to delve into this feature in greater detail. But as we mentioned earlier, that is the subject for other books—ones that have already been written, and written well.

CHAPTER THIRTEEN

Preparing Images for Print and the Web

The simple act of printing is just that—simple. So long as your printer is in working order and hooked up properly, it's a matter of choosing the Print command and letting the computer and printer do their things. We imagine that 19th Century printing press operators would have wept with joy if they had been miraculously presented with—and taught how to use—today's tools. More to the point, if Deke had had these tools a mere 15 years ago when he directed a service bureau, he would undoubtedly be a more sane person today.

It likewise takes little effort to post an image on the Internet. It's mostly just a matter of attaching an image file to an e-mail message or copying the image from your computer to a remote server using FTP.

Naturally, you're going to run into occasional problems with both printing and posting. We've spent more time than we care to admit wrestling with printers and maintaining our small Web sites. But there are thousands of folks more qualified than we who can help you troubleshoot. The company that sold you your printer can help you make it work; your Internet Service Provider (ISP) can help you transfer images over the Net.

The trick, then, is not to get images onto paper or the Web. The trick is to get the photographs to look the way you intend them to look, with accurate colors and as much clarity as possible. So rather than addressing specific technologies—as we have in other parts of this book—this chapter examines the fundamentals of preparing images for print and the Web. We cover color-matching issues that will help turn your RGB imagery into accurate printed output. We also look at the

CMYK color space, which is used in commercial offset printing. Finally, we explain how to export images to the common Internet file formats and point out which format—JPEG or GIF—is most likely to serve your needs.

If your printer or ISP isn't working properly, this chapter isn't going to make it work any better. However, if your larger concern is finessing your images so that they look their absolute best, then we're here to help.

MIXING PIGMENTS ON PAPER

Printing a color image on paper is a very different process than displaying a color image onscreen. Whereas images on a monitor are created by mixing colored lights, print images are created by mixing inks or other pigments. When you mix one light with another, the resulting color becomes lighter. For example, red and green light mix to form yellow. But when you mix one ink with another, the resulting color becomes darker. Red and green pigment mix to form a brown.

For this reason, colored lights are called *additive colors* and colored pigments are called *subtractive colors*. Additive colors become brighter as light is added; subtractive colors grow brighter as pigments are subtracted.

If the additive and subtractive color models sound like direct opposites, it's because they are. In fact, the primary pigments used to output color images from virtually every kind of printer in use today are based on the opposites of the additive primaries, red, green, and blue. The next section explains how these opposites work.

RGB to CMY

Suppose we want to print a digital photograph that comprises the red, green, and blue color channels pictured in Figure 13-1. When the channels are colorized, like the inset images in Color Plate 13-1 on page C30, the white pixels in the channel become red, green, or blue; the black pixels remain black. It's as if red, green, and blue transparencies were laid over the grayscale images shown in Figure 13-1. This means each channel starts out quite dark. But as one channel is mixed with another—as illustrated incrementally in Color Plate 13-1—the image becomes progressively lighter.

Red   Green   Blue

Figure 13-1 The 8-bit contents of the red, green, and blue color channels from an image captured with a Minolta Dimage EX. Color Plate 13-1 shows the channels in color.

Printing works in an opposite manner, so opposite colors have to be employed. The best example of color opposites in action is Photoshop's Variations command, introduced in Chapter 12. The Variations dialog box positions colors that produce diametrical effects across from each other, as in Figure 13-2. Across from More Red, for example, is More Cyan. This means that cyan ink absorbs red light and reflects green and blue. Hence, cyan appears greenish blue in color. Magenta ink absorbs green light and reflects red and blue, which is why magenta is a pinkish purple. Finally, the opposite of blue is a color that reflects red and green light—in other words, yellow.

Therefore, the exact opposites of red, green, and blue are cyan, magenta, and yellow, or *CMY* for short. Color Plate 13-2 on page C30 shows what happens if we take the exact content from the red, green, and blue channels from Figure 13-1 and print them using cyan, magenta, and yellow ink. This time, the white pixels in the channels remain white, while the black pixels take on the color of the ink. The channels start out very light, but as one layer of ink mixes with another, the photograph becomes progressively darker.

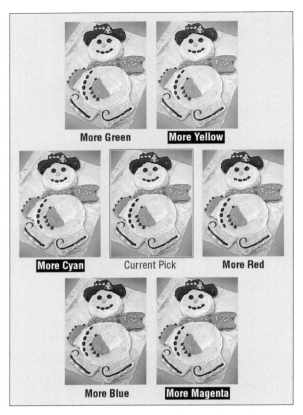

Figure 13-2 This enhanced detail from Photoshop's Variations dialog box shows how cyan, magenta, and yellow serve as complementary opposites for red, green, and blue.

Key Color and Characterization

If this were a perfect world, cyan, magenta, and yellow would be all the colors we needed to print an RGB image. Unfortunately, the world is—in polite vernacular—*perfection-impaired*. RGB and CMY images may look pretty similar when shown on separate pages, but when displayed side by side, as in Color Plate 13-3 (page C31), the images appear remarkably different. The CMY photograph is significantly less saturated, with some pronounced color drift and a generally dingy cast.

One problem is that light is an infinitely purer color source than pigment on paper. White light can be divided into its primary components using filters or even a simple prism. But there's no way to divide the antithesis of white light—black pigment—into its components. So rather than being extracted from a pure source—as in the case of colored lights—ink colors have to be fabricated chemically according to subjective standards. Meanwhile, different paper stocks vary both in color and in the degree to which they absorb and spread ink. There's simply too much room for variation to measure up to the standards set by your monitor (which is by no means perfect in its own right).

Second, even if CMY could be trusted to reflect light every bit as well as RGB projects it, there's the problem of calibration. In order for CMY to exactly match the specific RGB of your monitor, you would have to calibrate the printer to your screen display. Not only would this be very difficult—we've been at this for a quarter century between us and we couldn't tell you how to begin to accomplish it—but it would work for just one monitor at a time. If you switched to a different machine, you would have to recalibrate your printer. Likewise, your commercial print shop would have to calibrate its presses to your monitor, making for a highly inefficient color-matching system.

Naturally, two problems require two solutions. The first is to add a fourth "key" color to compensate for the impurity of the other three. If you look at the second image in Color Plate 13-3, you'll notice that the color that the CMY inks have the most problem creating is black. Whites are not a problem, as demonstrated by the superimposed snowflake, but the black of the hat, eyes, and buttons is a murky brown. The best ink to correct this problem is black, known by the letter K for key—hence the common professional standard term *CMYK*. Color Plate 13-4 on page C31 illustrates the progression of a CMYK image.

The second solution is flexibility. CMYK channels are not slavishly converted from RGB according to a hard and fast formula. After *characterizing* the display capabilities of your monitor (or, at the very least, a standardized RGB workspace) and the output capabilities of your printer, your system can generate a tailor-made recipe of cyan, magenta, yellow, and black inks. This recipe is designed to accurately reproduce color from one and only one printer. So just as RGB is a screen-dependent color space, CMYK is a printer-dependent space.

Figure 13-3 shows the conversion of the RGB channels for the snowman image to CMYK channels for reproduction in this book. The shifts in brightness values are most noticeable in the gloves and scarf, which grow lighter in the cyan channel and darker in the magenta channel, meaning that less cyan ink is applied and more magenta. The blue background grows shades darker in the cyan channel as well.

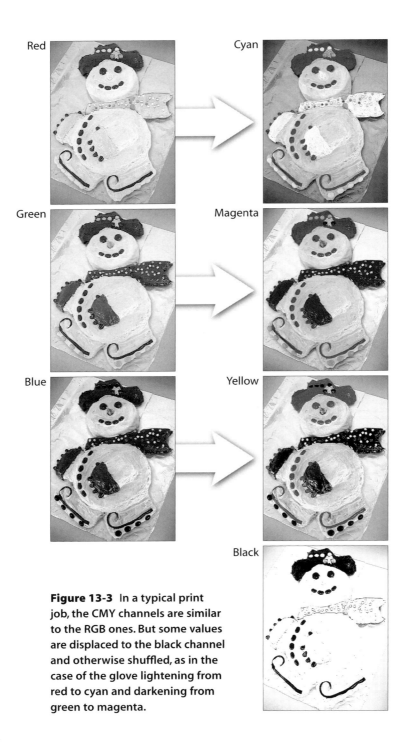

Red   Cyan

Green   Magenta

Blue   Yellow

Black

Figure 13-3 In a typical print job, the CMY channels are similar to the RGB ones. But some values are displaced to the black channel and otherwise shuffled, as in the case of the glove lightening from red to cyan and darkening from green to magenta.

Color is removed from all the black areas in the CMY channels to generate the contents of the black channel. Called *gray component removal*, or GCR, this routine is designed to mitigate the amount of ink on the page. Paper can only absorb so much ink, after which point it smears. This book in particular is set to a *total ink limit* of 320 percent, meaning that if a section of the image is printed in 100 percent black, that leaves just 220 percent for the other three inks to split between them. (In point of fact, the actual recipe for fully saturated black in this book is 75 percent each cyan, magenta, and yellow plus 95 percent black. 75 + 75 + 75 + 95 = 320.)

Even Then, Some Colors Won't Print

None of this is to say that a CMYK print can render an image as brightly and colorfully as it appears on screen. While characterization goes a long way toward ensuring better-looking output, RGB and CMYK are fundamentally different color spaces. There are some colors CMYK simply can't represent because it has a smaller *gamut*—that is, it can print a smaller variety of colors. We'd love to show you those colors, but we can't—as with any print media, the figures in this book are limited to CMYK. But we can tell you that the colors that most commonly drop out in a print image are vivid blues, purples, and reds.

Some image editors let you preview how an image will look when printed. Assuming that you've properly set up your CMYK space to match the printer you'll be using, you can preview the CMYK image in Photoshop by choosing View » Preview » CMYK. You can also identify which colors fall outside the CMYK gamut by choosing View » Gamut Warning. If you aren't happy with the way the image looks, you can adjust the image while the CMYK preview is active using Levels, Variations, and the other options we discussed in Chapter 12.

USING A PERSONAL PRINTER

Personal color printers such as inkjets, dye-subs, and others in the $1,000 and under range vary widely in the number of inks they use. Some are limited to CMY, most are CMYK, and a few offer one or two extra inks to fill in the gamut. (Notice we didn't say *expand* the gamut. The personal printers we've seen— including the six-ink Epson Stylus Photo series—are confined to the CMYK gamut. The additional inks merely help to better print colors that fall inside the CMYK space.)

Every color printer includes a *printer driver*, which is piece of software that communicates the photograph from the image editor or other application to the printer. The driver is designed to translate colors directly from a specified RGB space. In other words, you don't have to first convert the photograph to CMYK inside the image editor. In fact, converting to CMYK is very likely a bad idea. Many combinations of image editors and drivers ironically do a worse job of printing preconverted CMYK images than they do straight RGB. This is because a typical driver insists on running an RGB-to-CMYK color conversion, and that conversion may double-convert colors that start off as CMYK in the first place (or work from the RGB screen version of an image instead of the actual CMYK image itself). You're better off leaving the image set to RGB and using the driver to control how the CMYK image looks in print.

Page Setup

The driver software manifests itself to the user in two ways—the Page Setup command and the Print command, both under the File menu. The Page Setup dialog box lets you specify the paper size, orientation, and other issues that control how the image sits on the page. Figure 13-4 shows a sample Page Setup window that combines options from the Epson Stylus Photo EX driver with Photoshop's default halftoning and registration mark options.

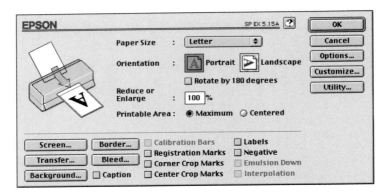

Figure 13-4 Use the Page Setup command to specify how the image fits on the page.

It's a good idea to confirm that the image and page are in alignment before printing the image. In Photoshop for Windows, click and hold down the mouse button on the portion of the status bar that lists the size of the image in memory, as indicated in the top example of Figure 13-5. (If the status bar does not appear at the bottom of the Photoshop window, choose Show Status Bar from the Window menu.) A page thumbnail with a dummy image will appear, as in the bottom example in Figure 13-5. In Photoshop for the Mac, you confirm the image size by clicking on the document size indicator in the lower left corner of the image window, as shown in Figure 13-6.

Figure 13-6 In Photoshop for the Mac, click and hold on the document size indicator in the lower left corner of the image window.

Figure 13-5 To see how this Canon PowerShot A5 snapshot fits on the page in Photoshop for Windows, click and hold on the document size indicator in the status bar.

Both on the PC and the Mac, the box with an X indicates the size of the printed image. If the X exceeds the boundaries of the page thumbnail, then some of the outer edges of the image will be cropped away. To make the image better fit the page—whether you want the image to be larger or smaller—choose the Image Size command from Photoshop's Image menu. Assuming that you want to change the size of the image without affecting the number of pixels (which is recommended), turn off the Resample Image check box at the bottom of the Image Size dialog box, as highlighted in Figure 13-7. Then change the Width, Height, or Resolution value to taste. All three values are linked to each other, so changing one will automatically affect the other two. The result is a larger or smaller image that contains the same number of pixels as it did before.

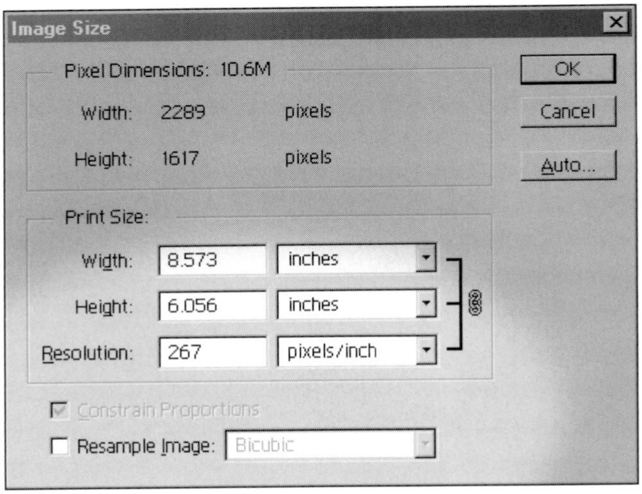

Figure 13-7 To resize an image in Photoshop, turn off the Resample Image check box and then change the Width, Height, or Resolution values.

NOTE: *Don't get hung up on the resolution. In Chapter 4, we recommend a handful of common resolution settings, but these are merely guidelines. If your primary reason for printing an image is to have a nice color print, then use any resolution you like. If the image looks jagged when printed, try raising the resolution (shrinking the image) and print it again. No rules here—feel free to go with the settings that look best to you.*

Printing Quality

The options that appear when you choose the Print command depend almost entirely on the printer driver. This means that, although the options shown in Figure 13-8 are fairly typical, yours are sure to differ.

Virtually all Print dialog boxes let you specify how many copies you want to make, which pages you want to print (most image editors are limited to a single page per document), whether you want to print in color or use only black ink, and so on. Most drivers let you change the print quality as well. Lower quality settings print faster and—in the case of ink-jet printers—use less ink. This is an ideal setting for confirming how colors look when printed. But always be sure to output the final image on good paper (so-called "photo quality" paper, if you have it) and the best quality setting. If there's no sense in shooting photographs at anything but the highest resolution offered by your camera, then there's certainly no sense in printing them at low quality.

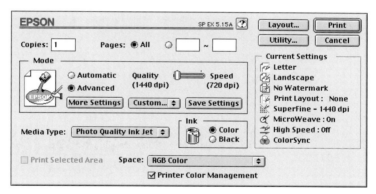

Figure 13-8 The Macintosh Print dialog box for a typical $500 ink-jet printer, complete with color and quality settings.

Note that under Windows 95 and 98, you may have to do a little digging to find some of your printer's most essential options. For example, to raise the quality setting for a Stylus Photo EX, you have to click on the Setup button to access the Page Setup options and then click on Properties to bring up the Main Properties panel, as illustrated in Figure 13-9. By default, most printers are set to the lowest quality setting, so this is an awful lot of work to go to every time you print. Fortunately, you can change the default setting:

1. Double-click on the My Computer icon in the upper left corner of your screen.

2. Locate the Printers folder and double-click on it.

3. Right-click on the icon for the printer you want to use.

4. Choose Properties from the pop-up menu.

5. Hunt around inside the Properties dialog box for the Quality option. Its placement varies from printer to printer.

6. Change the Quality setting, as well as the settings of any other options you like.

7. Press Enter or click on the OK button. The default setting is now changed.

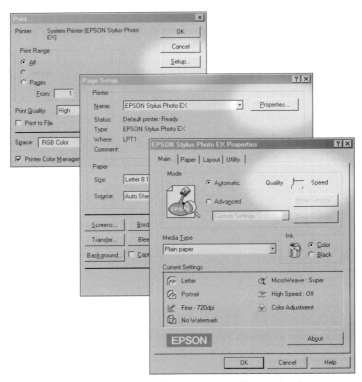

Figure 13-9 Driver software isn't always well organized, so you may have to hunt through one or two nested dialog boxes to find essential options.

Color Matching

Typically, the driver software automatically manages the RGB to CMYK translation to make sure that the printed colors match those you see on screen. If you purchased your printer in the last two or three years, it works like this: The driver assumes you're working in a standardized RGB space, such as the appropriately dubbed *sRGB* defined by Hewlett-Packard and Microsoft. Equally prevalent under the Mac OS and Windows, sRGB includes specific definitions of RGB colors so that the print driver is aware of the precise nature of the color environment that it will be converting from. It's up to the image editor and operating system to ensure that sRGB colors are displayed correctly on your screen (which you can characterize using the screen adjustment software outlined in the "Gamma Adjustment" section of Chapter 7). In other words, sRGB serves as an intermediary between the colors that you see onscreen and the colors that the printer prints.

But you are permitted a certain amount of control, which you may want to exercise in the event that your colors aren't printing as you had hoped. (If everything's looking okay, our motto is: leave well enough alone.) First of all, a few programs let you select RGB environments other than sRGB. If you're using Photoshop 5.0.2, for example, you can change color environments by choosing File » Color Settings » RGB Setup. Then choose a different option from the RGB pop-up menu at the top of the dialog box. If you plan on creating images for commercial printing, then we recommend you select the Adobe RGB (1998) option, as in Figure 13-10. Adobe RGB is a larger color space than sRGB, capable of rendering so many more colors that is likely to make a subtle difference in the quality of your commercial and dye-sublimation prints. It's even possible you may notice better color transitions in your ink-jet output.

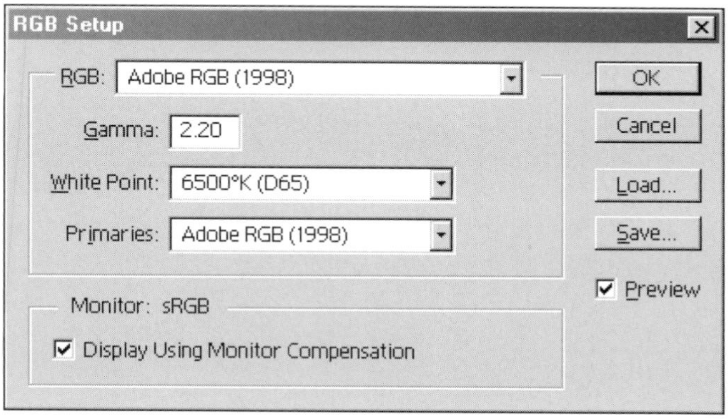

Figure 13-10 In Photoshop, choose the RGB Setup command and select Adobe RGB (1998) from the RGB pop-up menu.

Changing the RGB color space is a tweak, not a major adjustment. If your colors are printing inaccurately, you'll need to do more to fix them. The most likely culprit is your screen setup. If your screen isn't characterized properly, then the system software may think your monitor is projecting colors differently than it is and thus inaccurately convert colors from the sRGB or Adobe RGB space to your screen space. It's as if the software is talking to your screen in French when the screen really speaks Spanish. Get ahold of Adobe Gamma (included with Photoshop) or one of the other utilities mentioned in Chapter 7 and adjust your screen according to the information provided. The monitor colors will update according to your adjustments, so you may want to keep a copy of the image that you're trying to match open in the background so that you can double-check that the colors are beginning to better match the print.

You may also want to experiment with different color management settings. For example, after spending a little time sifting through our Stylus Photo EX options, we came across the Color options highlighted in Figure 13-11. By default, Epson's automatic color management system (CMS) is active. But we can select different options, such as Apple's system-wide ColorSync or Microsoft's ICM. We can also edit the settings manually using the Brightness, Contrast, Saturation, and other slider bars. Or we can simply turn off the CMS.

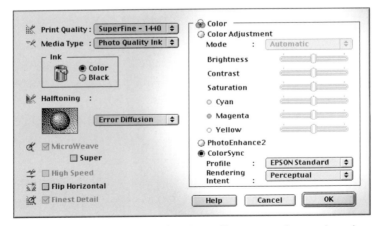

Figure 13-11 The highlighted options allow you to change the color management system that is used when printing to an Epson device.

To test these options, we printed the garish photographic composition shown in Color Plate 13-5 on page C32. The image contains a wide range of brightness values and highly saturated colors, so it serves as a good subject for a print test. We then printed the image to a Stylus Photo EX using Epson's own CMS, Apple's ColorSync, and with the CMS turned off. Color Plate 13-6 on page C32 compares a detail from the original to the prints. None of the settings was exactly on target, but ColorSync came the closest to getting it right. By comparison, Epson's Automatic setting fared slightly worse than no CMS at all.

(Incidentally, the printed images were scanned using a professional-level Umax PowerLook III flatbed scanner, which provides finely tuned color matching controls. So rest assured that Color Plate 13-6 comes as close to exactly representing the ink-jet output as is reasonably possible.)

Color management is an inexact science. In fact, with so many variables—monitor, image editor, driver software, operating system, printer, inks, paper—it's a unique example of Chaos Theory in action. There's no magic recipe for getting colors to print exactly right, and your experience will undoubtedly vary from the specific examples presented in Color Plate 13-6. But remember that solutions are available. Before you resort to turning down the brightness knob on your monitor to match some dreadful print, give the software options at your disposal a try.

PREPARING FOR PROFESSIONAL OUTPUT

Preparing a digital photograph for professional output is a different story. Whether you plan to print the photograph independently from an image editor or import it into a document created with a page-layout application such as QuarkXPress or Adobe InDesign, it's essential that you convert the image to the CMYK color space so that it's ready for separation.

> **NOTE:** The one exception is if you intend to print to color film and have someone else deal with the separation. Many artists and photographers prefer to work this way because it permits them to focus on the creative aspects of a job and let qualified technicians take over the nitty gritty production work. You can point to the film and say, "I want the image to look like this" and avoid a lot of miscommunication. Color film is a rare example of RGB output, so you can—and should—leave the photograph set to its native RGB color space.

Converting an Image to CMYK

Most image editors let you convert an RGB image to CMYK and continue to color correct, sharpen, and otherwise manipulate the image more or less to the same degree you could before. In Photoshop, for example, you create a CMYK image by choosing Image » Mode » CMYK Color. From that point on, some of the commands under the Filter menu become dimmed, but all other functions—including essential filters such as Unsharp Mask and Median—remain available.

But while you can adjust a CMYK image to your heart's content, the image editor's responsiveness may slow down a bit. Two reasons for this: First, your monitor is forever and always an RGB device. So to display the CMYK image on screen, the image editor has to continuously convert each and every pixel in the image—on the fly—from CMYK to RGB. This takes some extra calculation time to each and every operation, which slows the program down.

Second, a CMYK image is larger than the same image in RGB mode. As you may recall from Chapter 4, a grayscale image like the one in Figure 13-12 contains just one channel of information. This means each pixel consumes 8 bits, or one byte, of space in memory. An RGB image contains three channels of data, hence each pixel consumes 24 bits, or 3 bytes, of RAM. When you convert to CMYK, the image editor adds yet another channel—black—so each pixel expands to 32 bits, or 4 bytes. This means an RGB image automatically grows one third again larger when you convert to CMYK, and a third more data means the image editor has to work that much harder to keep up.

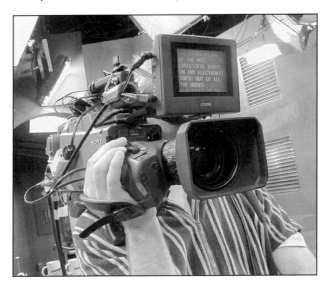

Figure 13-12 A grayscale image contains a single channel of information. Each pixel in this channel consumes 8 bits of data.

Red

Cyan

Green

Magenta

Blue

Yellow

Figure 13-13 An RGB image contains three grayscale channels (left), for a total of 24 bits per channel. A CMYK image adds a fourth channel (right), making 32 bits per channel.

Black

Defining CMYK

Except for the slowdown, converting an image to CMYK is an easy operation. Converting an image *properly*, however, is another matter. As we mentioned earlier, CMYK is a printer-specific color space. If you don't take the time to characterize the printer, then the colors you see onscreen will not match the final output.

Sadly, few image editing applications give you much in the way of control over how the CMYK conversion occurs. A notable exception—and the model by which others are measured—is the tried-and-true industry standard, Photoshop. In fact, Photoshop's color management functions are one of the leading reasons the program is held in such high regard among working professionals.

Prior to converting the image from RGB to CMYK, you should characterize the print environment that you intend to use. There are three ways to do this:

• **Photoshop profile** Contact the commercial print shop that you are working with and ask whether they have a Photoshop CMYK *profile* or *separation table* for the press that your image will be printed to. Photoshop profiles are entirely cross-platform, so don't worry if they say they only have it for the Mac or only for Windows—the same file will work on either machine. Just make sure that, if you're working under Windows, the filename ends with the three-letter extension API. (If it doesn't, just go ahead and add *.api* to the end.) Then inside Photoshop 5 or later, choose File » Color Settings » CMYK Setup to display the dialog box shown in Figure 13-14. Click on the Load button and open the profile.

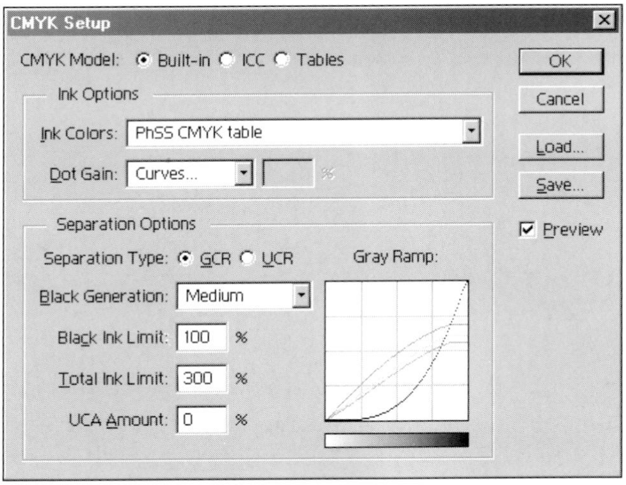

Figure 13-14 Photoshop's CMYK Setup dialog box provides all the controls you need to characterize your printing environment.

• **ColorSync/ICM profile** If your print shop is really on the ball, they may tell you they have a ColorSync or ICM profile. (Thy might also call it an ICC profile—same diff for our purposes.) Again, the file can be used on either platform; if you use Windows, makes sure the filename ends with the extension ICM. (Again, if it doesn't, add it.) On the PC, copy the ICM profile to the Windows\System\Color directory on your C: drive. On the Mac, copy it to the ColorSync Profiles folder, which resides in the Preferences folder inside the System Folder (System Folder\Preferences\ColorSync Profiles). Quit Photoshop and then restart Photoshop to make the program aware of the new profile. Then choose the CMYK Setup command and select the ICC option at the top of the dialog box. You should see three pop-up menus, like the one in Figure 13-15. Select the profile that you just copied from the first pop-up menu, labeled Profile.

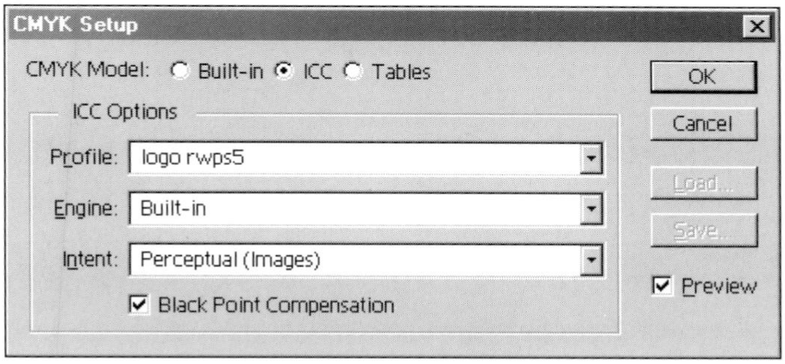

Figure 13-15 Select the ICC option and choose the ColorSync or ICM profile from the Profile pop-up menu. Shown here is the official *Real World* press profile created by Bruce Fraser.

• **Wing it** Naturally, every print shop on earth should be able to profile its presses. But you'd be surprised how many won't have the vaguest idea what you're talking about when you request a profile. In that case, you'll have to wing it. It's not the optimal solution, but we've had to do it more often than not and we generally manage to arrive at moderately predictable colors.

Winging it requires a bit more explanation than loading a predefined profile. Although we can't teach you everything there is to know about profiling a CMYK device, we can give you an idea of how to approach the subject:

1. First, you need some output from your print shop, along with the exact CMYK image that was used to create that output. Make sure the output was created with the press and paper you'll be using. (You can also use a test page created with a proofing printer, provided that the commercial print house is willing to warrant that the proofing device is accurately calibrated to the press.) This way, you have the CMYK file and the CMYK print to compare side-by-side.

2. Open the CMYK image in Photoshop. Does it look like the output? If so, you're done. By some miraculous accident, Photoshop's default CMYK space matches the capabilities of your print shop's press. If the onscreen image and printed output look different (far more likely), keep going.

3. Choose File » Color Settings » CMYK Setup to display the dialog box shown in Figure 13-14. This dialog box offers a lot of intimidating options, but don't worry—some are more important than others.

4. Turn on the Preview check box. This way you can see how your changes affect the CMYK image that you have open. Any and all changes made to the CMYK Setup settings will modify the CMYK image onscreen in real time.

5. The Dot Gain value is your single most valuable tool for tailoring Photoshop's onscreen display to match the printed CMYK output. The term *dot gain* refers to how much the halftone dots grow when they absorb into the paper. The default setting is 20 percent, meaning the dots grow roughly 20 percent in size and darken colors accordingly. If the printed image looks lighter than your screen display, select the Dot Gain value and nudge it downward by pressing the down arrow key. If the printed image appears darker (more likely), raise the value with the up arrow key. Small nudges result in significant changes, so give the screen time to refresh between each press of the arrow key.

6. If you're lucky, you can get a reasonable match with this one value. If not—or if you simply feel like finessing the colors until they look just right—click on the pop-up menu next to Dot Gain and select the Curves option. Photoshop displays the Dot Gain Curves dialog box shown in Figure 13-16.

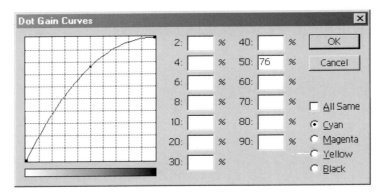

Figure 13-16 Change the curve settings for the Cyan, Magenta, Yellow, and Black channels to finesse how Photoshop displays the four inks on screen.

7. If the All Same option is checked, turn it off. Then use the Cyan, Magenta, Yellow, and Black options to switch between the four color channels and modify their display independently. This permits you to color correct the CMYK screen display, just as you might switch between channels in the Levels dialog box to color correct an image (as discussed in Chapter 12).

8. Modify the curve for each of the color channels. To do this, locate the lone point in the center of the curved line in the graph on the left side of the dialog box. Drag this point up to darken the display; drag it down to lighten the display. If you need more control, you can add points to the graph by clicking on the curved line. You may initially find these controls difficult to use, and it takes a while to get colors you like. But with patience, you'll get the hang of it. If you are in a patient mood, press the Escape key to return to the numeric Dot Gain value and do the best you can with it.

That's basically it. You can fine-tune the colors further using the settings at the bottom of the CMYK Setup dialog box (those in the Separation Options section), but you'll need your print shop's help to make the proper adjustments. The default settings are pretty widely representative, so if you can't get your print shop's attention, you're better off leaving these values as they are.

As we said at the outset, winging it isn't the ideal solution, so try to get a professionally produced profile if you can. But if you can't, at least you have a backup technique that works in a pinch.

> **NOTE:** Whatever you do, don't use Adobe Gamma or some other monitor characterization utility to deform your screen display so that it doesn't look natural but it matches your CMYK output. That is the purpose of CMYK Setup, and only CMYK Setup is meant to accommodate the display of CMYK images.

CREATING IMAGES FOR THE WEB

Compared to printing, creating images for the Web is a walk in the park. The output device for an Internet image is the computer screen, which is an RGB device. So there's no need to convert the image from the color space in which it was originally captured. And there are just two file formats that are commonly supported, GIF and JPEG. (Other formats such as PNG show signs of promise, but have yet to receive wide support from the two prominent Web browsers, Netscape Navigator and Microsoft Internet Explorer.)

What makes this topic even easier is that we've already covered the most salient points in Chapter 4. The section "Conserving Disk Space with JPEG" explains how the JPEG format permits you to save 24-bit RGB images using lossy compression. In "8-Bit Images Choose GIF," we tell you how GIF applies lossless compression—thus ensuring no pixels are changed—but is incapable of recording more than 256 colors per image. Both formats help minimize file size, but both likewise compromise the appearance of the image. The trick is to determine which compromise results in a small image that still manages to look great onscreen.

Putting the Squeeze on File Size

The number one rule of the Web is: keep it small. Although 56Kbps modems are the norm these days, phone companies are not required to optimize their lines for Internet traffic. So whatever the speed of your modem, you're lucky to connect at rates above 28Kbps—several times slower than the sluggish serial connections we lamented in Chapter 5. Even if you enjoy a speedier connection scheme such as ISDN, cable modem, or a corporate T1 line, you're limited by the ability of the Web site's server to respond to your browser's requests, which during peak hours may reduce the speed to below 28Kbps. And, of course, if you're posting images to your Web site, consider that most people loading your images have slow modem connections, regardless of your connection.

So let's assume for the moment that the average rate of Internet data exchange hovers around 28Kbps (though, frankly, we wouldn't be surprised to learn that it's much slower). This means it takes one second to transfer 28 kilobits, or a measly 3.5K. In a minute, you can download a 210K file. Naturally, nobody has the patience to wait for an entire minute to see your image load. Most commercial Web sites limit the total size of a page—including text, graphics, everything—to 30K to 40K. This way, the page loads in about 10 seconds, about the longest a typical surfer is willing to tolerate.

Unfortunately, 30K to 40K is obscenely small where digital photography is concerned. Take Figure 13-17, for example. Despite the fact that the bird is merely a fraction of a megapixel image, as shown in Figure 13-18, this RGB bird consumes 518K in RAM. At 28Kbps, that's a 2:45 download. Take our word for it, no one wants to tie up their computer for nearly 3 minutes waiting to see your image—not strangers randomly checking out your site, not a prospective client interested in your work, not even Grandma hoping to take a look at the newborn. Nobody.

Figure 13-17 This low-resolution bird consumes 518K in memory when viewed in full color.

Figure 13-18 Forget about posting the entire megapixel image from which the bird was cropped. This one consumes 3.52MB in memory and wouldn't even fit on your visitor's monitor.

TIP: *Don't even think about posting an entire megapixel image on a Web site. First of all, it's too large. But more importantly, modern browsers always show images at 100 percent view size, so you see every pixel. (The exception occurs if you specify a different size in the HTML code, which downloads all the pixels but only shows off some of them—a dumb idea.) A typical modern screen shows 1,024 by 768 pixels, older models are limited to 800 by 600 pixels or even less. So a megapixel image would completely fill the screen and then some. Always downsample or crop, and be brutal about it.*

If we downsample the image to 50 percent, we get it down to 130K. That leaves the bird with fewer pixels, as in the 60 ppi Figure 13-19. But at 206 by 215 pixels, it's more likely to fit comfortably with some text and other elements on a visitor's screen.

Figure 13-19 By resampling the photo to 50 percent, we throw away 75 percent of the pixels, making the bird a much more manageable screen image.

After that, it's just a matter of deciding which file format to use.

- **JPEG for photos** When saving standard photographs like the bird, JPEG is your best bet. It retains all the colors in your image, plus it gives you more flexibility than GIF in reducing file size. By saving the bird at one of Photoshop's lowest JPEG Quality settings, 2, we get the file size down to 12K. And as shown in Figure 13-20, the compression makes no perceivable change in the appearance of the image. There are differences, but the only way to find them is to compare the numerical values of the pixels in an image editor. Judging by looks, Figures 13-19 and 13-20 are virtually the same.

Figure 13-20 Thanks to a low-quality JPEG setting, the size of this image on disk drops to 12K. And yet, to look at it, you would swear it was almost identical to Figure 13-19.

- **GIF for high contrast** But JPEG can break down when working with high-contrast images. Suppose we remove the bird from its background, as in Figure 13-21. It looks very elegant. Save it to a JPEG file again using a Quality of 2, and we get the file size down to 6.5K. (Because the white background is one big area of flat color, it compresses very small.) Unfortunately, if we close the image and then open it again to see how the JPEG has been applied, we can see a halo of artifacts surrounding the edges, as in Figure 13-22. The solution is to use GIF. The GIF file shown in Figure 13-23 weighs in at 9K, but its edges are razor sharp. Any time you have high-contrast edges—whether you subjects are birds, sharp lines, or text—GIF is the better way to go.

> **TIP:** *Whether you select the JPEG or GIF format, make sure that the filename ends with the appropriate three-letter extension. This happens automatically on the PC, but Mac users have to enter the .jpg or .gif extension manually. (Lowercase extensions are preferred.) In Photoshop, you can automatically append the proper extension by holding down the Option key when select JPEG or GIF from the Format pop-up menu in the Save dialog box.*

Figure 13-21 By removing the bird from its background, we create high-contrast edges.

Figure 13-22 When applied to high-contrast images, JPEG surrounds the edges with a halo of artifacts.

Figure 13-23 Saving the bird as a GIF image sacrifices color but keeps the sharp edges.

Indexing Colors for GIF

A JPEG image doesn't require any special preparation. As we discussed in Chapter 4, you are asked to specify a Compression or Quality setting when saving the image, but that's the extent of it.

A GIF image, however, is a different matter. Before saving a GIF file, you should index the colors in the image from 16 million down to a scant 256 or fewer. The fewer colors you use, the smaller the file gets. This step isn't absolutely necessary; you can, if you want, save a 24-bit image to GIF directly and let the Save command automatically index the colors for you. But then you sacrifice control and you have no idea how the GIF image saved to disk looks until you close the image and reopen the file. By indexing manually, you know exactly what you're getting ahead of time.

In Photoshop, you can reduce the number of colors in an RGB image by choosing Image » Mode » Indexed Color. Although the specific dialog box shown in Figure 13-24 is unique to Photoshop, the options it contains are common to most image editors. Here's how the most important of these options work:

- **Palette** As discussed in Chapter 4, a GIF file communicates exactly which 256 or fewer colors an image contains by creating an index. This index refers to colors in a *palette*. The Palette pop-up menu determines how that palette is created. Only two options, Adaptive and Web, are applicable to Web images. The Adaptive setting selects the most common colors in the image. This produces the best looking results, but the image looks good only when displayed on a 24-bit monitor. If you're worried that many of your visitors may be armed with old-style 8-bit monitors, select the Web setting instead. The Web palette is a collection of 216 colors that are common to the Mac and Windows operating systems. This setting ensures wide compatibility, but the image quality may suffer.

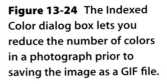

Figure 13-24 The Indexed Color dialog box lets you reduce the number of colors in a photograph prior to saving the image as a GIF file.

- **Color Depth** By default, the Color Depth option is set to its highest value, 8 bits/pixel, or 256 colors. You can shave a few K off the file size by removing colors from the palette. Each setting halves the number of colors while reducing the file size incrementally. The 7 bits/pixel setting lowers the number of colors to 128, 6 bits/pixel takes it down to 64, and so on. Turn on the Preview check box and keep an eye on the previewed image in the background to see how low you can go.

- **Dither** To produce the effect of more colors than there actually are, Photoshop can randomize neighboring pixels. Like grains of colored sand, these pixels mix to create the appearance of other colors. This techniques is called *dithering*. The None option turns off the dithering; the Diffusion option turns it on. (Avoid the Pattern setting—it just makes the dithering ugly.) Dithering makes for a better-looking image, but it also increases the file size slightly because it interferes with GIF's lossless compression scheme. So if an image looks okay without dithering, turn it off. But if you find you absolutely need dithering to achieve a successful effect, select the Diffusion setting.

Those are the most essential options. The other ones you can ignore. Color Matching and Preserve Exact Colors produce such minimal effects that even the most seasoned Web artists won't have the vaguest idea of whether you're using them or not.

Eliminating Unnecessary Data

One final note before we set you free to explore the wonders of archiving that wait for you in Chapter 14. Photoshop and other image editors have a habit of attaching small image previews and other extra data when you save the file to disk. This data is helpful when editing photographs, and it only slightly increases the size of the file. However, even a slight increase in file size slows down the transfer rate of an image, so when that image is bound for the Web, the extra data must go.

To jettison image fluff in Photoshop, choose File » Save a Copy. After selecting a file format and naming the image, turn on the Exclude Non-Image Data check box, which appears highlighted in Figure 13-25. That's all there is to it. Every spare byte of data is tossed overboard so only the pixel data remains.

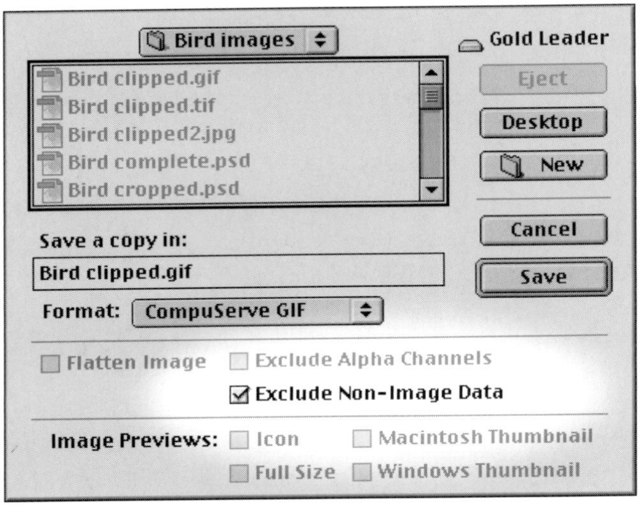

Figure 13-25 To get the smallest file size possible, choose File » Save a Copy and select the Exclude Non-Image Data check box.

CHAPTER FOURTEEN

Archiving Digital Images

A few years back, Deke refinanced the loan on his studio. The appraiser who came out to assess the building's value brought with her a Sony DSC-F1, a 640 by 480-pixel digital camera that was once one of the best models in its class. Deke needed the studio to appraise high, so he thought he might gain a little favor by striking up a conversation about the camera. Instead, he gained a little insight into one professional's bewildering use of the device.

The appraiser's workflow went a little something like this: After filling the camera's memory with pictures, she would copy the files to her hard disk and output the photos she liked to her ink-jet printer. Then she'd throw away all the JPEG files without ever bothering to back them up. At this, Deke's ears pricked up. Didn't she have a Zip or even a floppy that she could copy the files to? Yes, she had a Zip drive. Did she know that a single 100MB cartridge could hold 1,000 images from a DSC-F1? Sure, but it takes too much time to back up the files. But what if she ever needed to refer back to one of the pictures? She would scan the printout, of course. Then she'd make a new printout and throw away the file again. But didn't she spend more time scanning the prints than she would have spent copying the files? She didn't know, and come to think of it, she didn't seem to appreciate being asked.

We sincerely hope you aren't thinking, "You know, I like the way that appraiser thinks!" But there is a certain demented logic to it. After all, this is the kind of person who probably throws away her negatives when she gets them back from the developer—an inadvisable but widely practiced custom. If she needed a copy of a photograph, she'd scan it into her computer and make a new one. So what works for film must work for digital, right?

The problem is, this technique doesn't work for film photography either. The purest source for a film-based photograph is a transparency—negative or slide. The print is merely a copy, and every copy made from the print drifts farther and farther from the original. If you can't find the transparency for a treasured heirloom, that's one thing; but if you have the negative or slide in your possession, you should hold onto it and store it in a safe place.

This goes double for digital. The one and only source for a digital photograph is the image file on disk. Although you can copy that file as many times as you want— with the assurance that every copy is every bit as good as the original—anything other than an electronic file is an imitation, and often times a poor one at that. With an image file, you can take advantage of future output technologies; with a print, you're locked into the technology you used at the time. Given that a single disk can hold hundreds or even thousands of photographs and that a single drawer can hold hundreds of disks, storage space is a minor concern. And assuming you're willing to make multiple backups and check those backups over time, you can make an image file last a lifetime.

Not everyone wants to hear about the importance of archiving. For example, although we can't prove that digital photography was to blame, Deke's appraiser did end up low-balling his studio. But the truth is, the time you spend archiving is every bit as important as the time you spend shooting the photographs in the first place. Neglect either process, and you have nothing to show for your efforts.

HOW ARCHIVING WORKS

The idea behind archiving is simple: copy your files to disks and put those disks in a safe place. But we've seen so many people struggle with this issue (the appraiser is just one story out of a hundred) that we figured a brief overview is in order. Here's how we approach the process, from copying the files from a camera to getting them into long-term storage:

1. **Copy the digital images to your hard disk** Flash memory is not the most stalwart of storage media, so it's a good idea to get your images transferred to disk as quickly as possible. Clearly, if you're out of town, this may take a week or more, but if you have a computer handy, copy the images the same day you shoot them. A hard disk is the best repository for images, being both fast and

reliable. Besides, your hard disk is always accessible, so you can easily edit images and make additional copies at your leisure.

2. **Duplicate the images to another disk** If there's one overarching rule to archiving, it's this: *one copy is never enough*. The question is not if a piece of media will go bad, but when, and your hard disk is no exception. So the moment you finish copying the images to your hard disk, copy them from the hard disk to another disk. We like to keep one set of images on the hard disk of a portable computer, and another set on the hard disk of a desktop computer. But you can just as easily use a Zip, SuperDisk, Jaz, or some other medium.

3. **Delete the images from the camera memory** Now that you've made two copies of the images, it's safe to erase the camera memory so you can take more pictures. But be sure the files are copied before you erase. Once you delete a file from any kind of Flash RAM—including SmartMedia or CompactFlash—it's gone for good. Deke learned this the hard way. After returning from a remote dive vacation, he confused two cards and deleted images from the wrong one. After consulting some professional data retrieval companies, he learned that the images are actually zapped away—permanently. He might as well have shot a roll of film and tossed it in the ocean.

4. **Organize and name your image files** God knows, it takes enough time to shoot the pictures, copy them to your hard disk, make backups, and erase the camera's memory without having to sift through all the images and give them meaningful names. But sift you must. Without proper organization, you don't stand a chance of finding an image you shot a month ago, much less a year ago. We name each and every photograph and organize it into a folder that lists the date the picture was shot and the camera used to shoot it. When naming, be sure to observe cross-platform naming conventions. Mac users should avoid symbols prohibited under Windows (including @, ?, *, <, >, /, \, and both double and curly quotes). Also be sure to add file extensions, such as .jpg, .tif, and .gif. Windows users should keep filenames under 31 characters, including extensions, for maximum compatibility with Macs.

> **WARNING:** *Virtually every camera under $1,000 stores images as JPEG or TIFF files. But more expensive professional models—including those from Kodak, MegaVision, PhaseOne, Leaf, and others—save images in proprietary formats, many of which preserve colors that are outside the range of RGB or CMYK. Each time you open the proprietary file, the software converts the colors according to your specifications. It's like developing the photo with a fresh batch of chemicals. The upshot is that you should hang on to the original file produced by the camera. This goes for cameras that capture JPEG and TIFF*

files as well. Although a photograph may look better after you crop or correct it, only the original contains the raw data captured by the camera. If you decide to modify the image, be sure to save it under a different name—and feel free to archive it too. But whatever you do, keep all original files.

5. **Duplicate the images to a long-term storage medium** You can't keep files on your computer's hard disk forever. And as you permit your hard disk to fill up, you leave less and less room for applications and virtual memory, which can make your system unstable. Therefore, when you finish editing the images, printing them out, posting them on Web sites, and doing all the other things you plan to do with your images, you need to get them off the hard disk and into long-term storage. Our favorite long-term storage is CD-ROM. We make at least three CDs of all our images, two that we keep in our respective offices and another that we put in a safety deposit box as a backup against theft or natural disaster. If this sounds extreme, imagine coming into work one morning and finding that every disk, print, and file you had ever created was flooded as a result of a burst water pipe from the floor above you. Unfortunately, this very thing happened to a friend of ours, Glenn Mitsui. If you've ever seen his work, you know what a shame it is that many of his files were lost for good.

6. **Delete the images from your hard disk** First make sure that you have *at least* two copies of the images on CD-ROM and/or some other storage medium. Then delete the images from your hard disk.

The final step is always the hardest for us. The images have often resided on our hard disks for a few months before we do a long-term backup. But freeing up hard disk space is an eternal struggle, so at some point, you have to decide that your images are no longer part of your regular regimen and are ready to go to a bookshelf or drawer. So, rest assured, as long as your images are backed up, it's safe to erase.

TIP: To maintain a smooth-working system, never permit a hard disk to get more than 90 percent full. This means leaving 10 percent of the space open at all times. So if you have a 2GB hard disk, leave at least 200MB open. If the hard disk holds 4GB, leave 400MB open.

To check the size of a Windows hard disk and the amount of room available, double-click on the My Computer icon. Then right-click on the icon for the hard disk (or partition) in question and choose Properties. Highlighted in Figure 14-1, the Free Space value tells how much of the hard disk is open; the Capacity value shows the total amount of data that the hard disk can hold.

On the Mac, select the desired hard disk icon in the upper right corner of the screen and choose File » Get Info or press ⌘-I. The Capacity value shows the size of the hard disk; the Available value tells how much of the hard disk is open. Both values appear highlighted in Figure 14-2.

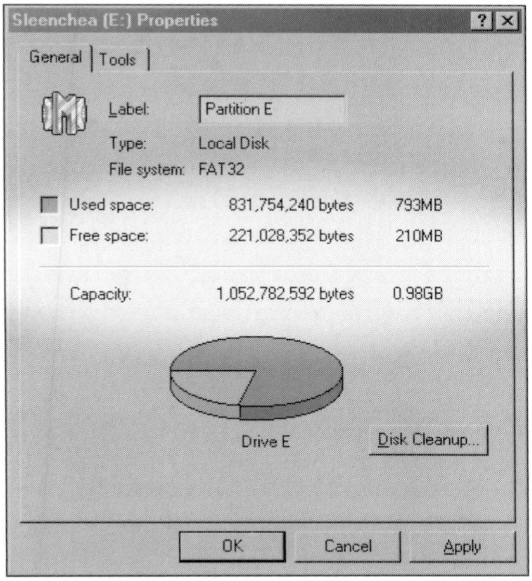

Figure 14-1 To check out the size and free space on a PC hard disk, right-click on the hard disk icon in the My Computer window and select Properties.

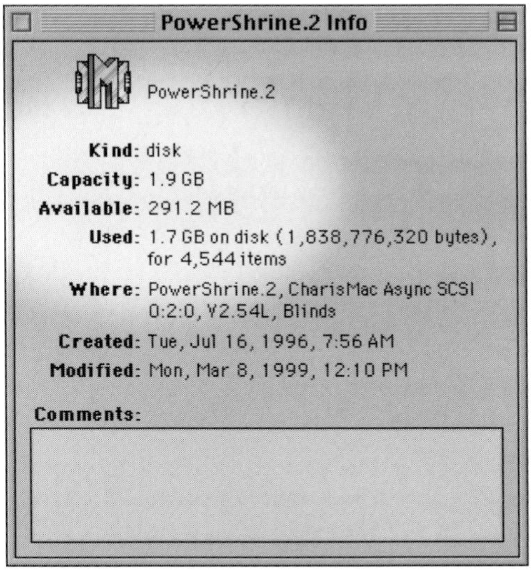

Figure 14-2 On the Mac, you can inspect a hard disk by clicking on it and then pressing ⌘-I.

BURNING CD-ROMS

A CD-ROM is far and away the least expensive and most durable backup medium for digital photography. (TDK claims its CDs "will maintain their data integrity for a minimum of 100 years." Naturally, given that CDs haven't been around for 100 years, this is highly speculative.) And, given the fact that virtually every computer manufactured these days can read a CD-ROM without requiring you to purchase additional hardware, the CD-ROM is the most universally compatible format around.

But just because your computer can read a CD doesn't mean it can write one. You have to purchase an additional CD-R drive to do that, which costs about $400. Also worth noting: copying data to a CD is not a simple matter of drag-copying files, as it is with floppies, Zips, and other disks. You have to use special software, included with the drive, and you have to plan your approach fairly carefully.

Unless you're using a rewritable CD (CD-RW)—which costs several times more than a standard blank CD-R disk—you can't update or replace an image once you copy it. The data is permanently etched into the surface of the disk, which is why the act of writing a CD is often called *burning*. And although you can create a *multisession* CD, in which you burn a second and third group of images at later periods of time, the additional sessions are unlikely to work properly except when the CD is used with the specific drive that created it. To ensure compatibility from one computer to the next, you're better off copying all your images to the CD in one fell swoop.

When burning a typical CD, you have one shot to get it right, or else start over with a fresh disk. So a little bit of planning goes a long way. Here are a few things to know up front:

- **Be aware of your limits** A CD-ROM holds 650MB of data (or 74 minutes of music) and uses just one side of the disk. Strangely, every piece of CD-burning software we've used lets you select as many files for backup as you want. If the files add up to more than 650MB, though, the CD will fail during testing.

- **Always start with a fresh CD** You probably get multiple copies of free software in the mail. When that happens with a floppy disk, you can write over the disk. But with CDs, you can't. We receive literally hundreds of CDs that we can't use over the span of a year—you can throw them in the trash or convert them to coasters.

- **Allow time.** A typical 4x CD-R drive takes about 30 minutes to test and burn a CD. If you're in a hurry, you can cut that time in half by skipping the testing phase. But only skip this step when you're really in a jam. The testing phase can find errors in your setup that would otherwise render the CD unusable.

- **Don't interrupt the burn.** Your CD-burning software may permit you to switch applications and continue working. But a single interruption can cause an error that ruins the disk. The only way to guarantee smooth sailing is to let the machine work unhindered. We usually set a CD to burn as the last thing we do before leaving the office for the day.

- **Be prepared for the occasional CD to fail.** As cheap as they are—about $1 apiece— you can afford to lose a CD every once in a while. When a CD does fail, check your settings and try again with a fresh disk. It may just be a bad CD—we've found that about 1 in 20 just don't work.

If you have access to both a PC and a Mac equipped with CD-R drives, we heartily encourage you to back up your images to both Windows- and Macintosh-formatted CDs, as in Figure 14-3. (Alternatively, Macintosh users can burn a single *hybrid* disk, as discussed in the upcoming section "Making a Macintosh CD.") This way, you'll be prepared to use your images on just about every brand of personal computer on the market. Not only does this make you more marketable today, it also ensures that you'll be able to access your photographs from whatever kind of computer you decide to use in the future. Whether or not you have CD-R drives on both platforms—admittedly an unlikely occurrence even in a well-equipped studio—the following sections explain how to format CD-ROMs for optimum compatibility.

Figure 14-3 The ideal situation is to back up your images to both a Windows CD and a Mac CD. That way, you're ready for anything.

NOTE: *Macs can read CDs and other disks formatted on PCs with the help of a control panel called PC Exchange. And a program called MacOpener from DataViz lets you read Macintosh-formatted media on a PC. However, be aware that both platforms open images more quickly—and with fewer problems— from native disks (disks that are formatted for that specific platform).*

Making a Windows CD

If you use a PC, then the CD-R drive probably included a piece of software called Easy CD Creator from Adaptec. As shown in Figure 14-4, the Easy CD Creator window is divided into two halves. The top half shows the contents of your hard disk and other drives, and the bottom half shows the contents of the CD you intend to burn. Adding an image to the CD is a simple matter of dragging the file from the top half of the window to the bottom half.

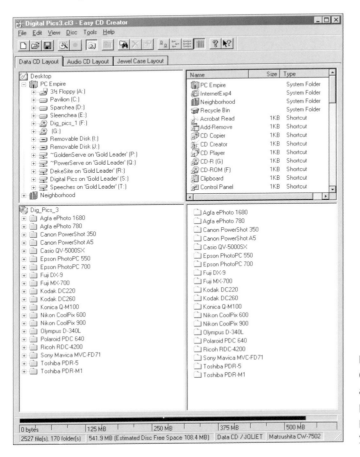

Figure 14-4 Easy CD Creator shows the files available to your computer at top and the proposed contents of your CD at bottom.

TIP: *As you add files, keep an eye on the progress strip at the bottom of the window. It shows how many megabytes of data you've compiled so far and how many more you can add before the CD is full. If you look at the bottom of Figure 14-3, you can see that our CD so far contains 2,527 files for a total of 541.9MB, leaving 108.4MB free. Easy CD Creator will let you go beyond 650MB, but don't unless you want the CD to fail.*

When you create your first CD, it may take you back to the old days of DOS and Windows 3.1 when filenames were limited to just eight characters. This is because, by default, Easy CD Creator and other programs truncate longer filenames. For example, the file TRexSkeleton.jpg becomes !TREXSKE.JPG. The culprit is ISO 9660, a long-standing CD-ROM standard supported by all computers, regardless of operating system. Although we recognize the universality of the eight-dot-three naming convention, it just doesn't hack it for identifying digital images. Luckily, you can preserve long filenames using an ISO 9660 variant called Joliet. To activate this variant in Easy CD Creator, choose File » CD Layout Properties, click on the Data Settings tab and select Joliet from the File System pop-up menu. This option appears highlighted in Figure 14-5.

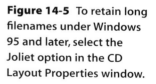

Figure 14-5 To retain long filenames under Windows 95 and later, select the Joliet option in the CD Layout Properties window.

NOTE: *A Macintosh computer can read a Joliet-formatted CD, but it will truncate the filenames to the eight-dot-three standard, as illustrated in Figure 14-6. This isn't an ideal solution, but it's no worse than it would be if you had formatted the CD using ISO 9660 and let Easy CD Creator do the truncating. So you might as well use Joliet and preserve long filenames on the PC at least.*

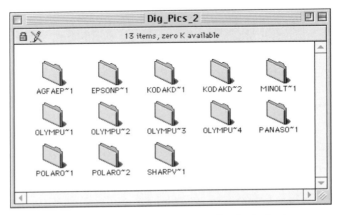

Figure 14-6 If you take a Windows CD that includes long, Joliet-style filenames (top) and open it on the Mac (bottom), the filenames get truncated, but the images remain readable.

After you get all your files in order, click on the Record button or choose File »
Create CD to burn the images onto a blank CD. But before you press Enter to
initiate the burn, click on the Advanced tab and select the Close Disc option highlighted in Figure 14-7. This creates a single-session CD and ensures wide
compatibility with just about any CD-ROM drive ever manufactured.

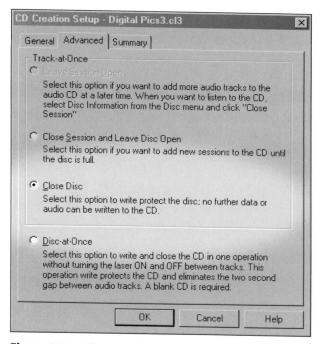

Figure 14-7 Select the Close Disc option to create a
universally compatible single-session CD.

Making a Macintosh CD

Creating a CD on the Mac is at once more difficult and more versatile than it is
on the PC. This is because the Mac lets you do something that Windows doesn't—
you can create a CD that works equally well on either platform. This kind of CD
is called a *Mac/ISO hybrid*, and we very much recommend you use this standard
whenever possible.

> **NOTE:** *Contrary to popular misconception, a Mac/ISO hybrid CD does not cut
> in half the amount of space available on the CD. Data is shared between both
> platforms, not copied twice. This makes hybrid CDs uniquely efficient.*

Every Macintosh CD-R drive we've ever seen ships with a utility called Toast. Like Easy CD Creator, Toast is distributed by Adaptec, but it works very differently. For starters, you can determine exactly how the CD window will look when opened at the Macintosh Finder desktop (something you can't control when creating a CD for the PC). To do this, first choose Utilities » Create Temporary Partition to section off a part of your hard disk that will serve as the mock-up window for the CD. Shown in Figure 14-8, a dialog box asks how big you want to partition to be and where you want to put it. If you plan on creating a Mac/ISO hybrid, set the size of the partition to 640MB or smaller to leave some space free for the special ISO 9660 data. Naturally, Toast requires 640MB of free space on your hard disk. If the hard disk is too full, you'll need to delete some files before proceeding.

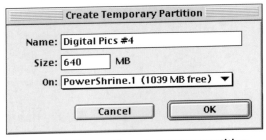

Figure 14-8 By creating a temporary partition, you can specify exactly how a CD will look when opened on a Mac.

The partition appears as a new disk icon on the Finder desktop. Double-click on the icon to open the partition and then drag-copy images to the partition just as if it were a disk. You can align the files and folder exactly the way you want them, as demonstrated in Figure 14-9, and expect them to appear in exactly this same manner on the final CD. You can even create a custom 32 by 32-pixel icon and paste it into the Get Info dialog box, as in Figure 14-10.

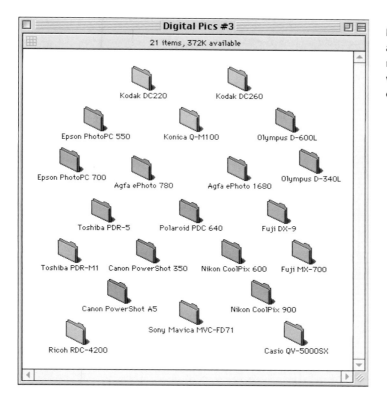

Figure 14-9 Copy the files and folders to the temporary CD partition just as if it were a separate hard disk or other drive.

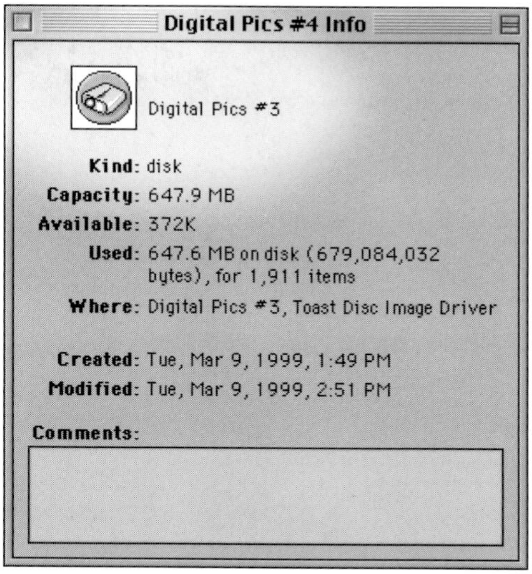

Figure 14-10 Use the Get Info command to create a custom icon for your CD.

When you finish setting up the temporary CD partition, return to the Toast program and choose Format » Mac/ISO Hybrid. Toast presents you with two buttons, Mac and ISO. The first controls the files you see on the Mac; the second affects the files that appear on the PC. Drag the CD partition icon from the Finder desktop onto the Mac button, as in Figure 14-11. This completes the Macintosh half of the CD.

Figure 14-11 To complete the Macintosh half of the hybrid CD, drag the temporary partition icon onto the Mac button in the Toast window.

To specify the contents of the CD when viewed on a PC, click on the ISO button. Inside the ISO 9660 dialog box, click on the Settings tab and select Joliet from the Naming pop-up menu, as in Figure 14-12. The Joliet option preserves long filenames, just as it does on the PC. Next, click on the Files tab. Then drag and drop folders from the Finder into the ISO 9660 window to add the images to the PC half of the CD. Assuming that you want the same images to appear on the PC as you see on the Mac, you merely copy those same images again. For example, we would drag and drop the 21 folders pictured in Figure 14-9. Any files that appear to both Mac and PC users are copied to the CD only once and shared between the platforms.

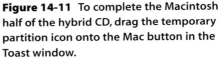

Figure 14-12 The Joliet option preserves long filenames when the images are viewed under Windows.

When you are finished, click on the Done button. If any filenames violate the Windows 95/Joliet naming conventions, you will see an error message. When this occurs, check the folders in the ISO 9660 window to find those filenames that end with three red exclamation points. Assuming you're naming your images properly—with three-letter extensions and no illegal characters—custom icons are the most common culprits, as highlighted in Figure 14-13. Either rename or delete the offending files.

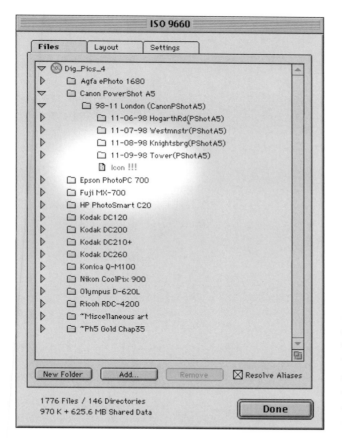

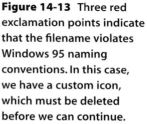

Figure 14-13 Three red exclamation points indicate that the filename violates Windows 95 naming conventions. In this case, we have a custom icon, which must be deleted before we can continue.

When you finish setting up files and confirming names, click on the Write CD button. The software asks for a blank CD-R disk, and away you go. If you encounter any other error messages, consult the manual that came with your drive. But chances are good that the drive will write the hybrid CD and eject it when it's done.

COMPRESSION UTILITIES

One of the most common misconceptions in digital imaging—second only to the idea that any kind of compression is harmful—is that any kind of compression is helpful. Designers and photographers regularly use compression utilities such as Aladdin's StuffIt on the Mac and Nico Mak's WinZip for Windows to stuff and zip their image files. But in point of fact, these programs have very little effect on the size of digital images. StuffIt and WinZip can be very helpful in emailing images in bulk, they are nothing but trouble when archiving images.

StuffIt and WinZip in Action

If you aren't familiar with StuffIt, WinZip, or other programs of their ilk, here's how they work: Most programs—Microsoft Word, QuarkXPress, Adobe Illustrator, and just about every other program that's not an image editor—save data to disk in an uncompressed format. This means that their files may take up as much room on disk as they do in memory—sometimes even more—quite in contrast to image files. This uncompressed strategy permits the program to open and save its files more quickly, but it also means you're saving a lot of unnecessary data to disk.

StuffIt and WinZip cut the fat out of these files by applying lossless compression. Both programs employ the very same LZW and Huffman Encoding schemes that we explained in the "Preserving Image Quality with TIFF" section of Chapter 4. These simple schemes have a tremendous effect on your everyday average bloated computer files. Figure 14-14 shows how StuffIt and WinZip are able to compress five Word documents. StuffIt was able to reduce 2,703K of data down to 1,191K, a 56 percent savings. WinZip got the file size down to 1,273K, saving 53 percent. If you look more closely, you can see that one file in particular—Chap03.doc—shrinks by as much as 75 percent, all without losing a single scrap of information. As a result, we almost never email a Word file or similar document without first stuffing or zipping it.

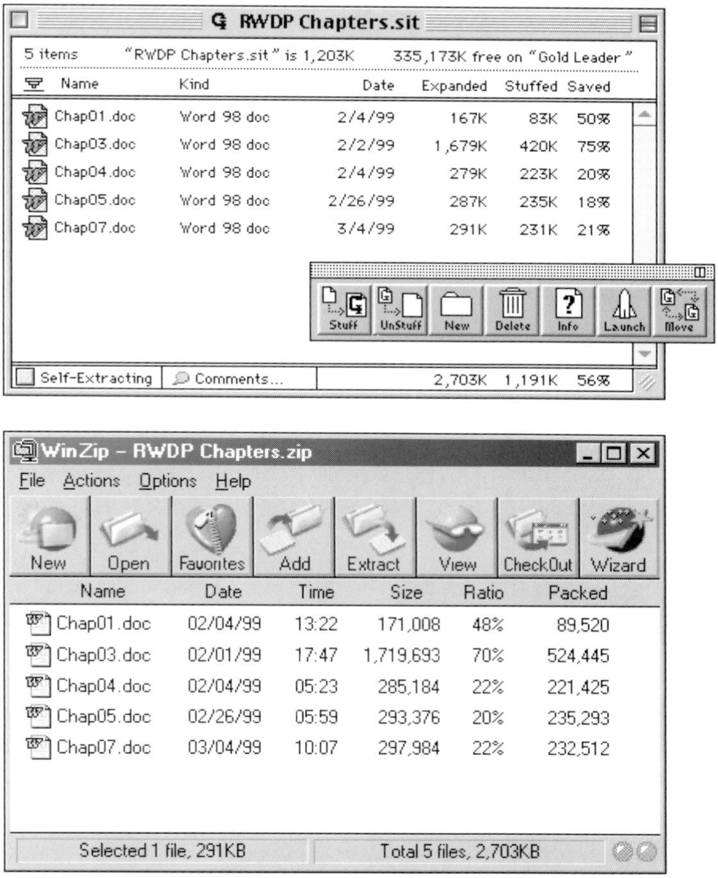

Figure 14-14 Both StuffIt (top) and WinZip (bottom) do a fantastic job of compressing "fatty" files, like these Microsoft Word documents.

One Compression Is Enough

If you save an image using JPEG, GIF, or TIF with LZW compression—as explained in Chapter 4—then the image is already compressed. Applying another level of compression simply doesn't do any good. Back in the old days, StuffIt would complain if you tried to stuff a file that had already been stuffed with the message, "You can't stuff a StuffIt file! (Why would you want to?)" As Figure 14-15 illustrates, the same holds true for compressed images. The result of compressing five JPEG images is a 0.4 percent savings in StuffIt and a 0.8 percent savings in WinZip.

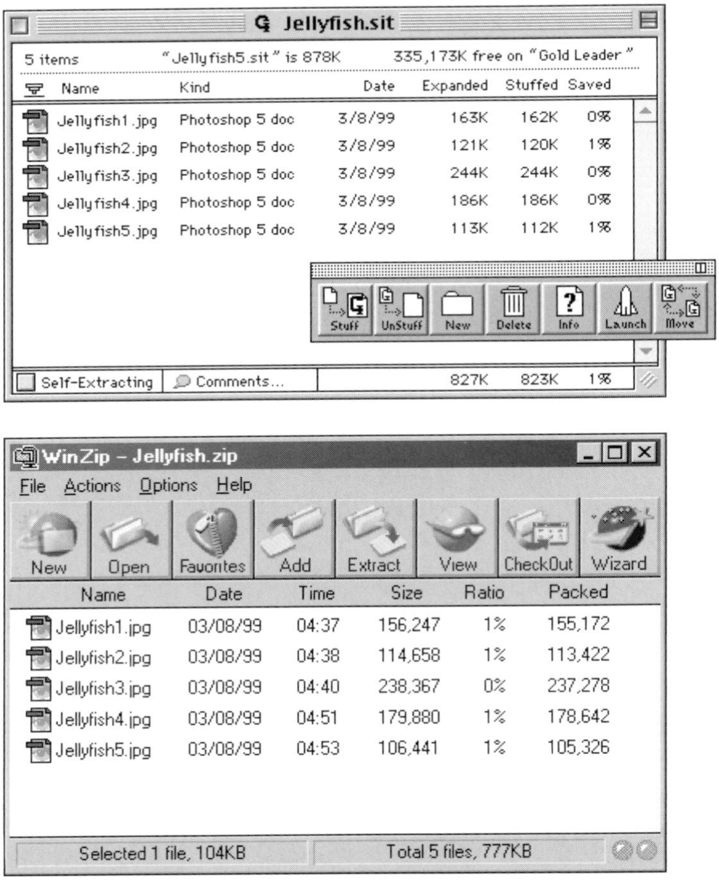

Figure 14-15 But neither StuffIt nor WinZip fares well when compressing photographs that have already been compressed, such as these JPEG images.

This is not to say StuffIt and WinZip don't have their uses. Both programs let you combine several images into a single file, which comes in handy when transferring images via email. They may also have a big impact on uncompressed native files, such as layered PSD files created with Photoshop. And both StuffIt and WinZip let you split a file into two or more pieces, helpful when an image is too big to fit on a floppy disk, for example.

But do *not* stuff or zip images and then burn them to a CD or other long-term storage medium. This merely adds another layer of complexity to the file, and can in rare instances result in corrupt data. By copying images to disk in their original format, you often use no more disk space, you save time, and you ensure your photographs are immediately accessible to an image editor or other program.

> *TIP: Some digital cameras save images as uncompressed TIFF files. In this case, StuffIt and WinZip will be able to compress the files significantly. But you're better off opening the image in an image editor and saving the image as TIFF with LZW compression. A few image editors, including Photoshop and Jasc Software's Paint Shop Pro, let you convert entire folders of files using batch processing. Again, you save room on disk, you save time, and you ensure immediate accessibility.*

CATALOGING YOUR ARCHIVES

After a few years of shooting digital photographs, you're liable to amass a fairly considerable library—at least a few hundred pictures and possibly several thousand. As we can attest from personal experience, a handful of the pictures stand out in your mind, but the vast majority slip out of memory weeks after you shoot them. Fill up a few CDs, and you'll be hard-pressed not only to remember what you shot, but to find what little you can remember.

That's where cataloging becomes essential. Whereas meaningful filenames are critical when performing searches using your operating system's Find command, a preview of an image goes even farther in communicating the gist of the photograph. You can browse your images visually as well as by name.

Thumbnail Previews

In Photoshop, for example, you can view a thumbnail for a selected file in the Open dialog box, as in Figure 14-16. But this only works if a Photoshop-compatible thumbnail was saved with the file. On the Mac, you can generate a thumbnail on the fly by clicking on the Create button below the thumbnail. But on the PC, the only way to create a thumbnail is to open the image and resave it. Photoshop on the Mac also lets you save icon-sized previews with an image, which you can view from the Finder desktop, as in Figure 14-17. Under Windows, only Photoshop's native PSD files include icon previews.

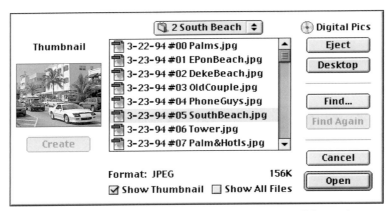

Figure 14-16 If an image contains a Photoshop-compatible preview, you can click on the filename and view a thumbnail of the image in Photoshop's Open dialog box.

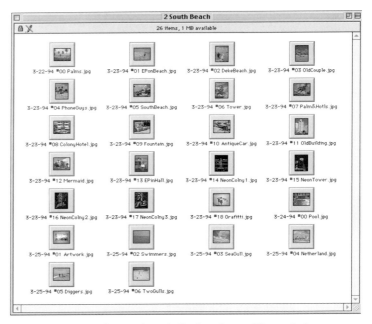

Figure 14-17 At the Macintosh Finder, choose View » As Icons or View » As Buttons to see 32 by 32-pixel previews of images generated by Photoshop.

But although Windows users get a bit of a raw deal from Photoshop, the operating system comes to the rescue. Later versions of Windows 95 and all versions of Windows 98 let you preview an image directly from the desktop. Choose View » As Web Page, then click on a filename to see a thumbnail preview. As you can see in Figure 14-18, this preview is several times larger than the dinky icons available on the Mac. Unfortunately, this feature applies only to the Web image formats, JPEG and GIF; Windows is unable to peer into TIFF files.

Figure 14-18 Choose View » As Web Page to see thumbnail previews of image files from the Windows desktop.

Being able to preview one image at a time is nice, but seeing many images at once is even better. Some image editors include built-in browser functions that provide large previews of several images at a time, regardless of file format. In Micrografx Picture Publisher, for example, the open dialog box shows you thumbnail previews for ten images at a time (see Figure 14-19).

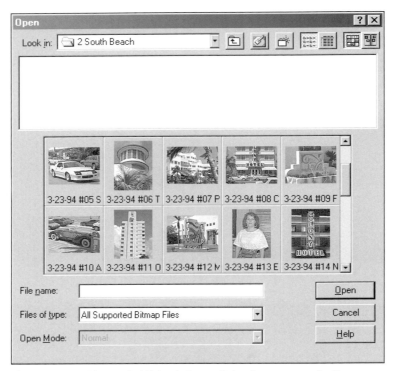

Figure 14-19 Picture Publisher's Open dialog box automatically generates thumbnail previews of your photographs and displays up to ten at a time.

Paint Shop Pro takes this concept one step farther. Choose File » Browse to bring up the window shown in Figure 14-20. Not only can you preview as many images as you like—subject only to the physical constraints of your monitor—you can also change the order in which the images appear. In Figure 14-20, for example, the images are sorted by size—a common feature at the desktop level but uncommon inside an application. You can keep the browser window open even when editing images, great for those times when you need to inspect a few photographs before deciding exactly which one to use. All in all, this browser function is sufficiently excellent to justify the $99 price of Paint Shop Pro on its own. (You can preview the program for 60 days by downloading it from *www.jasc.com*.) Sadly, neither Picture Publisher nor Paint Shop Pro is available for the Mac.

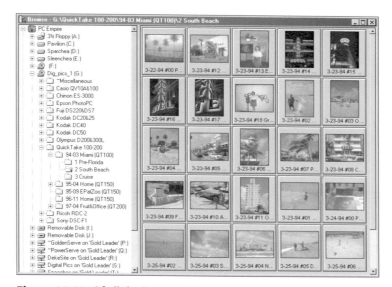

Figure 14-20 Of all the image editor browsing features, Paint Shop Pro's is the best, capable of showing you as many thumbnails as your monitor will hold.

Cataloging Utilities

If you're really feeling motivated, you can use a cataloging utility to organize your photo collection. The advantage of creating a catalog is that it permits you to search more precisely for a specific image—whether or not the disk that contains the image is currently available to your computer. You can enter keywords, search multiple archives, and even add security checks if you want to protect confidential or copyrighted photographs.

One of the best and most reasonably priced cataloging utilities is the cross-platform Portfolio from Extensis (available for a 30-day trial from *www.extensis.com*). Creating a catalog in Portfolio is a simple matter of dragging folders or files from a disk and dropping them into a new document. As shown in Figure 14-21, the program then asks you what size thumbnails you want it to create and whether you want it to automatically generate keywords based on file and folder names. After you confirm these settings, Portfolio spends a few minutes importing images, generating thumbnails, and otherwise building the catalog. Figure 14-22 shows the progress window that Portfolio uses to keep you apprised of its actions as it processes your files.

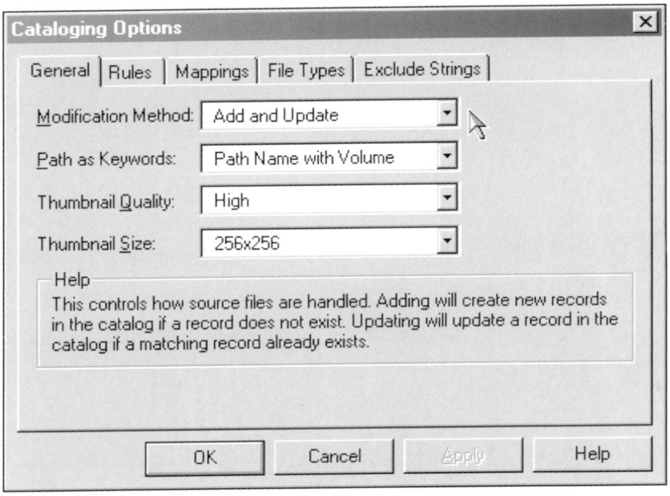

Cataloging Options   ☒

General | Rules | Mappings | File Types | Exclude Strings

Modification Method: Add and Update   ▼

Path as Keywords: Path Name with Volume   ▼

Thumbnail Quality: High   ▼

Thumbnail Size: 256x256   ▼

Help
This controls how source files are handled. Adding will create new records in the catalog if a record does not exist. Updating will update a record in the catalog if a matching record already exists.

OK   Cancel   Apply   Help

Figure 14-21 When you add images to a catalog, Portfolio asks you how it should generate thumbnails and keywords.

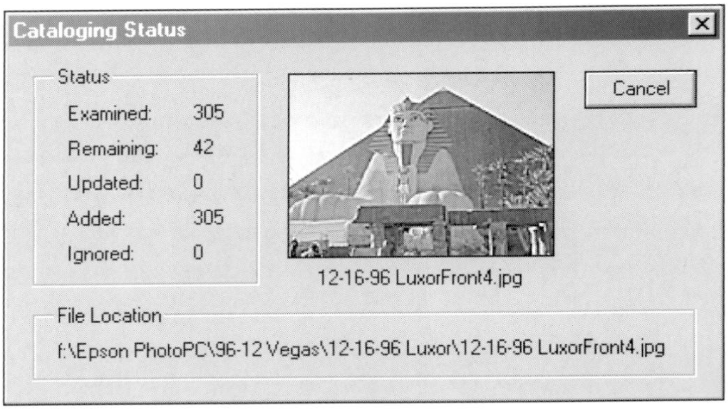

Cataloging Status   ☒

Status
Examined: 305
Remaining: 42
Updated: 0
Added: 305
Ignored: 0

Cancel

12-16-96 LuxorFront4.jpg

File Location
f:\Epson PhotoPC\96-12 Vegas\12-16-96 Luxor\12-16-96 LuxorFront4.jpg

Figure 14-22 As Portfolio builds the catalog, it displays a thumbnail of the image being processed and lists the number of images left to go.

After building the basic catalog, you can search images by keyword. For example, in Figure 14-23, we ran a search for the word fruit and came up with some images shot for a *Macworld* magazine layout a few years back using an Epson PhotoPC, Olympus D-300L, and a handful of other cameras. We can view the list by thumbnail previews, as in Figure 14-23, or by name, as in Figure 14-24.

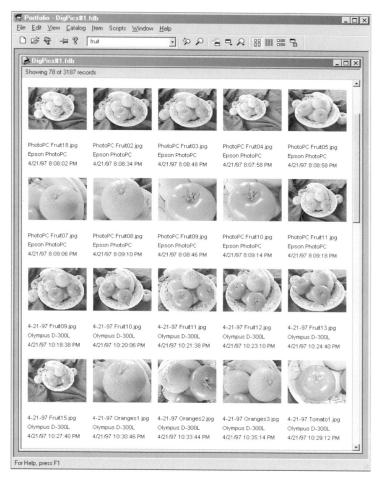

Figure 14-23 The result of searching a Portfolio catalog for all images containing *fruit*. The program isn't smart enough to recognize fruit, but it can find images whose file or folder names include *fruit*.

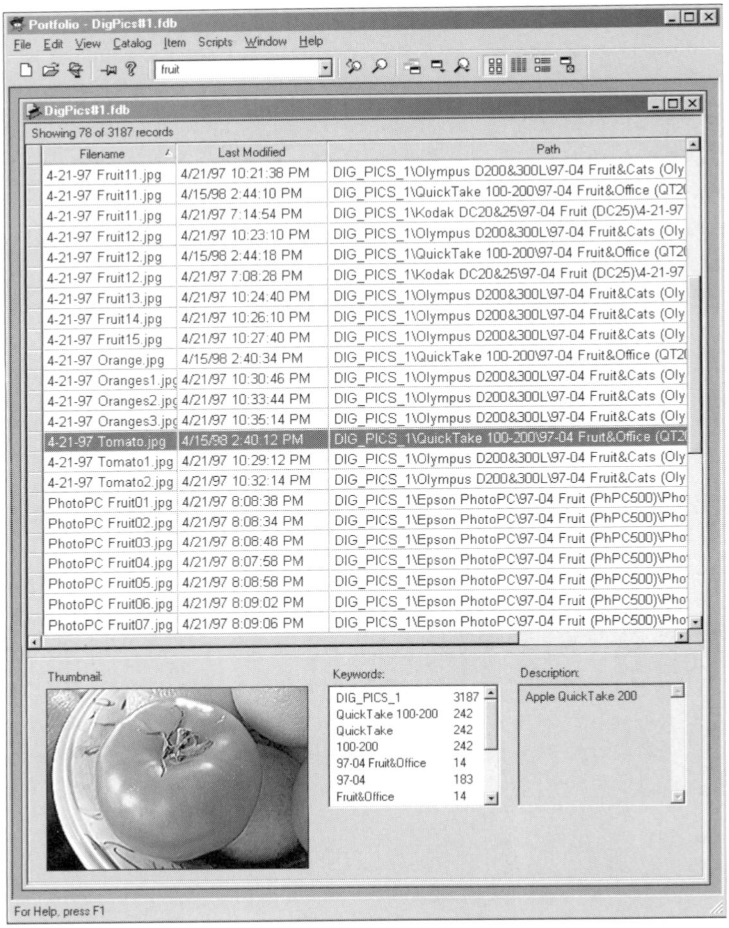

Figure 14-24 When viewing a catalog as a list, you can see keywords and description text for the selected image, which in this case was shot with an Apple QuickTake 200.

The bottom of Figure 14-24 shows a list of keywords for the selected image, all of which Portfolio generated automatically from the file and folder name. Even though this particular image is named *4-21-97 Tomato.jpg*, Portfolio picked up the word *fruit* from the folder name, *97-04 Fruit&Office*. You can add or subtract keywords as you see fit by right-clicking on a filename and selecting the Properties command. You can even create a list of commonly used *master keywords* to expedite the process of adding keywords to multiple images at a time.

Portfolio isn't the only image cataloger on the market. The German developer Canto makes an application called Cumulus that's designed specifically to hunt down photographs served over a network, making it a mainstay of stock agencies and large photographic studios. Some graphics applications include their own catalog programs. CorelDraw 9, for example, ships with a limited edition of Canto Cumulus. But whatever program you choose, give yourself time to get up and running—these programs tend to take some time to learn—and still more time to manage keywords, descriptions, and other image tags.

Printing Contact Sheets

The final way to keep track of your archived artwork is to print contact sheets, just like photographers have done for years. The difference is that you can print these kinds of contact sheets yourself using a personal ink-jet or dye-sub printer.

Starting with Version 5, Photoshop provides an automated contact sheet function that creates a document filled with thumbnail views of all images in a specified folder. To use this feature, choose File » Automate » Contact Sheet. This brings up the dialog box shown in Figure 14-25. Click on the Choose button to locate the folder of images you want to print. Enter the dimensions of the contact sheet into the Width and Height options. Use the Layout values to specify how many thumbnails print on a page.

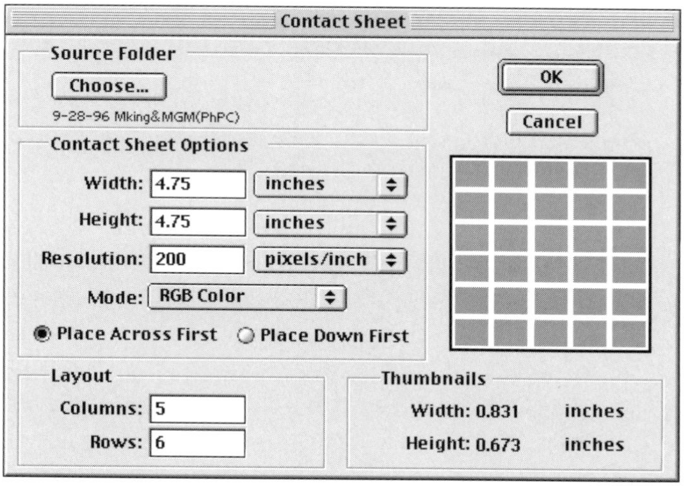

Figure 14-25 The Contact Sheet feature automatically generates a page filled with thumbnails of all images in a specified folder.

TIP: Katrin uses the Contact Sheet command to create covers for her CDs. The trick is to enter a value of 4.75 inches into both the Width and Height options, as in Figure 14-25. A resolution of 200 ppi is probably good enough, though you can go higher if you like. The printed file will fit exactly inside a CD case, as in Figure 14-26.

Figure 14-26 A 4.75 by 4.75-inch contact sheet looks great inside a CD case. A CD holds a lot more than 30 megapixel images, however, so you'll need several contact sheets to show all images.

After you fill in the dimension and layout values, press the Return or Enter key. Photoshop spends a minute or so opening images, resizing them, and pasting them into the contact sheet document. If one document fills up, Photoshop automatically creates a second one and starts adding thumbnails to it. Photoshop 5 isn't smart enough to rotate photographs that were shot vertically or add labels, like those shown in Figure 14-27, so you may need to edit the document manually after the Contact Sheet command completes (Photoshop 5.5 is able to automatically add labels). Then flatten the document by choosing Layer » Flatten Image and print it.

Color Plate 12-1 On left we have an image as it originally appeared when captured with a Ricoh RDC-2. The colors are grossly inaccurate, and the contrast is too extreme. But after 20 minutes of work with an image editor, you can restore the photograph as you remember it (right). (See page 283 for more information.)

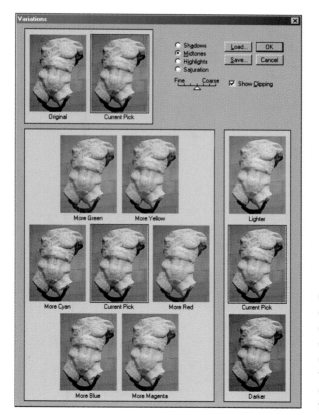

Color Plate 12-2 Photoshop's Variations dialog box hinges on the concept of opposites. To correct a dark image, click on Lighter. To correct a green cast, click on More Magenta. If you go too far with a correction, you can back it off by clicking on an opposite. (See page 297 for more information.)

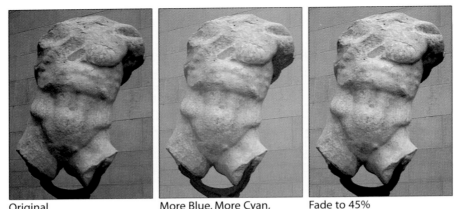

Original   More Blue, More Cyan,   Fade to 45%
                   Lighter

Color Plate 12-3 Shot with a Kodak DC260, the first image is a little dark and orange from the warm museum lighting. Choosing Variations and applying the More Blue, More Cyan, and Lighter buttons cooled the image down, but went a bit too far in the opposite direction (middle). By averaging the original and corrected images, we achieved a neutral effect that better shows off the color of the stone (right). (See page 299 for more information.)

Color Plate 12-4 An Ionic temple shot under exactly the same conditions in the British Museum with the Ricoh RDC-4200 (top) and the Kodak DC260 (bottom). Though the Ricoh's colors are completely out of control, they can be fixed by backing off the saturation. (See page 300 for more information.)

Color Plate 12-5
After removing the orange cast and lightening the image (top), we clicked on the Less Saturation thumbnail three times to mute the intensity (bottom). (See page 300 for more information.)

Color Plate 12-6 Because he shot this gavial in a glass tank, Deke had to disable the fill flash on an Olympus D-340L. Relying on natural light, the image comes out dark and murky, with a pronounced green cast from the water. (See page 301 for more information.)

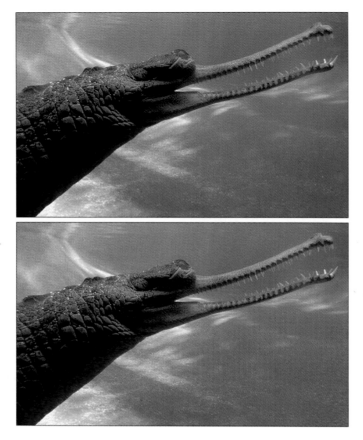

Color Plate 12-7 By applying different Levels settings to each of the three color channels, we were able to increase the brightness and downplay some of the green in the image (top). To finish things off, we boosted the saturation using the Hue/Saturation command (bottom). (See page 301 for more information.)

Color Plate 12-8 A Kodak DC200 captured the colored areas in a grape iMac as deep blue (top). Fortunately, this gaffe was a cinch to put right (bottom) with the help of the Edit pop-up menu in the Hue/Saturation dialog box. (See page 305 for more information.)

Color Plate 12-9 If you sharpen a digital photograph that includes lots of noise, the Unsharp Mask filter enhances the noise as it enhances the focus (left). The solution is to first suppress the noise with the Median command and then apply Unsharp Mask (right). (See page 319 for more information.)

Color Plate 12-10 For a low-resolution camera, Kodak's DC40 produces some surprisingly good images. But in this case, it missed out on color saturation (top). We can boost the colors with Hue/Saturation, but that has the unfortunate effect of drawing out compression artifacts (bottom). (See page 320 for more information.)

Color Plate 12-11 Before boosting the saturation of an image, copy it to a new layer. Then choose the Median command to quell the JPEG artifacts. In our case, we set the Radius value to 8 pixels (top). Finally, select the Color blend mode from the Layers palette (bottom) and merge the two layers into one. (See page 320 for more information.)

Color Plate 13-1 A screen image is formed by mixing a red channel (left) with a green channel (middle) and a blue channel (right). The inset images show each channel by itself. (See page 324 for more information.)

Color Plate 13-2 When outputting a color image, the printer mixes a cyan channel (left) with a magenta channel (middle) and a yellow channel (right). The inset images show each channel on its own. (See page 325 for more information.)

Color Plate 13-3 An RGB image (left) compared with the same image separated directly to CMY inks (right). Not only are the CMY inks incapable of producing rich blacks, they also require calibration to generate better color saturation. (See page 326 for more information.)

Color Plate 13-4 Each ink in a CMYK image mixes with the next to create a full color photograph. Based on the printer characterization, colors have been shifted in the cyan and magenta channels, as compared with Color Plate 13-2. Ink density has also been removed from the hat, eyes, and buttons in the CMY channels to fund the black channel. The result is a much closer match to the original RGB photograph. (See page 327 for more information.)

Color Plate 13-5 Created in Photoshop using a combination of photos captured with an Olympus D-400Zoom, this image contains a wealth of vivid colors and brightness values. (See page 337 for more information.)

Original   Epson Automatic   ColorSync Perceptual   None

Color Plate 13-6 A detail from the original image (left) compared with three samples printed from an Epson Stylus Photo EX ink-jet device. Of the CMS settings tested, ColorSync's Perceptual rendering provides closest match, with the yellow of the face printing a bit too orange and the red around the eyes printing a bit blue. Epson's default Automatic setting is a disappointment, looking worse than no color management at all. (See page 337 for more information.)

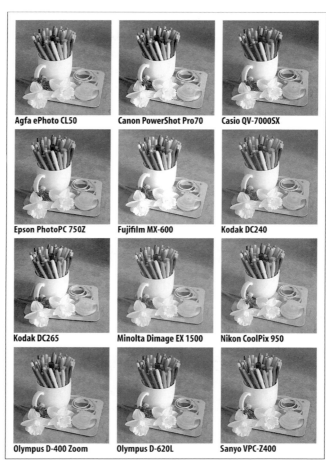

Figure 14-27 Deke printed this contact sheet to help him evaluate comparative images he shot for *Macworld* magazine. In Photoshop 5, he had to insert the camera names manually.

If you follow all the suggestions in this chapter, you should be able to access and enjoy your digital photographs for years to come. With any luck, you may find that your digital image library takes up less room, costs less, is better organized, and lasts longer than a film library half its size.

INDEX

Get up and running quickly...

...with these *Visual QuickStart Guides* covering the latest digital graphics and Web publishing tools.

HTML 4 for the World Wide Web
Elizabeth Castro
ISBN 0-201-69696-7
336 pages
$17.95 U.S.

Illustrator 8 for Windows and Macintosh
Elaine Weinmann & Peter Lourekas
ISBN 0-201-35388-1
396 pages
$19.99 U.S.

Dreamweaver 2 for Windows and Macintosh
J. Tarin Towers
ISBN 0-201-35435-7
400 pages
$19.99 U.S.

DHTML
Jason Teague
ISBN 0-201-35341-5
256 pages
$17.95 U.S.

Fireworks 2 for Windows and Macintosh
Sandee Cohen
ISBN 0-201-35458-6
304 pages
$18.99 U.S.

QuarkXPress 4
Elaine Weinmann
For Macintosh:
ISBN 0-201-69623-1
376 pages
For Windows:
ISBN 0-201-69699-1
368 pages
$18.95 U.S.

Photoshop 5 for Windows and Macintosh
Elaine Weinmann & Peter Lourekas
ISBN 0-201-35352-0
400 pages
$19.95 U.S.

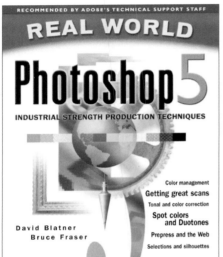